Catholicism: East of Eden

Insights into Catholicism for the 21st Century

by
Richard (Peter) Bennett
former Roman Catholic priest

Berean Beacon Press

Catholicism: East of Eden
Insights into Catholicism for the 21st Century
by Richard Bennett

ISBN: 0-9774229-0-9

Cover design by Mel Climer
Book design by Layne Moore
Photography by Tom Cockrem

Printed in the United States of America.

Table of Contents

Chapter 1

From Tradition To Truth: A Priest's Story[1]

Born Irish, in a family of eight, my early childhood was fulfilled and happy. My father was a colonel in the Irish Army until he retired when I was about nine. As a family, we loved to play, sing, and act, all within a military camp in Dublin. We were a typical Irish Roman Catholic family. My father sometimes knelt down to pray at his bedside in a solemn manner. Most evenings we would kneel in the living room to say the Rosary together. No one ever missed Mass on Sundays unless he were seriously ill. By the time I was about five or six years of age, Jesus Christ was a very real person to me—but so also were Mary and the saints. I can identify easily with others in traditional Catholic nations in Europe and with Hispanics and Filipinos who put Jesus, Mary, Joseph, and other saints all in one boiling pot of faith.

The catechism was drilled into me at the Jesuit School of Belvedere, where I had all my elementary and secondary education. Like every boy who studies under the Jesuits, I could recite before the age of ten five reasons why God existed and why the Pope was head of the only true Church. Getting souls out of Purgatory was a serious matter. The often quoted words, "It is a holy and a wholesome thought to pray for the dead that they may be loosed from sins," were memorized even though we did not know what these words meant. We were told that the Pope as head of the Church was the most important man on earth. What he said was law, and the Jesuits were his right-hand men. Even

---

[1] Used by permission. Second edition published in *Far from Rome, Near to God: Testimonies of Fifty Converted Roman Catholic Priests*, Richard Bennett and Martin Buckingham, eds. (Edinburgh and Carlisle, PA: Banner of Truth Trust, 1997; Webpage: www.banneroftruth.co.uk).

though the Mass was in Latin, I tried to attend daily because I was intrigued by the deep sense of mystery that surrounded it. We were told that it was the most important way to please God. Praying to saints was encouraged, and we had patron saints for most aspects of life I did not make a practice of that, with one exception: St. Anthony, the patron of lost objects, since I seemed to lose so many things.

When I was fourteen years old, I sensed a call to be a missionary. This call, however, did not affect the way in which I conducted my life at that time. Age sixteen to eighteen were the most fulfilled and enjoyable years a youth could have. During this time, I did quite well both academically and athletically.

I often had to drive my mother to the hospital for treatments. Once while waiting for her, I found quoted in a book these verses from Mark 10:29-30, *"And Jesus answered and said, Verily I say unto you, There is no man that hath left house, or brethren, or sisters, or father, or mother, or wife, or children, or lands, for my sake, and the gospel's, But he shall receive an hundredfold now in this time, houses, and brethren, and sisters, and mothers, and children, and lands, with persecutions; and in the world to come eternal life."* Not having any idea of the true salvation message, I decided that I truly did have a call to become a missionary.

Trying to earn salvation

I left my family and friends in 1956 to join the Dominican Order. I spent eight years studying what it is to be a monk, the traditions of the Church, philosophy, the theology of Thomas Aquinas, and some of the Bible from a Catholic standpoint. Whatever personal faith I had was institutionalized and ritualized in the Dominican religious system. Obedience to the law, both Church and Dominican, was put before me as the means of sanctification. I often spoke to Ambrose Duffy, our Master of Students, about the law being the means of becoming holy. In addition to becoming "holy," I wanted also to be sure of eternal salvation. I memorized part of the teaching of Pope Pius XII in which he said, "...the salvation of many depends on the prayers and sacrifices of the mystical body of Christ offered for this intention." This idea of gaining salvation through suffering and prayer is also the basic message of Fatima and Lourdes, and I sought to win my own salvation as well as the salvation of others by such suffering and prayer. In the Dominican monastery in Tallaght, Dublin, I performed many difficult feats to win souls, such as taking cold showers in the middle of winter and beating my back with a small steel chain. The Master of Students knew what I was doing, his own austere life being part of the inspiration that I had received from the Pope's words. With rigor and determination, I studied, prayed, did penance, and tried to keep the Ten Commandments and the multitude of Dominican rules and traditions.

Outward pomp—inner emptiness
Then in 1963 at the age of twenty-five, I was ordained a Roman Catholic priest and went on to finish my course of studies of Thomas Aquinas at the Angelicum University in Rome. But there I had increasing difficulty with both the outward pomp and the inner emptiness. Over the years I had formed, from pictures and books, images in my mind depicting the Holy See and the Holy City. Could Rome be this same city? At the Angelicum University I was also shocked that hundreds of others who poured into our morning classes seemed quite disinterested in theology. I noticed *Time* and *Newsweek* magazines being read during classes. And many of those who were interested in what was being taught seemed only to be looking for either degrees or positions within the Catholic Church in their homelands.

One day I went for a walk in the Colosseum so that my feet might tread the ground where the blood of so many Christians had been poured out. I walked to the arena in the Forum. I tried to picture in my mind those men and women who knew Christ so well that they had been joyfully willing to be burned at the stake or devoured alive by beasts because of His overpowering love. The joy of this experience was marred, however, for as I returned by bus to our quarters I was insulted by jeering youths shouting words meaning "scum or garbage". I sensed that their motivation for such insults was not because I stood for Christ as the early Christians had done, but because they saw in me

7

the Roman Catholic system. Quickly I put this contrast out of my mind; yet what I had been taught about the present glories of Rome now seemed very irrelevant and empty.

One night soon after that, I prayed for two hours in front of the main altar in the church of San Clemente. Remembering my earlier youthful call to be a missionary and the hundredfold promise of Mark 10:29-30, I decided not to take the theological degree that had been my ambition since beginning study of the theology of Thomas Aquinas. This was a major decision, but after long prayer I was sure I had decided correctly. The priest who was to direct my thesis did not want to accept my decision. In order to make attainment of the degree easier, he offered me a thesis written several years earlier. He said I could use it as my own if only I would do the oral defense. This turned my stomach. It was similar to what I had seen a few weeks earlier in a city park: elegant prostitutes parading themselves in their black leather boots. What he was offering was equally sinful. I held to my decision, finishing at the University at the ordinary academic level without the degree.

On returning to Ireland from Rome, I received official word that I had been assigned to do a three year course at Cork University. I prayed earnestly about my missionary call. To my surprise, I received orders in late August 1964 to go to Trinidad, West Indies, as a missionary.

Pride, fall, and a new hunger
On October 1, 1964, I arrived in Trinidad, and for seven years I was a successful priest in Roman Catholic terms, doing all my duties and increasing substantially the number of people who came to Mass. By 1972 I had become quite involved in the Catholic Charismatic Movement. Then, at a prayer meeting on March 16th of that year, I had the temerity to thank the Lord that I was such a good priest and requested that if it were His will, He humble me that I might be even better. Later that same evening I had a freak accident, splitting the back of my head and injuring my spine in many places. Without coming close to death, I doubt that I would ever have risen out of my self-satisfied state. Set, rote prayer showed its emptiness as I cried out to God in my pain.

In the suffering that I went through in the weeks after the accident, I began to find some comfort in direct personal prayer. I stopped saying the Breviary (the Roman Catholic Church's official prayer for clergy) and the Rosary and began to pray using parts of the Bible itself. This was a very slow process. I did not know my way through the Bible and the little I had learned over the years had taught me more to distrust it rather than to trust it. My training in philosophy and in the theology of Thomas Aquinas had left me helpless, so that coming into the Bible now to find the Lord was like going into a huge dark woods without a map.

When assigned to a new parish later that year, I found that I was to work side-by-side with a Dominican priest who had been like a brother to me over the years. For more than two years we were to work together, fully seeking God as best we knew in the parish of Pointe-a-Pierre. We read, studied, prayed, and put into practice what we had been taught in Church teaching. We built up communities in Gasparillo, Claxton Bay, and Marabella, just to mention the main villages. In a Catholic religious sense we were very successful. Many people attended Mass. The Catechism was taught in many schools, including government schools. I continued my personal search into the Bible, but it did not much affect the work we were doing; rather it showed me how little I really knew about the Lord and His Word. It was at this time that Philippians 3:10 became the cry of my heart, *"That I may know him, and the power of his resurrection...."*

About this time, the Catholic Charismatic Movement was growing, and we introduced it into most of our villages. Because of this movement, some Canadian Christians came to Trinidad to share with us. I learned much from their messages, especially about praying for healing. The whole impact of what they said was very experience-oriented but was truly a blessing insofar as it got me deeply into the Bible as a source of authority. I began to compare scripture with scripture and even to quote chapter and verse! One of the texts the Canadians used was Isaiah 53:5, *"...and with his stripes we are healed."* Yet in studying Isaiah 53, I discovered that the Bible deals with the problem of sin by means of substitution. Christ died in my place. It was wrong for me to try to expedite or try to cooperate in paying the price of my sin. *"If by grace, it is no more of works, otherwise grace is no more grace..."*[2] *"All we like sheep have gone astray; we have turned every one to his own way; and the LORD hath laid on him the iniquity of us all."*[3]

One particular sin of mine was getting annoyed with people, sometimes even angry. Although I asked forgiveness for my sins, I still did not realize that I was a sinner by the nature that we all inherit from Adam. The Scriptural truth is, *"As it is written, There is none righteous, no, not one"*[4], and *"For all have sinned, and come short of the glory of God."*[5] The Catholic Church, however, had taught me that the depravity of man, which is called "original sin," had been washed away by my infant baptism. I still held this belief in my head, but in my heart I knew that my depraved nature had not yet been conquered by Christ. *"That I may know him, and the power of his resurrection..."*[6] continued to be the cry of my heart. I knew that it could be only through His power that I could live the Christian life. I posted this text on the dashboard of my car and in other places. It became the plea that motivated me, and the Lord Who is faithful began to answer.

The ultimate question
First, while I was visiting in Seattle and in Vancouver, British Columbia, I discovered that God's Word in the Bible is absolute and without error. I had been taught that the Word is relative and that its truthfulness in many areas was to be questioned. Now I began to understand that the Bible could, in fact, be trusted. With the aid of *Strong's Concordance*, I began to study the Bible to see what it says about itself. I discovered that the Bible teaches clearly that it is from God and is absolute in what it says. It is true in its history, in the promises God

---

[2] Romans 11:6
[3] Isaiah 53:6
[4] Romans 3:10
[5] Romans 3:23
[6] Philippians 3:10

has made, in its prophecies, in the moral commands it gives, and in its direction as to how to live the Christian life. *"All scripture is given by inspiration of God, and is profitable for doctrine, for reproof, for correction, for instruction in righteousness: That the man of God may be perfect, thoroughly furnished unto all good works."*[7]

Later during that same visit, I was asked to talk to the prayer group in St. Stephen's Catholic Church. I took as my subject the absolute authority of God's Word. It was the first time that I had understood such a truth or talked about it. From there, I returned to Vancouver, B.C., and in a large parish Church before about four hundred people, I preached the same message. Bible in hand, I proclaimed that "the absolute and final authority in all matters of faith and morals is the Bible, God's own Word." Three days later, the Archbishop of Vancouver, B.C., James Carney, called me to his office. I was then officially silenced and forbidden to preach in his archdiocese. I was told that my punishment would have been more severe, were it not for the letter of recommendation I had received from my own archbishop, Anthony Pantin. Soon afterwards I returned to Trinidad.

Church-Bible dilemma

While I was still parish priest of Point-a-Pierre, Ambrose Duffy, the man who had so strictly taught me while he was Student Master, was asked to assist me. The tide had turned. After some initial difficulties, we became close friends. I shared with him what I was discovering. He listened and commented with great interest and wanted to find out what was motivating me. I saw in him a channel to my Dominican brothers and even to those in the Archbishop's house. When he died suddenly of a heart attack, I was stricken with grief. In my mind, I had seen Ambrose as the one who could make sense out of the Church-Bible dilemma with which I so struggled. I had hoped that he would have been able to explain to me and then to my Dominican brothers the truths with which I wrestled. I preached at his funeral and my despair was very deep.

---

[7] II Timothy 3:16-17

I continued to pray Philippians 3:10, "*That I may know him, and the power of his resurrection....*" But to learn more about Him, I had first to learn about myself as a sinner. I saw from the Bible (I Timothy 2:5) that the role I was playing as a priestly mediator—exactly what the Catholic Church teaches but exactly opposite to what the Bible teaches—was wrong. I really enjoyed being looked up to by the people and, in a certain sense, being idolized by them. I rationalized my sin by saying that after all, if this is what the biggest Church in the world teaches, who am I to question it? Still, I struggled over the conflict within. I began to see the worship of Mary, the saints, and the priests for the sin that it is. But while I was willing to renounce Mary and the saints as mediators, I could not renounce the priesthood, for in that I had invested my whole life.

Tug-of-war years
Mary, the saints, and the priesthood were just a small part of the huge struggle with which I was working. Who was Lord of my life—Jesus Christ in His Word or the Roman Church? This ultimate question raged inside me especially during my last six years as parish priest of Sangre Grande (1979-1985). That the Catholic Church was supreme in all matters of faith and morals had been dyed into my brain since I was a child. It looked impossible ever to resolve the dilemma. Rome was not only supreme but always called "Holy Mother." How could I ever go against "Holy Mother", all the more so since I had an official part in dispensing her sacraments and keeping people faithful to her?

In 1981, I actually rededicated myself to serving the Roman Catholic Church while attending a parish renewal seminar in New Orleans. Yet when I returned to Trinidad and again became involved in real life problems, I began to return to the authority of God's Word. Finally the tension became like a tug-of-war inside me. Sometimes I looked to the Roman Church as being absolute, sometimes to the authority of the Bible as being final. My stomach suffered much during those years; my emotions were being torn. I ought to have recognized the simple truth that one cannot serve two masters. My working position was to place the absolute authority of the Word of God under the supreme authority of the Roman Church.

This contradiction was symbolized in what I did with the four statues in the Sangre Grande Church. I removed and broke the statues of St. Francis and St. Martin because the Second Commandment of God's Law declares in Exodus 20:4, *"Thou shalt not make unto thee any graven image...."* But when some of the people objected to my removal of the statues of the Sacred Heart and of Mary, I left them standing because the higher authority, i.e., the Roman Catholic Church, said in its law Canon 1188: "The practice of displaying sacred images in the churches for the veneration of the faithful is to remain in force." I did not see that what I was trying to do was to make God's Word subject to man's word.

My own fault

While I had learned earlier that God's Word is absolute, I still went through this agony of trying to operate as though the Roman Catholic Church holds more authority than God's Word, even in issues where the Church of Rome was saying the exact opposite to what was in the Bible. How could this be? First of all, it was my own fault. If I had accepted in both theory and practice the authority of the Bible as supreme, I would have been convicted by God's Word to give up my priestly role as mediator. My role as mediator, however, was too precious to me to even consider giving up, being the major part of my identity and my whole source of income. Second, no one ever questioned what I did as a priest. Christians from overseas came to Mass, saw our sacred oils, holy water, medals, statues, vestments, rituals, and never said a word! The marvelous style, symbolism, music, and artistic taste of the Roman Church was all very captivating. Incense not only smells pungent, but to the mind it spells mystery.

Turning point

One day, a woman challenged me (the only Christian ever to challenge me in all my twenty-two years as a priest), "You Roman Catholics have a form of godliness, but you deny its power." Those words bothered me for some time because the lights, banners, folk music, guitars, and drums were dear to me. Probably no priest on the whole island of Trinidad had as colorful robes, banners, and vestments as I had. Clearly I was unable to apply the Scripture to my life where it mattered most.

In October 1985, God's grace was greater than the lie that I was trying to live. I went to Barbados to pray over the compromise that I was forcing myself to live. I felt truly trapped. The Word of God is absolute indeed. I ought to obey it alone; yet to the very same God, I had vowed obedience to the supreme authority of the Catholic Church. In Barbados I read a book in which was explained the biblical meaning of Church as "the fellowship of believers." In the New Testament there is no hint of a hierarchy; "clergy" lording it over the "laity" is unknown. Rather, it is as the Lord Himself declared "...*one is your Master, even Christ; and all ye are brethren.*"[8] Now to see and to understand the meaning of church as "fellowship" left me free to let go of the Roman Catholic Church as supreme authority and depend on Jesus Christ as Lord. It began to dawn on me that in biblical terms, the bishops I knew in the Catholic Church were not biblical believers. They were for the most part pious men taken up with devotion to Mary and the Rosary and loyal to Rome, but not one had any idea of the finished work of salvation—that Christ's work is done, that salvation is personal and complete. They all preached penance for sin, human suffering, religious deeds, "the way of man" rather than the Gospel of grace. But by God's grace I saw that it was not through the Roman Church nor by any kind of works that one is saved, "*For by grace are ye saved through faith; and that not of yourselves: it is the gift of God: Not of works, lest any man should boast.*"[9]

New birth at age forty-eight

I left the Roman Catholic Church when I saw that life in Jesus Christ was not possible while remaining true to Roman Catholic doctrine. In leaving Trinidad in November 1985, I only reached neighboring Barbados. Staying with an elderly couple, I prayed to the Lord for a suit and necessary money to reach Canada, for I had only tropical clothing and a few hundred dollars to my name. Both prayers were answered without making my needs known to anyone except the Lord.

From a tropical temperature of 90 degrees, I landed in snow and ice in Canada. After one month in Vancouver, I came to the United

[8] Matthew 23:8
[9] Ephesians 2:8-9

States of America. I now trusted that He would take care of my many needs, since I was beginning life anew at forty-eight years of age, practically penniless, without an alien resident card, without a driver's license, without a recommendation of any kind, having only the Lord and His Word.

I spent six months with a Christian couple on a farm in Washington State. I explained to my hosts that I had left the Roman Catholic Church and that I had accepted Jesus Christ and His Word in the Bible as all-sufficient. I had done this, I said, "absolutely, finally, definitively, and resolutely." Yet far from being impressed by these four adverbs, they wanted to know if there was any bitterness or hurt inside me. In prayer and in great compassion, they ministered to me, for they themselves had made the transition and knew how easily one can become embittered. Four days after I arrived in their home, by God's grace I began to see in repentance the fruit of salvation. This meant being able not only to ask the Lord's pardon for my many years of compromising but also to accept His healing where I had been so deeply hurt. Finally, at age forty-eight, on the authority of God's Word alone, by grace alone, I accepted Christ's substitutionary death on the Cross alone. To Him alone be the glory.

Having been refurbished both physically and spiritually by this Christian couple together with their family, I was provided a wife by the Lord, Lynn, born-again in faith, lovely in manner, intelligent in mind. Together we set out for Atlanta, Georgia, where we both obtained jobs.

A real missionary with a real message
In September 1988, we left Atlanta to go as missionaries to Asia. It was a year of deep fruitfulness in the Lord that once I would never have thought was possible. Men and women came to know the authority of the Bible and the power of Christ's death and resurrection. I was amazed at how easy it is for the Lord's grace to be effective when only the Bible is used to present Jesus Christ. This contrasted so sharply with the cobwebs of church tradition that had so clouded my twenty-one years in missionary garments in Trinidad—twenty-one years without the real message.

To explain the abundant life of which Jesus spoke and which I now enjoy, no better words could be used than those of Romans 8:1-2: *"There is therefore now no condemnation to them which are in Christ Jesus, who walk not after the flesh, but after the Spirit. For the law of the Spirit of life in Christ Jesus hath made me free from the law of sin and death."* It is not just that I have been freed from the Roman Catholic system, but that I have become a new creature in Christ. It is by the grace of God—and nothing but His grace—that I have gone from dead works into new life.

The present day

My present task: the good work that the Lord has prepared for me to do is as an evangelist situated in central Texas, U.S.A. What Paul said about his fellow Jews I say about my dearly loved Catholic brothers: my heart's desire and prayer to God for Catholics is that they may be saved. I can testify about them that they are zealous for God, but their zeal is not based in God's Word but rather in their church tradition. If you understand the devotion and agony that some of our brothers and sisters in the Philippines and South America have put into their religion, you may understand my heart's cry, "Lord, give us a compassion to understand the pain and torment of the search our brothers and sisters have made to please You. In understanding pain inside the Catholic hearts, we will have the desire to show them the Good News of Christ's finished work on the Cross."

My testimony shows how difficult it was for me as a Catholic to give up Church tradition, but when the Lord demands it in His Word, we must do it. The "form of godliness" that the Roman Catholic Church has makes it most difficult for a Catholic to see where the real problem lies. Everyone must determine by what authority we identify truth. For Papal Rome, the ultimate authority lies in the decisions and decrees of the reigning Pope. In her own words, "The Supreme Pontiff, in virtue of his office, possesses infallible teaching authority when, as supreme pastor and teacher of all the faithful...he proclaims with a definitive act that a doctrine of faith or morals is to be held as such".[10] Yet according to the Bible, it is God's Word itself which is the authority by which truth is known. It was man-made traditions which caused the Reformers to demand "the Bible only, faith only, grace only, in Christ only, and to God only be the glory."

The reason why I share

I share these truths with you now so that you can know God's way of salvation. Our basic fault as Catholics is that we believe that somehow we can of ourselves respond to the help God gives us to be right in His sight. This presupposition that many of us have carried for years is aptly defined in the latest *Catechism of the Catholic Church*, "Grace is the help God gives us to respond to our vocation of becoming his adopted sons...."[11]

With that mindset, we were unknowingly holding to a teaching that the Bible continually condemns. Such a definition of grace is man's careful fabrication, for the Bible consistently declares that the believer's right standing with God is *"without works"*[12] , *"without the deeds of the Law"*[13] , *"not of works"*[14] , *"It is the gift of God,"*[15] . To attempt to make the believer's response part of his salvation and to look upon grace as "a help" is to flatly deny Biblical truth, *"...if by grace, then is it no more of works: otherwise grace is no more grace..."*[16] .

The simple biblical message is that "the gift of righteousness" in Christ Jesus is a gift, resting on His all-sufficient sacrifice on the cross, *"For if by one man's offence death reigned by one; much more they which receive abundance of grace and of the gift of righteousness shall reign in life by one, Jesus Christ"*[17] . So it is as Christ Jesus Himself said, He died in place of the believer, the One for many[18] , His

---

[10] *Code of Canon Law*, Latin-English ed. (Washington, DC: Canon Law Society of America, 1983) Canon 749

[11] *Catechism of the Catholic Church* (Mahwah, NJ: Paulist Press, 1994) Para. 2021

[12] Romans 4:6

[13] Romans 3:28

[14] Ephesians 2:9

[15] Ephesians 2:8

life a ransom for many. As He declared, "...*this is my blood of the new testament, which is shed for many for the remission of sins*"[19]. This is also what Peter proclaimed, "*For Christ also hath once suffered for sins, the just for the unjust, that He might bring us to God...*"[20]. Paul's preaching is summarized at the end of II Corinthians 5:21, "*For he hath made him to be sin for us, who knew no sin; that we might be made the righteousness of God in him....*" This fact is presented clearly in the Bible. Acceptance of it is now commanded by God, "...*Repent ye, and believe the gospel*"[21].

The most difficult repentance for us dyed-in-the-wool Catholics is changing our mindset from thoughts of "meriting", "earning", "being good enough", simply to accepting with empty hands the gift of righteousness in Christ Jesus. To refuse to accept what God commands is the same sin as that of the religious Jews of Paul's time, "*For they being ignorant of God's righteousness, and going about to establish their own righteousness, have not submitted themselves unto the righteousness of God.*"[22] Repent and believe the Good News! ◆

---

[16] Romans 11:6

[17] Romans 5:17

[18] Mark 10:45

[19] Matthew 26:28

[20] I Peter 3:18

[21] Mark 1:15

[22] Romans 10:3

Chapter 2

The Lord Gave His Word: Unshakable Authority

Regarding the subject of the unshakable authority of the Scripture, I understand the turmoil and doubt that can go on inside the Catholic heart. For many years I was also in turmoil over this very topic. It is of supreme importance that one comprehend that there is the unshakable authority—the written Word of God—because saving faith and the Scriptures are inseparable. One who counts on the power and fidelity of God shall be confident that he will receive the things He has promised, *"Now faith is the substance of things hoped for, the evidence of things not seen."*[1]   The Word of God is the objective foundation on which such a one's hope rests. Faith based on this secure authority is the expectation that the Lord God will perform all that He has promised to us who are in Christ, *"we believe and are sure."*[2] Because of this enduring link between the Scriptures and true faith, the Word must be studied in regards to its truthfulness. Call to remembrance, if you will, the lovely words of the Apostle Paul,*"[Love] rejoiceth not in iniquity, but rejoiceth in the truth."*[3]

Truth and the Scripture
The Lord Jesus Christ, in His great high priestly prayer, declared clearly the truth of God's Word. He said, *"Sanctify them through thy truth: thy word is truth."* God's Word not only contains the truth but is Truth itself. This is consistent with the declarations throughout the Old Testament in which the Holy Spirit continually proclaimed that the revelation from God is truth. The Lord Himself identified truth with the Written Word.

---

[1] Hebrews 11:1

[2] John 6:69

[3] I Corinthians 13:6

There is no source other than written Scripture alone, to which the statement, *"thy word is truth"*, can apply. That source alone—the Scripture—is the believer's standard of truth.

In the New Testament, it is the Written Word of God—and that alone—to which the Lord Jesus Christ and His apostles refer as the final authority. In the Temptation, the Lord Jesus three times resisted Satan, saying, *"It is written."*[4] In stating, *"it is written"*, the Lord showed His complete acceptance of the authority of the written Word. This is also evident in His words, *"Think not that I am come to destroy the law, or the prophets: I am not come to destroy, but to fulfill. For verily I say unto you, till heaven and earth pass, one jot or one tittle shall in no wise pass from the law, till all be fulfilled."*[5]

Other sources of authority condemned

Christ Jesus continually castigated and rebuked the Pharisees because they placed their tradition on a par with the Word of God. He condemned them because they were attempting to corrupt the very basis of truth by equating their traditions with the Word of God. He declared to them that they were *"making the word of God of none effect through your tradition, which ye have delivered."*[6] These traditions of the Pharisees were precepts, ordinances, and rules of religious belief and practice that had been developed over time by learned religious teachers. They had been passed on by word of mouth and by selectively edited writings. These traditions, both oral and written, formed a body of cultural material that became an official set of interpretations and guidelines for religious life. Even the clear teaching of the Holy Scripture was being sifted by them and modified to suit men's tastes and preferences. Furthermore, in refuting the errors of the Sadducees, the Lord declared, *"Ye do err, not knowing the Scriptures, nor the power of God."*[7]

---

[4] Matthew 4:4, 7, 10.

[5] Matthew 5:17-18

[6] Mark 7:13

[7] Matthew 22:29

Since the Scripture alone is inspired, it alone is the ultimate authority. It alone is the final judge of all human traditions and reasoning. The Word of the Lord teaches, "*Every word of God is pure: he is a shield unto them that put their trust in him.*"[8] It then immediately commands in the next verse, "*Add thou not unto his words, lest he reprove thee, and thou be found a liar.*" This teaching and command shows emphatically that it is God's Word alone that is pure and uncontaminated. The truth is this: since God alone breathes out His written Word, it—and it alone—is the sole rule of faith. It cannot be otherwise. Any church that contradicts Scripture or attempts to assign to it an inferior position in the life of faith may safely be accounted as a liar and deceiver bent on moving God off His throne so that she may occupy the position of absolute authority herself.

The expression "Scripture alone"
From the time of the giving of the Ten Commandments on Mount Sinai (when the Holy God wrote with His finger on the tablets of stone[9]) until this present day, the written Word of God has been in existence in the world. The term "Sola Scriptura" or "the Scripture alone" is short hand for saying that Scripture is the only point of reference for finding out what is to be believed about God and what God requires of man. The very phrase "Scripture says" means that it is exclusively transcribed, and not hearsay. The command to believe what is written means we are to receive only the pure Word of God. It separates out from all other sources that body of truth which a person is to believe. At stake is God's incorruptible truth. For men, what is at stake is certainty, which is revealed in the words of Proverbs 22:21, "*[To] know the certainty of the words of truth.*" Certainty is needed for the salvation of immortal souls. In the very last commandment in Scripture, God resolutely commands that no one is to add to and no one is to take away from His Written Word. *"For I testify unto every man that heareth the words of the prophecy of this book, if any man shall add unto these things, God shall add unto him the plagues that are written in this book: and if any man shall take away from the*

---

[8] Proverbs 30:5

[9] Exodus 24: 12, 31:18, 32:15-16

words of the book of this prophecy, God shall take away his part out of the book of life, and out of the holy city, and from the things which are written in this book."[10]

Principle of interpretation

The principle of "Scripture alone" is consistent with the very way in which the word of truth that comes from God says it is to be interpreted, as Psalm 36:9 explains, *"For with thee is the fountain of life: in thy light shall we see light."* God's truth is seen in the light of God's truth. This is exactly the same as the Apostle Paul says, *"Which things also we speak, not in the words which man's wisdom teacheth, but which the Holy Ghost teacheth; comparing spiritual things with spiritual."*[11] It is precisely in the light shed by God's truth that His truth is seen. Scripture provides its own rule of interpretation. The Apostle Peter, under the impulse of the Holy Spirit, declares, *"Knowing this first, that no prophecy of the scripture is of any private interpretation. For the prophecy came not in old time by the will of man: but holy men of God spake as they were moved by the Holy Ghost."*[12] Peter makes it clear that in order to maintain the purity of Scripture, the source of interpretation must be from the same pure source as the origin of the Scripture itself. It is only with the Holy Spirit's light that Scripture can be comprehended correctly. The Holy Spirit causes those who are the Lord's own to understand Scripture. Since the Spirit does this by Scripture, the same principle is at work: Scripture itself is the rule of interpretation of its own truth, *"and it is the Spirit that beareth witness, because the Spirit is truth."*[13]

Those sincerely desiring to be true to the Lord in this very matter of the standard of "Scripture alone" must obey His command, *"Turn you at my reproof: behold, I will pour out my spirit unto you, I will make known my words unto you."*[14] One who is yearning for truth in

---

[10] Revelation 22:18-19

[11] I Corinthians 2:13

[12] II Peter 1:20, 21

[13] I John 5:6

[14] Proverbs 1:23

22

this essential matter must take the attitude of Psalm 51:17, "*a broken and a contrite heart, O God, thou wilt not despise.*" The Lord God will not despise but rather reveal the basic foundational truths of the Lord Christ Jesus and the Apostles. In the words of the Apostle John, "*This is the disciple which testifieth of these things, and wrote these things: and we know that his testimony is true.*"[15] The Apostle John wrote, as did Peter and Paul, in order that those who are made right with God should know that His testimony is true.

Sufficiency and clarity of Scripture

The total sufficiency of Scripture is declared by the Apostle Paul, "*All scripture is given by inspiration of God, and is profitable for doctrine, for reproof, for correction, for instruction in righteousness: that the man of God may be perfect, thoroughly furnished unto all good works.*"[16] For final truth and authority, all that is needed is the Scripture. This is because the Word of God bears its own spiritual rule of historical-grammatical interpretation. Parts of Scripture in which the meaning is plain clarify sections that initially appear obscure. The Holy Spirit Himself is given to the believer so that by prayer and diligent comparative study, both knowledge of the Gospel and the will of God are made clear to him. By comparing Scripture with Scripture under the illuminating ministry of the Holy Spirit, the renewed reader is safeguarded from the danger of imaginative, self-centered, mystical deceit and from religious fanaticism and cultic heresies. Natural men, those not made alive by the Holy Spirit and indwelt by Him, have only their darkened understandings to guide them. Of them the Scripture says, "*But the natural man receiveth not the things of the Spirit of God: for they are foolishness unto him: neither can he know them, because they are spiritually discerned.*"[17]

The Scriptures are so plain that even a child can come to faith through the written Word. The Apostle Paul writes to Timothy, "*From a child thou hast known the holy scriptures, which are able to make*

---

[15] John 21:24
[16] II Timothy 3:16, 17
[17] I Corinthians 2:14

thee wise unto salvation through faith which is in Christ Jesus."[18]
Much of the Scripture is quite plain and straightforward. For example,
John 3:36 says, "*He that believeth on the Son hath everlasting life:
and he that believeth not the Son shall not see life; but the wrath
of God abideth on him.*" The meaning in this verse is clear and to the
point, as is most of Scripture.

The claim that "Scripture alone" was not possible

In an attempt to justify tradition as an authority, an appeal is often made
to the very last verse in John's gospel where it is stated, "*and there are
also many other things which Jesus did, the which, if they should
be written every one, I suppose that even the world itself could not
contain the books that should be written.*"[19]   Of course, there were
many deeds and sayings of the Lord that are not recorded in Scripture.
But Scripture remains the authoritative record that the Holy Spirit has
given to His people. We do not have a single sentence that is authori-
tatively from the Lord outside of what is in the written Word of the New
Testament. To appeal to a tradition for authority that the Holy Spirit
has not given is futile. The idea that somehow sayings and events from
the Lord had been passed on by word of mouth and are preserved
reliably in tradition is simply not true. Given the fluid nature of language,
the fragility of verbal communication, and the unstable nature of human
memory, such a claim is ludicrous. To believe in the traditions of men
requires a superstitious naivety of spirit and irrational gullibility. The
Scripture even gives an example of a false tradition already at work at
the time of John's writing of his Gospel. John refutes the false tradition,
"*then went this saying abroad among the brethren, that that
disciple should not die.*"[20]   That rumor, that the Lord would return
before John died, was not the written Word of truth; nevertheless it had
gone around the church in John's time.

Another desperate attempt to justify tradition is the claim that
the early Church did not have the New Testament. However, the Apostle

---

[18] II Timothy 3:15
[19] John 21:25
[20] John 21:23

Peter speaks about the writings of the Apostle Paul when he states, "...*even as our beloved brother Paul also according to the wisdom given unto him hath written unto you; As also in all his epistles, speaking in them of these things; in which are some things hard to be understood, which they that are unlearned and unstable wrest, as they do also the other scriptures, unto their own destruction.*"[21] Peter also declares that he was writing so that the believers could remember what he said. So he wrote, "*Wherefore I will not be negligent to put you always in remembrance of these things, though ye know them, and be established in the present truth.*"[22]

From the earliest times, a substantial part of the New Testament was available. Under the inspiration of the Lord, the Apostle Paul commands his letters to be read in other churches besides those to which they were sent. This clearly shows that the written Word of God was being circulated even while the Apostles lived. The Lord's command to believe what is written has always been something that the believers could and did obey. In this matter one must have the humility "*not to think above that which is written.*" In the words of the Apostle, "*And these things, brethren, I have in a figure transferred to myself and to Apollos for your sakes; that ye might learn in us **not to think of men above that which is written***, *that no one of you be puffed up for one against another.*"[23]

The absurd rationale that tradition is needed because the early Church did not have the New Testament ignores two very simple facts concerning God's provision for the early Church.[24] Before the canon of the New Testament was complete, the Apostles were present as Christ's personally commissioned ambassadors, endowed with His authority. Then even during the transitional stage, the Apostles had neither difficulty in preaching the Gospel from the Old Testament Scriptures nor in using

---

[21] II Peter 3:15, 16

[22] II Peter 1:12

[23] I Corinthians 4:6

[24] Appendix I deals more fully with the topic of the Scripture given to the early church.

them as an authoritative guide for all matters of faith and morals.[25] The New Testament writings were incorporated and received into the canon of Holy Scripture when the last surviving Apostle had completed his work. Written revelation was at an end because the final prophetic word on salvation had been given, in and from the Lord Jesus Christ.

The Regulation and the believer's love of God

The believer cannot say he loves the Lord Jesus Christ unless his trust is totally in the very words of Christ. This again underscores the importance of Scripture. *"Jesus answered and said unto him, if a man love me, he will keep my words: and my Father will love him, and we will come unto him, and make our abode with him. He that loveth me not keepeth not my sayings: and the word which ye hear is not mine, but the Father's which sent me."*[26] And again, *"Heaven and earth shall pass away, but my words shall not pass away."*[27] Living His own life in this world to the glory of His Father, the Lord Jesus could say, *"And he that sent me is with me: the Father hath not left me alone; for I do always those things that please him."*[28] In His supreme aim to please His Father, Christ Jesus looked to the authority and direction of the Scriptures. He confirmed the very message of the Old Testament, *"the law of the LORD is perfect, converting the soul: the testimony of the LORD is sure, making wise the simple."*[29]

The believer is to be true to the way of the Lord by holding only to what is written: *"thy word is truth."* All true disciples must acknowledge that there is an absolute measure by which a thing may be judged to be truth or falsehood, as well as pleasing or displeasing to God. In times past, that standard was called "the rule of faith" or "the basis of truth", meaning the measure by which truth is known. This principle, clearly demonstrated in both the Old and New Testaments, is that the written Word of God *itself* is the basis of truth. It is not

---

[25] Acts 17:2- 18:28, 28:23; Galatians 3:8; Romans 9:17

[26] John 14:23, 24

[27] Matthew 24:35

[28] John 8:29

[29] Psalm 19:7

possible to own the Lord Jesus Christ as Master and then refuse the rule of the Father's Word in and by Him. There is no "halfway house" here in which the pretense of an anti-Scriptural piety can find safe-haven. It is a clear choice. If you love God you love His Word alone, not His Word plus the words of men. You cannot say you love God and despise His Word, for the marks of authentic spiritual affection are patent in the Word itself, *"to this man will I look, even to him that is poor and of a contrite spirit, and trembleth at my word."*[30]

Catholic Church's source of authority

With heaviness of heart I now address the Catholic Church's source of authority, remembering all the many years when I likewise instructed men, women and children in the doctrine that is to follow.

The Catholic Church is forthright in stating where her certainty regarding doctrine lies. She officially teaches,
"As a result the [Catholic] Church, to whom the transmission and interpretation of Revelation is entrusted, 'does not derive her certainty about all revealed truths from the holy Scriptures alone. Both Scripture and Tradition must be accepted and honored with equal sentiments of devotion and reverence.'"[31]
This statement is a formal denial of the sufficiency of Scripture. And it is a repudiation of the Scripture's unique authority—for Scripture alone is vested with all the moral authority of God over His creatures. That a Church claims to be Christian while simultaneously affirming her equal love for Tradition and the Scripture is to make the Scripture to be of no worth. It is like a husband who declares that he loves his wife while he at the same time states that he also loves equally his secretary. Even as such love is adulterous, so also is the Vatican's "equal sentiments of devotion and reverence" for her Tradition. This "devotion and reverence" translates into an unfaithfulness and rejection of Scripture as the final authority.

---

[30] Isaiah 66:2
[31] *Catechism of the Catholic Church,* Second Ed. (United States Catholic Conference, Inc—Libreria Editrice Vaticana, 1997) Para. 82. All catechism quotations taken from this edition unless otherwise stated.

Superior position of tradition in Catholicism

The very nature of any authority is that it is self-governing. The life of faith must have a sovereign authority. If two authorities rule faith then it is destined for failure because one authority will dominate the other. The Vatican's pretense of an equal "devotion and reverence" for both Scripture and Tradition is merely the ecclesiastical equivalent to the authority principle of Orwell's famous barnyard where it was declared that all animals are equal, but with the qualifier that some animals are more equal than others. With the Vatican, Tradition is always the " committee chairman" with the deciding vote on matters of authority. That is how Rome lives out and continually enforces her rules. For example, in the "Profession of Faith", the Council of Trent, the formula for submission is given with these words,

> "The apostolic and ecclesiastical traditions and all other observances and constitutions of that same Church I most firmly admit and embrace. **I likewise accept Holy Scripture according to that sense which our holy Mother Church has held and does hold,** whose [office] it is to judge of the true meaning and interpretation of the Sacred Scriptures; **I shall never accept nor interpret it otherwise than in accordance with the unanimous consent of the Fathers**."[32]

Thus the seat of authority, or the rule of faith, is firmly in the hands of the Roman hierarchy. The men who make up the hierarchy are "holy Mother Church". They sit in judgment on the Scriptures. The end result is that the Catholic person ends up believing not the Almighty God and His written Word, but rather holy Mother Church and her Tradition. This way of thinking is drilled into the minds of "the Catholic faithful".

An example of how Holy Mother governs is found in the *Catechism of the Catholic Church*, "As a mother who teaches her children to speak and so to understand and communicate, the Church our Mother teaches us the language of faith in order to introduce us to the understanding and the life of faith."[33] However, on the most important

---

[32] Henry Denzinger, *The Sources of Catholic Dogma*, Tr. by Roy J Deferrari from *Enchiridion Symbolorum*, 30th ed. (St. Louis, MO: B. Herder Book Co., 1957) # 995. Throughout the book, bolding in any quotation indicates emphasis added by this author.

topic of trusting Christ alone, whom the Scriptures proclaim as the all-sufficient Savior, the same teaching authority requires that souls look to her maternal care rather than to fix their eyes on Christ Jesus alone. She officially declares,

"'Believing' is an ecclesial act. The Church's faith precedes, engenders, supports and nourishes our faith. The Church is the mother of all believers. 'No one can have God as Father who does not have the Church as Mother.'"[34]

The Lord Christ threatens those who offend His little ones or who willfully are the occasion of sin to them. Anyone who shall grieve souls, though they be of the weakest, by opposing their entrance into the ways of God, it would be better for him that a millstone were hung about his neck and he were cast into the sea, for his final end will be in the fire that never shall be quenched. What then is the destiny of a whole Church system that teaches, "Both Scripture and Tradition must be accepted and honored with equal sentiments of devotion and reverence"?

Claimed lordship of the Pope

Within Catholicism, the basis for truth, while absolute, is not the unqualified authority of God in Scripture; rather it is the authority of a man, the Pope of Rome. The ultimate authority lies in the decisions and decrees of the reigning Pope. This is seen in documentation from official Catholic sources, as Vatican canon law declares,

"The Supreme Pontiff, in virtue of his office, possesses **infallible teaching authority** when, as supreme pastor and teacher of all the faithful...he proclaims with a definitive act that a doctrine of faith or morals is to be held as such."[35]

The mandated response of "the Christian faithful" to this claimed infallible teaching authority is spelled out in Canon 752, "A religious respect of intellect and will, even if not the assent of faith, is to be paid to the teaching which the Supreme Pontiff...." Any entreaty against the

---

[33] *Catechism*, Para. 171

[34] *Catechism*, Para 181

[35] *Code of Canon Law*, Can. 749

totalitarian imposition of a claimed infallibility is silenced by the decree of Canon 333 Sec. 3, "There is neither appeal nor recourse against a decision or decree of the Roman Pontiff."

According to the Scripture, however, infallibility is an attribute of God and not that of any man or group of men. Eternity, omniscience, and infallibility are among God's attributes or properties of His Being that cannot be passed or delegated to creatures. God declares that He cannot lie and that "*before me, there was no God formed, neither shall there be after me.*"[36] Yet the papal claim to "infallible teaching authority" is essentially a claim to divinity. The Vatican's doctrine flaunts the claim that the Pope is "The Holy Father".[37] Nothing more strikingly displays the arrogance of the Papacy than this appalling claim to infallibility. The Pope, in setting himself up as supreme, has *de facto* denied the absolute authority of God!

Alleged infallibility and the facts of history
That a human power should claim infallibility to be "as God" defies imagination. In aping God's attribute of infallibility, the system of Rome not only mocks the Godhead and His truth, but it also denies the facts of history. Pope Honorious (625-638) was condemned as a heretic by the Sixth Ecumenical Council (680-681 A.D.). He was also condemned as a heretic by Pope Leo II, as well as by every other Pope until the eleventh century. So there were "infallible" Popes condemning another "infallible" Pope as a heretic. There was even one Pope who, himself, denied the infallibility of the office. The Catholic historian, August Bernard Hasler, writes, "but [Pope] John XXII did not want to hear about his own infallibility; he viewed it an improper restriction of his rights as a sovereign, and in the bull *Qui quorundam* (1324) condemned

---

[36] Titus 1:2, Isaiah 43:10

[37] *The Catholic Encyclopedia,* Robert Broderick, ed. (Nashville, TN: Thos. Nelson Inc., 1976) p. 217. Entry under Father: "Holy Father is a title of the pope alone. God the Father is the First person of the Blessed Trinity."

the Franciscan doctrine of papal infallibility as the work of the devil."[38]
The Vatican's declaration of claimed infallibility is demolished by the
Lord's commandment, "*I am the LORD thy God ... Thou shalt have
no other gods before me.*"[39] The same alleged infallibility is seen,
although in different terminology, in Rome's declaration that her tradition
is divinely inspired.

Rome claims her tradition is sacred

To maintain her pomp, ceremonies, and sacraments, Rome officially
states that her Tradition is sacred,

> "Sacred Tradition and Sacred Scripture, then, are bound closely
> together and communicate one with the other. For both of them,
> flowing out from the same divine wellspring, come together in some
> fashion to form one thing and move towards the same goal."[40]

Rome claims not only that Sacred Tradition has the same source as the
Scripture and forms "one thing" with it, also that her Holy Tradition
transmits in its entirety God's Word. She declares,

> "*Sacred Scripture* is the speech of God as it is put down in writing
> under the breath of the Holy Spirit. **And [Holy]** *Tradition* **transmits
> in its entirety** the Word of God which has been entrusted to the
> apostles by Christ the Lord and the Holy Spirit. It transmits it to
> the successors of the apostles so that, enlightened by the Spirit of
> truth, they may faithfully preserve, expound, and spread it abroad
> by their preaching."[41]

Such teaching dishonors God's Holy Name and is a profanity
against His Holy Word. The Scripture teaches that the Written Word
of God cannot be commingled with anything else. The Lord Jesus
Christ's himself said, "*the scripture cannot be broken.*"[42] "*Is not my*

---

[38] August Bernard Hasler, *How the Pope Became Infallible: Pius IX and the
Politics of Persuasion* (Garden City, NY: Doubleday & Co., Inc., 1981) pp. 36, 37.
Originally published in German under the title *Wie der Papst Unfehlbar Wurde*
(Verlag, Munchen: R. Piper & Co., 1979).

[39] Exodus 20:2-3

[40] *Catechism*, Para. 80

[41] *Catechism*, Para. 81, square brackets and italic in the original.

[42] John 10:35

word like as a fire? saith the Lord; and like a hammer that breaketh the rock in pieces?"[43]   The Catholic assertion that "Holy *Tradition* transmits in its entirety the Word of God" is literally a blasphemy against the Holy Spirit. The Holy Spirit himself communicates His Word to believers. It is not the Holy Spirit's endeavor to transmit an unholy Tradition that upholds idolatry, superstition, and necromancy. *"So shall my word be that goeth forth out of my mouth: it shall not return unto me void, but it shall accomplish that which I please, and it shall prosper in the thing whereto I sent it."*[44]   It is true faith that the Spirit of God seals in the hearts of believers, as He alone is the Spirit of truth. By His own divine light, efficacy, and power, the testimony of the Holy Spirit is given to all believers in the Written Word. The Holy Spirit's communication of His own light and authority to the Scripture is the evidence of its origin. The Holy Spirit brings His Word to believers.

Tradition as it is used in the Catholic storehouse
The Vatican's declaration that "Holy *Tradition* transmits in its entirety the Word of God" not only denigrates the divine Person of the Holy Spirit, but it also leads one to look to Tradition rather than on the divine Person of the Holy Spirit to open the Word to him or her. That this is the very desire of Rome is emphasized by her use of italics in the beginning of Paragraph 113 of her latest *Catechism*, *"Read the Scripture within the 'living Tradition of the whole Church.'"*   Then Rome goes so far as to reprimand those who stray because she states there is "…the tendency to read and to interpret Sacred Scripture outside the Tradition and Magisterium of the Church."[45]   The Church of Rome in her "Tradition and Magisterium" leaves room for paying divine honors to the supposed relics of martyrs, erecting altars, burning incense, consecrating images and temples, and making prayers and praises to the honor of saints departed, etc. Thus false worship is taught and practiced to the exclusion of the Holy Spirit's direct leading and teaching.

---

[43] Jeremiah 23:29

[44] Isaiah 55:11

[45] "DOMINUS IESUS" September 5th 2000 http://www.vatican.va/roman_curia/ congregations/ cfaith/documents/rc_con_cfaith_doc_20000806_dominus- iesus_en.html

The Vatican's instruction is literally soul damning in the words of the Lord, *"Woe unto you, lawyers! for ye have taken away the key of knowledge: ye entered not in yourselves, and them that were entering in ye hindered."*[46]

The Apostle Paul urges the believer to look to the *"...demonstration of the Spirit and of power: That your faith should not stand in the wisdom of men, but in the power of God."*[47] Just as a fresh supply of manna was given each day to the Israelites in the desert, so the Spirit of God ever breaks anew the Scriptures to those who hunger and thirst for righteousness. Therefore, it is incumbent on all who love Catholics to faithfully direct them away from the words of men, and toward the Scripture wherein they may find One Who said, *"He that believeth on me, as the scripture hath said, out of his belly shall flow rivers of living water."*[48]

Claim that apostolic succession upholds tradition

Under the heading *"The Apostolic Tradition"* and the sub heading *"...continued in apostolic succession"*, Rome claims the following,

> "In order that the full and living Gospel might always be preserved in the Church the apostles left bishops as their successors. They gave them 'their own position of teaching authority.' Indeed, 'the apostolic preaching, which is expressed in a special way in the inspired books, was to be preserved in **a continuous line of succession** until the end of time.' This living transmission, accomplished in the Holy Spirit, is called Tradition, since it is distinct from Sacred Scripture, though closely connected to it."[49]

Nowhere in Scripture is there reference to "a continuous line of succession" (which amounts to "apostolic succession"). In the New Testament the Apostles did not appoint other apostles but rather elders and deacons. Nonetheless Rome attempts to defend her position in the name of a continuous line of succession from the Apostles.[50] If one

---

[46] Luke 11:52

[47] I Corinthians 2:4, 5

[48] John 7:38

[49] *Catechism*, Para. 77, 78

wants to use the concept of "apostolic succession", the true successors of the Apostles are the saints of the household of God who "*are built upon the foundation of the apostles and prophets, Jesus Christ himself being the chief corner stone.*"[51] If that doctrinal foundation is destroyed, one does not have apostolic faith; rather he has apostasy. "Apostolic succession" without apostolic doctrine is a fraud. It is only scriptural doctrine that makes one wise unto salvation through faith that is in Christ Jesus.

Blasphemy against the Holy Spirit
A frank examination of the Catholic Church's doctrine of authority leads to the conclusion that her claim to authority is not simply without true biblical foundation, but it also is an attempt to usurp completely the divine authority of the Lord God in His Written Word. "Holy Mother Church" in biblical terms is neither holy nor strictly speaking a "church". She is rather the clear successor to the Imperial Roman Empire, the spirit and character of which is embodied in her arrogant law, traditions and pagan customs. (This we will more fully describe and document in Chapter Four.)

Calling her tradition sacred, accepted and honored on a par with the written Word of God while presumptuously assuming such preposterous claims as papal infallibility, is in the strict sense of the term a blasphemy against the Holy Spirit. That is why there can never be any negotiation, compromise, or alliance between the Vatican and the Bride of Christ. The "Temple curia" of the Pharisees, in the Lord's time, identified themselves with all that was good, upright, and holy. There was no question in their minds but that God worked wholly in, by, and through their teachings and administrations. Christ Jesus, however, proved them to be "*like unto whited sepulchres, which*

---

[50] The Pharisees of Jesus' time had their basic allegiance to a "living Torah". For them Scripture did not mean a finished revelation. Their real loyalty was to a living knowledge they claimed came through Tradition from Moses. In precisely the same way, the system of Rome claims a "living transmission" called Tradition by means of apostolic succession.

[51] Ephesians 2:20

indeed appear beautiful outward, but are within full of dead men's bones, and of all uncleanness."[52]   In a similar manner, the proud privileges and claims of the Roman system to be the very mouthpiece of God are shown by the Word of the Lord to be "*seducing spirits, and doctrines of devils*."[53]

The Holy Spirit, foreseeing all these things, as the guide and Comforter of the true Church, has graciously provided a divine answer for the dangerous, ubiquitous, and deceiving system of Rome and her fabricated authority base. God Himself, Who began the writing of the Word with His own finger, has in these last days spoken to us "*by his Son*."[54] This Son authenticated the writings of the Old Testament and, as the Alpha and Omega, having all authority in heaven and on earth, authorized the New Testament and commanded its writing in His words to the Apostle John, "*what thou seest, write in a book*."[55] The Lord Jesus Christ's mind and counsel come to the believers in writing. The Scripture is given as a merciful and steadfast relief against all that is confusion, darkness, and uncertainty, including the Catholic Church. In our precious Lord we truly praise God for the treasure and confidence that we have in the Scripture, which is truth, for "*all scripture is given by inspiration of God, and is profitable for doctrine, for reproof, for correction, for instruction in righteousness that the man of God may be perfect, thoroughly furnished unto all good works*."[56]

Faith, the written Word of God, and salvation
There is an inseparable bond between the certainty of the Scriptures and saving faith. Faith is the gift of God that comes by the Word of God, "*faith cometh by hearing, and hearing by the word of God*."[57] Faith must have a foundation on which to rest. That underpinning can be nothing else but the Word of Him that cannot lie. The heart must

---

[52] Matthew 23:27
[53] I Timothy 4:1
[54] Hebrews 1:2
[55] Revelation 1:11
[56] II Timothy 3:16, 17
[57] Romans 10:17

receive and act on what He says. The Holy Spirit makes the Word of God operative when through it He speaks to the soul. The Bible teaches that it is through faith that the believer is justified before God, "*a man is justified by faith without the deeds of the law.*"[58]   What is the arrangement or power by which a man is justified? The Scripture asks the same question, "*by what law? of works? nay: but by the law of faith.*"[59]   Believers are not left in confusion. It is the law of faith that is also the working of grace, excluding all boasting, bringing utter conviction and power. Faith is the conduit for a dependent, self-denying grace that casts away every doubt before the absolute certainty of God's Word. By faith—that is, by relying upon God's veracity—one enters into the reality of life in Christ Jesus "*with joy unspeakable and full of glory.*"[60]

We are constantly acting on the belief that what others say is true, such as believing what the members of our families say is true, and what is sworn to in courts of justice is true. The Apostle John reasons, "*if we receive the witness of men, the witness of God is greater: for this is the witness of God which he hath testified of his Son. He that believeth on the Son of God hath the witness in himself: he that believeth not God hath made him a liar; because he believeth not the record that God gave of his Son. And this is the record that God hath given to us eternal life, and this life is in his Son. He that hath the Son hath life; and he that hath not the Son of God hath not life.*"[61]   Faith, then, is the bond of union between the soul and the Lord. By believing on Christ, His righteousness is credited to us, and we are approved of by God.

The foolish are those who are "*slow of heart to believe all that the prophets have spoken.*"[62]   The foolish have misgivings about the written Word of God or place something else on a par with the

---

[58] Romans 3:28

[59] Romans 3:27

[60] I Peter 1:8

[61] I John 5:9-12

[62] Luke 24:25

written Word, and thus nullify to themselves its authority and power. Both errors miss the mark of having eternal life in Christ. What is extremely serious is a Church which claims that its people must love their church traditions as much as they love the written Word because purportedly the two are one. If such were the teaching of a Church, it would remove the very foundation on which saving faith is based. But at this point we rejoice in having seen the adequacy, truth, and certainty of God's written Word. *"The holy scriptures,"* declares the Apostle Paul, *"are able to make thee wise unto salvation through faith which is in Christ Jesus."*[63] There is no book that has so much power as the Bible. None is so capable of moving the hearts, consciences, and minds of mankind. *"For the word of God is quick, and powerful, and sharper than any two edged sword, piercing even to the dividing asunder of soul and spirit, and of the joints and marrow, and is a discerner of the thoughts and intents of the heart."*[64] The critical question is whether one has both trusted its absolute veracity and also the Lord of glory of whom it speaks. If so, we can together with joy say, *"Christ died for our sins according to the scriptures; and that he was buried, and that he rose again the third day according to the scriptures."*[65] *"For I know whom I have believed, and am persuaded that he is able to keep that which I have committed unto him against that day."*[66] ◆

---

[63] II Timothy 3:15

[64] Hebrews 4:12

[65] I Corinthians 15:3-4

[66] II Timothy 1:12

Chapter 3

The Mystique of the Catholic Priesthood

One might wonder what remains of the glory of the Catholic priesthood in face of the worldwide scandals, and in particular those that have occurred recently in the U.S.A. For example, on July 7th 2003 under the heading "Clergy Sex Abuse: Justice Must Come for the Bishops", the *San Francisco Chronicle* reported,

"That there are some sinful priests should not itself cause a crisis of faith. In fact, it is a matter of Catholic faith that all men and women are born sinners—and priests are not immune from sin or human nature. But the number of victims and the years that this abuse spans is simply staggering. The real outrage is that it took so long for these men to be brought to justice and that this abuse was allowed to go on for so long. And that is no accident…How does one begin to understand how such a problem could have been allowed to fester for so long? The nature of a celibate all-male clergy, the culture of secrecy and the inclination to protect their fellow priests certainly played a central role."[1]

On July 23rd 2003, the Massachusetts' Attorney General published a report stating that the Roman Catholic Church abuse scandal in Boston most likely involved more than one thousand victims, causing even more astonishment regarding the state of the Catholic priesthood. The summary report stated,

"The Attorney General's investigation revealed that the magnitude of the Archdiocese's history of clergy sexual abuse of children is staggering. Records produced by the Archdiocese reveal

---

[1] http://sfgate.com/cgi-bin/article.cgi?f=/c/a/2003/07/07/ED262205.DTL 7/21/03. *San Francisco Chronicle*, 7/7/03 by James Hammer, Assistant District Attorney in San Francisco and a former Jesuit seminarian (1988-95).

complaints regarding at least 789 victims. When information from other sources is considered, the number of alleged victims who have disclosed their abuse likely exceeds one thousand. The magnitude of the Archdiocese's history of clergy sexual abuse is equally shocking if evaluated in terms of the number of priests and other Archdiocese workers alleged to have sexually abused children since 1940. The investigation revealed allegations of sexual abuse of children made against at least 237 priests and thirteen other Archdiocese workers. Of these 250 priests and other Archdiocese workers, 202 allegedly abused children between 1940 and 1984, with the other forty-eight allegedly abusing children during Cardinal Law's tenure as Archbishop."[2]

Another report surfaced in August, 2003, in the *Dallas Morning News*, "Roughly two-thirds of top U.S. Catholic leaders have allowed priests accused of sexual abuse to keep working, a systematic practice that spans decades and continues today, a three-month *Dallas Morning News* review shows. The study—the first of its kind— looked at the records of the top leaders of the nation's 178 mainstream Roman Catholic dioceses, including acting administrators in cases where the top job is vacant…Most protected priests were accused of sexually abusing minors—primarily adolescent boys, but also younger ones, and a sizable number of girls of various ages. The newspaper's study also covered behavior that indicated a sexual attraction to minors, such as viewing child pornography or, in one case, trading sexually charged e-mails with someone a priest believed was a minor."[3]

While the U.S.A. is entangled in Catholic sex abuse scandals, similar events have despoiled families in other nations.

"From Canada to Australia, South Africa to Hong Kong, and across Europe from Ireland to Pope John Paul II's native Poland, clergy sex abuse cases and the ensuing cover-ups have proven to be a worldwide problem. This past spring, three leading bishops resigned in Europe. Scores of other clergy across the globe have

---

[2] "Summary report of Massachusetts Attorney General", p 2, posted on www.ago.state.ma.us 7/23/03

[3] www.dallasnews.com/cgi-bin/2002/priests.cgi 8/26/03

faced lawsuits, criminal cases, and public allegations of sexual abuse or cover-up....It is not about one man or one country, it is about an institution."[4]

While many Catholics in the U.S.A. have begun calling for the exposure of the facts, removal of corrupt bishops, reform, redress and compensation, the Vatican has for many years ordered strictest secrecy in child abuse cover-up cases.

"The order, written in Latin, was sent from the Vatican in 1962 and is marked with the seal of Pope John XXIII....The document states: **'Matters should be pursued in a most secretive way...they are to be restrained by a perpetual silence...**and everyone pertaining to the tribunal in any way...is to observe the strictest secret, which is commonly regarded as a secret of the Holy Office...under the penalty of excommunication.'"[5]

Under its strictest penalty—excommunication—Rome has since 1962 warned her cardinals, archbishops and bishops to keep the clergy sexual abuse secret. The press has begun to expose this clandestine legislation,

"The hierarchy of the Catholic Church has been instructed by the Vatican at least since 1962 to keep certain cases of clergy sexual abuse secret under pain of excommunication, according to Boston lawyer Carmen L. Durso. A copy of the directive was sent yesterday to U. S. Attorney Michael J. Sullivan at his Boston office by Mr. Durso, who said he believes the church has been obstructing justice. Mr. Durso said it might also explain why Cardinal Bernard F. Law and bishops of the Boston Archdiocese and elsewhere covered up sexual abuse of children by clergy...Paul Baier, president of Survivors First, a victims' advocacy group, who is also familiar with the document, called the church's action in concealing instances of sexual abuse 'a coordinated effort of conspiracy.' Bryan Smith of Hubbardston, Worcester area leader of Survivors Network of Those Abused by Priests, said people in the church who covered

[4] www.boston.com/globe/spotlight/abuse/ print3/121402_failings.htm 8/21/03
[5] www.telegraph.co.uk/news/main.jhtml?xml=/news/2003/0/8/ 18wvat18.xml&sSheet=/news/2003/08/18/ixnewstop.html 8/21/03 Bolding in any quote indicates emphasis added by this author.

up for priests 'should be prosecuted. If it were anyone else, they would be in jail by now,' he said."[6]

Claim for the excellence of the Catholic priesthood

Regarding prestige of the Catholic priesthood, what non-Catholics fail to realize is the continuing mystique, power and glory, which is to be given to her priesthood by Catholics. For example, Vatican Council II states,

> "**First, then, priests are to make it their most cherished object to make clear to people the excellence and necessity of the priesthood**. They do this by their preaching and by the personal witness of a life that shows clearly a spirit of service and a genuine paschal joy. Then they spare no trouble or inconvenience in helping both youths and older men whom they prudently consider suitable for so great a ministry to prepare themselves properly so that they can be called at some time by the bishops....However, it is emphatically not to be expected that the voice of the Lord calling should come to the future priest's ears in some extraordinary way....Therefore organizations for the promotion of vocations, whether diocesan or national, are recommended highly...In sermons, in catechetical instruction and in periodicals the needs of the Church both local and universal are to be made known clearly. The meaning and excellence of the priesthood is to be highlighted."[7]

Rather than teaching the Gospel and the Scripture, one of the primary jobs of the priest is to recruit other men for the priesthood; but even this is under tight control of the bishop.

Thus the excellence of the Catholic priesthood is a common theme within Catholicism. The glory of the priesthood is to be held up

---

[6] http://www.telegram.com/apps/pbcs.dll/frontpage 7/29/03

[7] *Vatican Council II: The Conciliar and Post Conciliar Documents,* No. 63, *Presbyterorum Ordinis*, 7 Dec. 1965, Austin Flannery, O. P., Gen. Ed., 1981 ed., 2 vols., (Northport, NY : Costello Publ. Co., 1975) Vol. I, §11, pp. 884-5.

before Catholic youth and their parents.[8]   Just what is this charm and nobility that is held up before Catholic youth and their parents by Rome? Rome declares quite emphatically that the priesthood, which is offered to her young men, is an identical priesthood with that of Christ Jesus himself. The actual words are the following:

"All priests share with bishops **the one identical priesthood and ministry of Christ.**"[9]

"The priest offers the Holy Sacrifice *in persona Christi;* this means more than offering 'in the name of' or 'in the place of Christ'. *In persona* means in specific sacramental identification with 'the Eternal High Priest'."[10]

---

[8] Former Roman Catholic A. J. Krause, who is now saved, testifies, "My Catholic school regularly challenged us to consider the possibility of becoming a priest or nun. Thoughts of dedicating my life to God in this way danced in my soul. What greater career path could I travel? So I spoke as someone who was inter-ested in the path of serving God. Because of my obvious devotion and love for the Catholic Church, the nuns and priests gave me special attention, especially because of my vocal desire to become a Catholic priest. I was taught that the priesthood is the highest calling for a man. I set out in a devoted path, desiring to do all that I thought pleased the Lord. After I received my first Holy Commun-ion I made a vow to God to never miss Mass on Sunday or any holy day of obligation…I was the talk of the school, making such sacrifices as a young boy. 'What a great priest he could be for the Church', people whispered. Local Jesuit priests courted me in my high school years giving me special attention. They enticed me with their private wine cellars in the basement of their rectory, and allowed me to play with their champion bird dogs. They explained to me how priests received salaries, retirement programs and ample vacations. They even took me bird hunting on weekends. This looked like a pretty good life to a high schooler considering a career. Yet Jesus had warned the top religious leaders of His day, '*Woe unto you, scribes and Pharisees, hypocrites! for ye compass sea and land to make one proselyte, and when he is made, ye make him twofold more the child of hell than yourselves.*' (Matthew 23: 15)…" See www.bereanbeacon.org for Mr. Krause's complete testimony.

[9] Flannery, Vatican Council II Document No. 63, *Presbyterorum Ordinis*, §7, p. 875

[10] Flannery, No. 77, *Dominicae Cenae,* 24 Feb 1980, in Vol. II, *Vatican Council II: More Post Conciliar Documents,* First Ed. (Northport, NY: Costello Publishing Co., 1982) §8, p. 74. Hereafter Flannery, *More Post Conciliar Documents.*

What is proposed before Catholic youth is that there is a specific identification between Christ and the priest. This is put in no uncertain terms, for even the *Catechism of the Catholic Church* states,

> "Now the minister, by reason of the sacerdotal consecration which he has received, is truly made like to the high priest and possesses the authority to act in the power and place of the person of Christ himself (*virtute ac persona ipsuis Christi*)."[11]

What devout Catholic youth, who really aspires to be good, noteworthy and successful in his religious life, would not want to be in such an office as to possess the authority, power and very priesthood of Christ Himself? This is what the official documents of the Church of Rome declare. In very attractive terms, this is what is put in the Pope's addresses, in magazines, articles and vocation lectures given in Catholic schools to bring the youth into priesthood.

The very work of redemption is also declared to be part of the priestly life. Thus Vatican Council II states, "In the mystery of the eucharistic sacrifice, in which priests fulfill their principle function, the work of our redemption is continually carried out."[12] Young people are instructed to aspire to an office in which they can continually carry out the work of redemption. What higher call could be presented before youth to which they would not wish in their youthful enthusiasm to achieve? They are told that all sacraments are the work of the priest. He is essential to the work of Christ in the modern world, thus in the official words of Rome,

> "By Baptism priests introduce men into the People of God; by the sacrament of Penance they reconcile sinners with God and the Church; by the Anointing of the Sick they relieve those who are ill; and especially by the celebration of the Mass they offer Christ's sacrifice sacramentally."[13]

---

[11] *Catechism of the Catholic Church* (1994), Para.1548

[12] Flannery, Vatican Council II Document No. 63, *Presbyterorum Ordinis*, Vol. I, §13, p. 888

[13] *Ibid.*, §5, p. 870

By far the most grandiose claim made for the Catholic priest is that he can bring down on the altar the same single sacrifice that Christ Jesus offered. This is the most sublime power alleged by Rome for her priests. Thus she teaches,

> **"The sacrifice of Christ and the sacrifice of the Eucharist are *one single sacrifice:* 'The victim is one and the same**: the same now offers through the ministry of priests, who then offered himself on the cross; only the manner of offering is different.' 'In this divine sacrifice which is celebrated in the Mass, the same Christ who offered himself once in a bloody manner on the altar of the cross is contained and **is offered** in an unbloody manner.'"[14]

Three things are claimed in the pronouncement just cited. First, it claims that Christ is contained in the elements of the Mass. Second, it claims that He is offered by a human being to God, and finally it claims that the offering is in an unbloody mode. None of these claims is true.

Priests are provided to the Catholic to perform rituals for him that will take him from the cradle to the grave—but especially he is needed to perform the supposed offering of Christ's own sacrifice. This is the appeal that the Catholic priesthood has to youth. It works even today as many young men go into the diocesan seminaries and into the religious orders (the Jesuits, Carmelites, Dominicans, Franciscans and others) so that they may have a share in the very priesthood of Christ and that they may claim this identity with the High Priest Who is Christ Jesus the Lord.

The one sacrificial Priest

In the New Testament, no sacrificial priests are mentioned, only elders[15] and pastors. There is utterly and entirely no biblical basis for the Catholic priesthood. In Christ Jesus, all believers are part of the royal priesthood of Christ in spiritual praise—but no one has a share in His sacrificial priesthood. Like the famous old parable of the King's

---

[14] *Catechism*, Para. 1367

[15] The terms overseer and elder/pastor are used interchangeably, Acts 20:17, 28; I Peter 5:1-4.

new suit, the pages of Scripture show that a biblical basis for Catholic priesthood simply does not exist!

The contrast between Christ's priesthood and the Old Testament priesthood is very clear. The Levitical priests were mere mortal men and, therefore, needed successors; Christ, in contrast, is an eternal Priest and His priesthood is untransferrable and needs no successor. *"And they truly were many priests, because they were not suffered to continue by reason of death: But this man, because he continueth ever, hath an unchangeable priesthood."*[16] Untransferrable expresses the sense of the passage. The concept strictly speaking was that it did not pass over into other hands. The Levitical priesthood had passed, as successive generations came, from one to another. This reasoning is designed to prove that the Priesthood of Christ is eternal; it does not pass from hand to hand.

The passage continues, *"Wherefore he is able also to save them to the uttermost that come unto God by him, seeing he ever liveth to make intercession for them."*[17] He does not die, as did the mortal Jewish priests. This is the reason He is able to save completely. The passage continues, *"who needeth not daily, as those high priests, to offer up sacrifice, first for his own sins, and then for the people's: for this he did once, when he offered up himself."*[18] Other priests before Christ were mere mortal men, and it was necessary that their office should pass to other hands. They were sinful men also, and it was necessary that sacrifices should be made for themselves as well as others. Christ Jesus did away with the Levitical priesthood and its many priests when He died on the cross, *"behold, the veil of the temple was rent in twain from the top to the bottom."*[19] The veil that hung in the Temple, separating the Holy of Holies from the Holy

---

[16] Hebrews 7:23-24 *"Unchangeable"* in Greek literally means "untransferrable," not passing on to others.

[17] Hebrews 7:25

[18] Hebrews 7:27

[19] Matthew 27:51

Place, was rent in two from top to bottom, signifying the end of the whole priesthood of the Old Testament. The office of the many priests of the Old Testament was done away with because the one Priest continues forever!

Of utter importance is the fact that Christ Jesus alone was qualified to offer Himself. He alone had the absolutely unique qualifications as the Holy Spirit teaches, *"for such an high priest became us, who is holy, harmless, undefiled, separate from sinners, and made higher than the heavens."*[20]   The Lord Jesus is the sole sacrificial priest of the New Testament.   He finished the work of our salvation by one sole offering. The Scriptures repeatedly establish this truth. The substance of this is found in the Lord's declaration from the cross, *"Tetelestai".* *"It is finished."*[21]

The One Sacrifice, once offered
Christ Jesus' sacrifice marked the fulfillment and end of the priestly ordinances of the Old Testament, *"there is no more offering for sin."*[22] Through His priestly offering on the cross, Christ Jesus *"when he had by himself purged our sins, sat down on the right hand of the Majesty on high."*[23]   It is clear that Christ's sacrifice was designed to be once for all, in contrast to the many sacrifices of the Old Testament. *"But this man, after he had offered **one sacrifice** for sins for ever, sat down on the right hand of God."*[24]   *"For by **one offering** he hath perfected for ever them that are sanctified."*[25]

The unique oneness of Christ's sacrifice is in the very fact that it was a single offering once made. The concept "once" is deemed so important that it is asserted seven times by the Holy Spirit in the New

---

[20] Hebrews 7:26

[21] John 19:30

[22] Hebrews 10:18

[23] Hebrews 1:3

[24] Hebrews 10:12

[25] Hebrews 10:14

Testament. The perfection of Christ's sacrifice is contrasted to the daily repeated sacrifices of the Old Testament. The truth of the excellence of Christ's sacrifice is highlighted by the word "once". For example, the Apostle Paul teaches, *"For in that he died, he died unto sin **once**: but in that he liveth, he liveth unto God."*[26] The Apostle Peter likewise declares, *"For Christ also hath **once** suffered for sins, the just for the unjust, that he might bring us to God, being put to death in the flesh, but quickened by the Spirit."*[27] The same truth is taught in the book of Hebrews five times with the conclusion, *"So Christ was **once** offered to bear the sins of many; and unto them that look for him shall he appear the second time without sin unto salvation."*[28]

True worship of God is in Christ Jesus, the eternal Priest
True worship of God is in Christ Jesus, the eternal Priest. He alone authenticates worship, since it is in His name and in accord with His Word. His own righteousness credited to the believer by grace through faith alone is the only basis of true worship. His restrictions in worship are most serious, *"God is a Spirit: and they that worship him must worship him in spirit and in truth."*[29] The greatest comfort believers have in true worship is that they have Jesus Christ, the Lord and Master in whom they are accepted, as their intercessor. He is their High Priest, *"now of the things which we have spoken this is the sum: we have such an high priest, who is set on the right hand of the throne of the Majesty in the heavens."*[30] This is the confidence in the presence of God that believers now have because they have one eternal Priest,

---

[26] Romans 6: 10

[27] I Peter 3:18

[28] Hebrews 9:28

[29] John 4:24

[30] Hebrews 8:1

who offered one sacrifice once and for all time! Without this truth, one does not have the Gospel or eternal life.

Life as it is lived in Catholic seminaries

Were it not documented in Catholic books[31] one would hardly believe the utter decadence in seminaries and in colleges that train men for the priesthood. The subculture of homosexuality is rampant across the U.S.A. Page after page of *Goodbye, Good Men* tells of the horrific influence of homosexuality that has permeated the youth in the Catholic seminaries. The ideals of youth are replaced by unnatural lusts that have become prevalent in major seminaries and colleges training men for the priesthood.[32]   Donald Cozzens, leading Catholic priest and rector of St. Mary's in Cleveland, Ohio (a leading U.S. seminary), states in his book on the priesthood that

> "An NBC report on celibacy and the clergy found that 'anywhere from 23 percent to 58 percent' of the Catholic clergy have a homosexual orientation.[33]   Other studies find that approximately half of American priests and seminarians are homosexually oriented…Moreover, the percentage of gay men among religious congregations of priests is believed to be even higher."[34]

Then nonchalantly he states, "At issue at the beginning of the twenty-first century is the growing perception—one seldom contested by those who know the priesthood well—that the priesthood is or is becoming a gay profession. And to the point is the question: Does it matter? Does not the question reveal still another form of homophobia?"[35]

Under the heading, "The Gay Crisis", Cozzens states, "Gay seminarians are likely to feel at home and at ease in a seminary with a

---

[31] Michael S. Rose, *Goodbye, Good Men, How Liberals Brought Corruption into the Catholic Church* (Wash. DC: Regnery Publ., Inc., 2002); also Donald B Cozzens, *The Changing Face of the Priesthood: A Reflection of the Priest's Crisis of Soul* (Collegeville, MN: The Liturgical Press, 2000).

[32] Rose, Chapter 4

[33] Timothy Unsworth, *The Last Priests in America* (New York: Crossroad, 1991) p. 248, in Cozzens, p. 99.

[34] Cozzens, p. 99

[35] Cozzens, p. 107

significant gay population. They feel they belong and their need for meaningful, deep relationships with other gay men is easily met, and because they instinctively recognize other gay seminarians, circles of support and camaraderie are quickly formed...The straight seminarian meanwhile, feels out of place and may interpret his inner destabilization as a sign that he does not have a vocation to the priesthood."[36]

In the concluding sentence of the book, Cozzens says, "Behind the changing face of the priesthood remains the saving face of Jesus the Christ."[37] He had already stated that saving souls through "the celebration of the sacraments is the primary function of the priest." (p. 8) Later he says, "The ritual, symbolic richness of the sacramental life of the Church, to a great extent, meets the human need for transcendence."(p. 30) The need for the esthetic may be met in the pageantry of the Catholic sacraments, but it does not meet the need to be right with God. To state that the saving face of Christ Jesus remains behind the priesthood is a lie. What Cozzens fails to see is that his own reliance on the "saving face of Jesus the Christ" is based not on the Gospel, which is *the power of God unto salvation*, but rather on the Catholic understanding of salvation through good works, a doctrine straight out of hell. Christ Jesus stands behind what is true and in accord with His written Word to the glory of His Father! The Catholic priesthood is a parody of all that for which Christ Jesus stands. The Lord Jesus Christ does not stand behind the Catholic make-believe; rather He is **the** High Priest who is holy, harmless, undefiled!

Continuing in a damning lifestyle

One wonders just how the men who are studying for the priesthood—having been presented with such high ideals as of their identity with Christ—can stay in the seminaries and colleges for religious formation when they meet the stark reality of a gay subculture and of abnormal sexuality. To answer that problem one has to consider the pressure put on sons by their mothers, in particular, and also the fact that youth,

---

[36] Cozzens, p. 135

[37] *Ibid.*, p.143

because of their inexperience, are more easily snared. Through this devastating experience and the horrendous guilt it engenders, they become trapped in the very vices they would have abhorred prior to entering the seminary. Two hooks catch the Catholic youth. First is the tradition of the Catholic Church, which teaches that celibacy is a way to sharing the rich experiences of Christ, and second is that through the tradition, which they are to hold as sacred, they are caught in a lifestyle that seems to be unbreakable.

Regarding the first of these hooks, the Catholic Church has declared it "unthinkable" that her tradition of celibacy is at fault. In her Vatican Council II documents she officially states,

"In any case, the [Catholic] Church of the West cannot weaken her faithful observance of her own tradition. And it is unthinkable that for centuries she has followed a path which, instead of favoring the spiritual richness of individual souls and of the People of God, has in some way compromised it, or that she has with arbitrary juridical prescriptions stifled the free expansion of the most profound realities of nature and of grace."[38]

The "unthinkable" has become an every day occurrence. Chapter 10 of *Goodbye, Good Men* begins with a quotation, "Complaints about doctrinal error, liturgical abuse and even personal misconduct in U.S. seminaries are now so common as to be routine."[39] Why then is it that we have a continuation of the Catholic priesthood and a continuation of the horrors that are being foisted on Catholics? The answer is that the Catholic Church is one huge monolithic dictatorial system that continues to plow forward in spite of what is apparent. She continues to uphold her teaching regarding the identity of Christ and the priest, and continues to say that priests are "other Christs". It is a continuation of the whole theme of Graham Greene's novel, *The Power and the Glory.*

This well-known novel by Catholic author Graham Greene shows the life of a Latino priest, sunk in sin. It was not just that he was

---

[38] Flannery, *More Post Conciliar Documents*, No. 95, *Sacerdotalis Caelibatus*, 24 June 1967, §41, p. 297

[39] This quotation is from Francis X. Maier, a former editor of the *National Catholic Register.*

drunk with liquor, immersed in immoral living and that his teeth were yellow with nicotine, but that he was still honored among the people as one who gave them Christ's forgiveness for sin in confession and baptized their babies to new life in baptism. In real life, the Catholic priesthood ideal continues even if tarnished. Young men are continually struck, as it were, in their vital organs by the "dual disease", lust for power and abnormal sexual lust. Graham Greene said it so well, *The Power and the Glory* is the name of the worldly game that is played by the Catholic Magisterium at the expense of so many ordinary Catholics. The claim that a priest's sinfulness does not obstruct the grace that flows through him and his sacraments is not simply the perspective of Graham Greene; it is the official teaching of Rome,

> "This presence of Christ in the minister is not to be understood as if the latter were preserved from all human weaknesses, the spirit of domination, error, even sin. The power of the Holy Spirit does not guarantee all acts of ministers in the same way. While this guarantee extends to the sacraments, so that even the minister's sin cannot impede the fruit of grace..."[40]

Men freed from the priesthood

Far From Rome, Near to God: the Testimonies of Fifty Converted Catholic Priests,[41] gives first-hand documentation that men from many different nations across the world were freed from the priesthood and from the Church of Rome. Why was it that they obtained their freedom and so many more did not? If you read the testimonies of these men, you will notice that some began inquiring in the book of Hebrews where they saw quite clearly that Christ's priesthood was unique to Him. Part of the way in which I saw the light was by reading one of our famous Catholic scholars, Raymond E. Brown. In his remarkable book, *Priest and Bishop: Biblical Reflections*, Brown declares,

> "When we move from the Old Testament to the New Testament, it is striking that while there are pagan priests and Jewish priests on

---

[40] *Catechism*, Para. 1550

[41] *Far from Rome, Near to God: The Testimonies of Fifty Former Roman Catholic Priests,* Richard Bennett and Martin Buckingham, Eds. (Carlisle, PA 17013: Banner of Truth Trust, 1997)

the scene, no individual Christian is ever specifically identified as a priest. The Epistle to the Hebrews speaks of the high priesthood of Jesus by comparing his death and entry into heaven with the actions of the Jewish high priest who went into the Holy of Holies in the Tabernacle once a year with a blood offering for himself and for the sins of his people (Hebrews 9:6, 7). But it is noteworthy that the author of Hebrews does not associate the priesthood of Jesus with the Eucharist or the Last Supper; neither does he suggest that other Christians are priests in the likeness of Jesus. In fact, the once-for-all atmosphere that surrounds the priesthood of Jesus in Hebrews 10:12-14 has been offered as an explanation of why there are no Christian priests in the New Testament period."[42]

Thus the noted Catholic author declared publicly that there were no Christian priests in the New Testament period of time. This came as a shock to me for, at the time I was reading the book, I was a Catholic priest. All my hopes, the investment of my whole life was in the priesthood. It was what I had sought after, it was what I had achieved; it was that in which I had my source of revenue. It was that in which I obtained honor and respect from people. I was utterly astounded that one of our famous Catholic authors could state that Christian priests did not exist in the New Testament and the only the priesthood was that of Christ Jesus the Lord.

I did not have the courage at that time to begin studying Hebrews 7:23-27 for myself. Some years later, however, I did study and I saw that the whole reason why there were many priests was because they died and had to be replaced (v. 23). I saw also that verse 24 differentiates the priesthood of Christ from the old Levitical priesthood (and every other "priesthood"), *"But this man, because he continueth ever, hath an unchangeable priesthood."* As pointed out above, it is interesting that the word "unchangeable" in Greek means literally "untransferrable"—not passed on to anyone else. The passage continues with the great news, *"wherefore he is able also to save them to the uttermost that come unto God by him, seeing he ever*

---

[42] Raymond E. Brown, *Priest and Bishop: Biblical Reflections* (New York: Paulist Press, 1970) p. 13

liveth to make intercession for them." Christ Jesus saves utterly and completely those who come to God by Him. The reason why is given as the passage continues, "*for such an high priest became us, who is holy, harmless, undefiled, separate from sinners, and made higher than the heavens.*"

Brown's book had certain repercussions in my life. It caused me to remember back to the year in which I studied as a priest in Rome. We had over three hundred young priests in my class. I could see that, for the most part, they were interested neither in a holy life nor in seeking to magnify Christ Jesus. Rather, most of these men were interested in getting high positions in different nations across the world. It was a real scandal to me to see with my own eyes men who had no interest whatsoever in the priesthood—except as a means for position and renown. I was horrified to the extent that outside of class, I chose to associate mostly with three other priests, one from Africa, another from Europe, and another from the United States, all of whom seemed to have my same ideals. However, this memory continued with me throughout the years of my own priesthood.

The Lord's call to ministry and marriage
The Catholic Church completely rules out marriage for its priests. She says emphatically,

> "A cleric who attempts even a civil marriage incurs an automatic (*latae sententiae*) suspension; but if he is given a warning and he does not have a change of heart and continues to give scandal, he can be punished gradually with various deprivations, even to the point of dismissal from the clerical state."[43]

Most serious for Rome is a priest attempting marriage, and she is arrogant enough to call this a scandal. In the Bible, marriage is honorable and undefiled.[44] Just as the sun overcomes the darkness, so the clear light of God's Word upholds marriage as honorable and anything but a scandal!

To desire the office of a bishop (that is, an elder or pastor), the Word of God says is good, "*if a man desire the office of a bishop, he*

---

[43] *Code of Canon Law*, Can. 1394, §1
[44] Hebrews 13:4

desireth a good work."[45]   The qualifications for someone who wishes such an office are then given,

> "*A bishop then must be blameless, the husband of one wife, vigilant, sober, of good behavior, given to hospitality, apt to teach; not given to wine, no striker, not greedy of filthy lucre; but patient, not a brawler, not covetous; one that ruleth well his own house, having his children in subjection with all gravity; (for if a man know not how to rule his own house, how shall he take care of the church of God?)*"[46]

The light of God's Word shows a man must be able to manage his own household before he attempts to oversee the believers in a Christian community. He is to be a man of one wife. Would to God that Catholics, and the Catholic clergy in particular, read these verses.

Gift of celibacy contrasted to Law of Priestly Celibacy

The gift of celibacy is spoken about by the Lord as a gift that given only to a few. The time and circumstances of that celibate life are solely between the Lord and the individual. "*For there are some eunuchs, which were so born from their mother's womb: and there are some eunuchs, which were made eunuchs of men: and there be eunuchs, which have made themselves eunuchs for the kingdom of heaven's sake. He that is able to receive it, let him receive it.*"[47]   It is to be noted that the celibate life is not a condition for ministry; rather, "*he that is able to receive it, let him receive it.*"   The Apostle Paul gave the same counsel as the Lord. He taught that it was fitting for the unmarried to remain single, if this was the "proper gift" one had from God, "*For I would that all men were even as I myself. But every man hath his proper gift of God, one after this manner, and another after that.*"[48]   He also gave the reasons why the single state was preferable, "*he that is unmarried careth for the things that*

---

[45] I Timothy 3:1

[46] I Timothy 3:2-5

[47] Matthew 19:12

belong to the Lord, how he may please the Lord: But he that is married careth for the things that are of the world, how he may please his wife."[49]   Yet the final word of caution given by the Apostle is utterly clear and forceful, "*But if they cannot contain, let them marry: for it is better to marry than to burn.*"[50]   This qualification is consistent with the Lord's own admonition, "*All men cannot receive this saying, save they to whom it is given.*"[51]   Therefore to make celibacy a law for those in ministry is utterly unbiblical. This, however, is precisely what the Church of Rome does.

While recognizing that virginity is not of the nature of ministry, the Vatican is bold enough to declare that priestly celibacy is a "sacred law. " The official teaching is the following,

"Virginity undoubtedly, as the Second Vatican Council declared, 'is not, of course, required by the nature of the priesthood itself. This is clear from the practice of the early Church and the traditions of the Eastern Churches.' But at the same time the Council did not hesitate to confirm solemnly **the ancient, sacred and providential present law of priestly celibacy**."[52]

Thus the Catholic Church contradicts the very Word of God and tempts the Lord God in what they do to their young men. The whole purpose of the Vatican, Pope, Cardinals, and Curia is to maintain control over the priests worldwide. They have imposed the law of priestly celibacy so that they can continue their control of men who, if they were married, would be responsible for their children, property, households, and most of all for their conscience. Rome has tempted God Himself in upholding an untrue priesthood and, additionally, bringing her youth into an atmosphere where they are waylaid by immoral lusts.

The wretchedness of this whole topic of a pretended priest-hood is a picture of the situation for all mankind. All have a bad record

---

[48] I Corinthians 7:7

[49] I Corinthians 7:32-33

[50] I Corinthians 7:9

[51] Matthew 19:11

[52] Flannery, *More Post Conciliar Documents*, No. 95, *Sacerdotalis Caelibatus*, §17, p. 290

and a bad heart. Each has a bad record because of personal sin. Each has a depraved human heart because of the original sin of Adam. All stand in need of the grace of God in Christ Jesus. Such was proclaimed over seven hundred fifty years before Christ Jesus had finished His priestly work on the cross. The prophet Isaiah declared, *"All we like sheep have gone astray; we have turned every one to his own way; and the Lord hath laid on him the iniquity of us all." "But he was wounded for our transgressions, he was bruised for our iniquities: the chastisement of our peace was upon him; and with his stripes we are healed."*[53] The Apostle Peter also declared, *"ye know that ye were not redeemed with corruptible things, as silver and gold, from your vain conversation received by tradition from your fathers."*[54] The believer is to look unto Christ Jesus, the Author and Finisher of his faith. In trusting on Christ Jesus alone, we have His righteousness credited to us, and though our sins are as scarlet, He makes them white as snow. This is the good news and we pray and plead in the Lord that those in the Catholic priesthood and those tempted by worldly power and its fleeting glory will hear the Word of God and live!

Who is your Priest?

The important question at the end of this chapter is this: who is your Priest? The priesthood of Christ is glorious, like Himself. It is the priesthood in which He has offered to the Father all that He is. It is His final finished work in which the glory of His person will shine forever. As priest, He had done all that was necessary to put away the sins of His people. He has provided for them both the forgiveness for their sins and His own perfect standing before God. *"It is finished,"* He declared. What was finished was the believer's slavery to sin and the true moral guilt that attends his sin! Paid was the price of the believer's redemption! Performed were all the requirements of God's law. In a word, complete satisfaction has been made to God for the believer. The Catholic priesthood, in contrast, is dust, smoke and mirrors. Like

---

[53] Isaiah 53:6, 5
[54] I Peter 1:18

the well-known allegory of the King's new suit, it simply does not legitimately exist! Believe on the Eternal Lord and know the Priest that gives life now, and forever! *"Having therefore, brethren, boldness to enter into the holiest by the blood of Jesus, By a new and living way, which he hath consecrated for us, through the veil, that is to say, his flesh; And having an high priest over the house of God...."*[55] This is the living way. It is death to attempt to come to God through earthly sacrificial priests who have no place in the New Testament. The way to the Eternal Father is through the Eternal Priest alone; His death is for us the way to life. To those who believe this He is precious beyond all understanding. ◆

---

[55] Hebrews 10:19-21

Chapter 4

The Papacy:
An Overview of Its History and Nature

The Papal Church is a magnificently rich, splendidly housed political and ecclesiastical power headquartered in Rome. It stands in stark contrast to what started there in the first century with some pastors ministering to small congregations. The differences are graphic. The early home churches under their pastors looked to the authority of the Word as received in the gospel accounts of the life of the Lord and the writings of the Apostles, together with the Old Testament.[1] These pastors and churches had a true and living faith in God's grace through the Gospel. From the letter of Paul to the Romans one sees that the Gospel was faithfully treasured in those early Roman congregations. At the beginning of his letter, the Apostle commends the believers at Rome for their faith, *"First, I thank my God through Jesus Christ for you all, that your faith is spoken of throughout the whole world. For God is my witness, whom I serve with my spirit in the gospel of his Son...."*[2] Such approvals are infrequent with the Apostle Paul. The faith of the churches of Rome continued to be well known and faithfully lived for two hundred fifty years more under very adverse situations, including extreme persecutions, the most famous of which took place under Emperor Nero in the 64 A.D. Totally unimaginable for these early believers in Rome would be the present concept of "the most holy Roman Pontiff." Unthinkable likewise would be the belief that rituals could confer the grace of the Holy Spirit and that Mary, the mother of the Lord, could be addressed in prayer as "the All Holy

---

[1] See Appendix I, "The Scripture Given to the Early Church".
[2] Romans 1:8-9

One".[3] In the fellowship of believers, a top heavy hierarchical system, from layperson to priest, from to priest to bishop, from bishop to cardinal and cardinal to Pope would have been totally abhorrent, as from the world and not from Christ who said, *"One is your Master, even Christ; and all ye are brethren."*[4]

The spread of the Christian faith during the first three centuries was extensive and rapid. In the providence of God, the main reasons for this were the fidelity and zeal of the preachers of the Gospel, the heroic deaths of the martyrs, and the translation of the Scriptures into the languages of the Roman world. Under Emperor Septimius Severus (193-211) Christians suffered appallingly. The most severe persecution was under the Emperor Diocletian and his co-regent, Galerius, during the years 303-311. The historian Philip Schaff states that, "all copies of the Bible were to be burned; all Christians were to be deprived of public office and civil rights; and last, all, without exception, were to sacrifice to the gods upon pain of death."[5] Yet far from exterminating the Christians and the Gospel, the persecution purified those who preached and increased their ability to give the Gospel message.

The persecution of Christians ended in 313 A.D. when the emperors Constantine in the West and Licinius in the East proclaimed the Edict of Milan. This decree established the policy of religious freedom for both paganism and Christianity. Four vice-prefects governed the Roman Empire under Constantine. Accordingly, under his authority the Christian world was to be governed from four great cities, Antioch, Alexandria, Jerusalem, and Rome. Over each city there was set a Patriarch, who governed all the elders of his domain. (This was later to be a called a diocese.) The mind of and purpose of Constantine was that the Christian churches were to be organized in a fashion similar to the government of the Empire.

---

[3] *Catechism of the Catholic Church* (1994), Para. 2677, "By asking Mary to pray for us, we acknowledge ourselves to be poor sinners and we address ourselves to the 'Mother of Mercy,' the All Holy One."

[4] Matthew 23:8.

[5] Philip Schaff, *History of the Christian Church*, Vol. 1, Second Period, p. 34

The respect enjoyed by the various Christian elders was usually in proportion to the status of the city in which they resided. Since Rome was the most powerful and prestigious city in the world at the time, it stood to unbiblical reason that the most prominent and influential bishop should be the Bishop of Rome. Gradually the honor and respect given to the Bishop of Rome grew, and these bishops in turn desired this adulation from bishops of other cities. The church was in such decline that with the passing of third and fourth centuries the bishops of Rome began to demand recognition for the exalted position they now considered their possession.

Gradual rise of papal Rome

In the fourth and fifth centuries as the true Gospel was watered down, its place was taken by ritualism and ceremony. The true worship of God and the inner conviction of the Holy Spirit gave way to formal rites and idolatry. Pagan practices were also introduced, white washed with an external form of Christianity.[6] From the beginning, the Gospel

---

[6] The history of the Vaudois, the Albigenses, the Waldenses, the Paulicians, and others shows that it is the Church of Rome that removed herself from the biblical faith. The history of the Papacy is the history of this removal and the profound effects thereof throughout the centuries from its genesis to the present. Nevertheless, the Lord has maintained a true witness to the Gospel throughout the centuries. See particularly George Stanley Faber, *The History of the Ancient Vallenses and Albigenses* (Fleet Street, London: Seeley & Burnside, 1838) Reprinted by Church History Research & Archives (CHRAA) (P O Box 38, Dayton, OH: 1990); also Peter Allix, *The Ecclesiastical History of the Ancient Church of Piedmont and of the Albigenses* (Oxford at the Clarendon Press, 1821) Reprinted by CHRAA. 1989; Jean Paul Perrin, *History of the Old Waldenses Anterior to the Reformation*, 1618 (Reprint by CHRAA, 1991); J. A. Wylie, *The History of Protestantism*, originally published in 1878 (Kilkeel, N. Ireland: Mourne Missionary Trust, 1985), re-published in four volumes by Hartland Publications, Rapidan, VA, 2002); J. H. Merle D'Aubigne, *History of the Reformation in the Sixteenth Century,* A New Translation (New York: John B. Alden, Publisher, 1883); Sir Samuel Morland, *The History of the Evangelical Churches of the Valleys of Piemont*, 2 vols.(London: 1658) Reprinted by The Baptist Standard Bearer, Inc., #1 Iron Oaks Drive, Paris, AR 72855, ISBN 1-5557978-541-7. See also Appendix excerpt from E. H Broadbent's *The Pilgrim Church.* Yet Vatican Council II Document No. 32 on Ecumenism holds to the old Roman Catholic view that it is the Evangelicals who first separated from Rome—in spite of the persistent clear historical facts to the contrary.

produced an internal unity among the believers, but with the substitution of ritualism for the Gospel came the insistence on an external, visible unity for the church. As the historian D'Aubigne relates,

"Various circumstances early contributed to originate and develop the idea of the necessity of an external unity. Men accustomed to the ties and political forms of an earthly country transferred some of their views and customs to the spiritual and eternal kingdom of Jesus Christ….The semblance of an identical and external organization was gradually substituted for the internal and spiritual unity which forms the essence of genuine religion. The precious perfume of faith was left out, and then men prostrated themselves before the empty vase which had contained it. The faith of the heart no longer uniting the members of the Church, another tie was sought, and they were united by means of bishops, archbishops, popes, mitres, ceremonies, and canons. The living Church having gradually retired into the hidden sanctuary of some solitary souls, the external Church was put in its place, and declared to be, with all its forms, of Divine institution….It was maintained that it [salvation] was transmitted by means of the forms which had been devised, and that no man could possess it if he did not receive it though this channel….As soon as the error as to the necessity of a visible unity of the Church was established, a new error was seen to arise— viz., that of the necessity of an external representative of this unity."[7]

The clergy-laity division of the church became the accepted base. This further devolved into a hierarchy of the ruling clergy. By the end of the fifth century, a sacrificing priesthood in which the priest presumed to mediate between God and men had replaced the early ministers of the Gospel who had taught the Scripture. The Church was no more the fellowship of believers under Christ Jesus, united by the Gospel, true worship, and indwelling of the Holy Spirit, but rather an institution dominated by a hierarchy of bishops and elders.[8]

---

[7] J. H. Merle D'Aubigne, *History of the Reformation in the Sixteenth Century,* A New Translation (New York: John B. Alden, Publisher, 1888) Vol. I, p. 3.

[8] J. A. Wylie, *The History of Protestantism*, originally published in 1878 (Kilkeel, N. Ireland: Mourne Missionary Trust, 1985) Vol. I, Book I, pp. 3-14. See also D'Aubigne, Book I, pp.1-34.

Simultaneously, from early to mid-fifth century, the city of Rome was beset first by Alaric the Goth, who captured it in 410 but did not stay to rule; Attila the Hun, who in 452 was persuaded by Leo, the then Bishop of Rome (440-461), to stop his advance and leave Italy altogether; and finally Genseric, leader of the Vandals, who captured the city, but was persuaded by Leo to spare the lives of Romans.[9] Leo's fame as Rome's protector grew enormously as a result.

The position of Imperial Roman emperor by now had become clearly vacant. A vacuum had been established because the Imperial leadership had left Rome and none of the barbaric leaders had tried to set himself up in that position. Leo, as the Bishop of Rome, saw the opportunity that lay in front of him,

> "Leo began to feel that the time had come to materialize the claims of Augustine regarding the temporal millennial kingdom of Christ, and with his avowed vested powers of loosing and binding openly to declare his right to the vacant throne as the fitting seat of Christ's universal kingdom. In this way the Roman church pushed its way into the place of the Western empire, of which it is 'the actual continuation.' Thus the empire did not perish; it only changed its form. The pope became Caesar's successor. This was a long stride forward."[10]

Bishop of Rome becomes the Pope

The removal of the seat of the Empire from Rome to Constantinople in 330 A.D. enhanced marvelously the Bishop of Rome's power. The ecclesiastical contest which had been going on for some time between Antioch, Alexandria, Jerusalem, and Rome as to which was the greatest was now for most part confined to the dioceses of Rome and the new contender, Constantinople.

The barbarian invasions of the Western Roman Empire helped immeasurably to build the whole structure of papal Rome. The ten

---

[9] LeRoy Edwin Froom, *The Prophetic Faith of Our Fathers: The Historical Development of Prophetic Interpretation* (Washington, DC: Review and Herald Publishing Assn., 1950) Vol. I, p. 498.

[10] *Ibid.*

barbarian kingdoms that were a serious threat were the Alamanni, Franks, Visigoths, Burgundians, Suevi, Anglo-Saxons, Lombards, Heruli, Vandals, and the Ostrogoths.[11] The Emperor of Rome now lived in Constantinople; yet his armies uprooted and destroyed the Vandals and the Heruli, while simultaneously contending with the Ostrogoths, who continued their siege of Rome.

Clovis, King of the Franks, was the first of the barbarian princes to accept the faith proposed by the Church of Rome. In fulfillment of a vow that he had made on the battlefield when he defeated the Allemanni, Clovis was baptized in 496 A. D. in the Cathedral of Rheims. The Bishop of Rome gave him the title of "the eldest son of the Church." In the sixth century, the Burgundians of Southern Gaul, the Visigoths of Spain, the Suevi of Portugal, and the Anglo-Saxons of Britain all followed suit in joining themselves to the religion of the Bishop of Rome. These barbaric kings and their peoples accepted easily the faith of Rome, which because it lacked the Gospel, was not very different in form and substance from their own pagan worship. All of these conversions advanced the power of the Roman Bishop. Then, too, these barbaric nations more easily accepted the religion of Rome because this city had traditionally been the seat of authority of the Caesars as masters of the world. The bishops of Rome now played their role as rightful heirs to the Caesars. The city that had been the seat of power for the Empire became the place for the Bishop to exercise his authority. More and more nations accepted his position.

Emperor Justinian I (527-565) was the one, more than anyone else, to establish the supremacy of the Bishop of Rome. He did it in a formal and legal manner by bringing purely ecclesiastical edicts and regulations under the control of civil law. Froom summarized,

"[One of Justinian's] great achievement[s] was the regulation of ecclesiastical and theological matters, crowned by the imperial Decretal Letter seating the bishop of Rome in the church as the

---

[11] The first seven are now known as Germany, France, Spain, Switzerland, Portugal, England, and Italy respectively.

'Head of all the holy churches,' thus laying the legal foundation for papal ecclesiastical supremacy."[12]

Justinian's official civil codex of law was to be enforced civilly throughout the Roman Empire, although that did not come about immediately.

"'Hence, in accordance with the provisions of these Councils, we order that the Most Holy Pope of ancient Rome shall hold the first rank of all the Pontiffs, but the Most Blessed Archbishop of Constantinople, or New Rome, shall occupy the second place after the Holy Apostolic See of ancient Rome, which shall take precedence over all other sees.'...Thus the supremacy of the Pope over all Christians received the fullest sanction that could be given by the secular master of the Roman world. From this time, then, is to be dated the secular acknowledgment of the Papacy's claims to ecclesiastical primacy, which became effective generally in 538, by the freeing of Rome from the Ostrogothic siege." [13]

Justinian's decree did not create the office of the Pope but rather set the legal foundation for advancement in ruling power by the bishops of Rome. The Emperor had his purposes,

"Justinian improved the advantage afforded by his reconquest of Italy to achieve his design of *a universal conformity in religious matters* that would exclude heresy and schism, as well as strengthen his own authority over the Western kingdoms. His object was to secure a unity of the church which should embrace both East and West. He considered that there was no surer way of reducing them all to one religion than by the advancement of the authority of ecclesiastical Rome, and by acknowledgment of the head of that church as the promoter of unity among them, whose business it should be to overawe the conscience of man with the anathemas of the church, and to enforce the execution of heavy penalties of the law. From about 539, the sovereign pontiff and the patriarchs began to have a corps of officers to enforce their decrees, as civil penalties began to be inflicted by their own tribunals."[14]

---

[12] Froom, Vol. I, p. 507.
[13] Novella 131 of Justinian, 9th collection, title 6, chap. 2 (numbered title 14, chap. 2 in Scott's tr. here quoted) in Froom, Vol. I, p. 513, including Froom's comment.
[14] Froom, Vol. I, p. 509. Italic is in the original.

Thus to allay the demise of the Imperial Empire, ecclestiacal unity was to be imposed by coercion if necessary, not the first time nor yet the last that religion would be used to buttress political positions. As proclaimed head of the Empire's church, the job fell to the Bishop of Rome. The title of "Pope" began to fit the one who sat as "Bishop of Rome", who now was free to use the civil sword of coercion given him by Justinian's decree. Formerly, ecclesiastical unity came by the moral persuasion of the Gospel and the Scripture alone to save individuals who then would be salt and light to their civil societies. But such unbiblical ideas and methods as the Bishops of Rome had so willingly sought after and received could hardly produce something other than worldly corruption. It is no surprise then that soon the Bishop of Rome desired to reign like a king with worldly pomp and worldly power. The very thing that the Lord had warned against was now transpiring. *And he said unto them, the kings of the Gentiles exercise lordship over them...but ye shall not be so....*[15]

The Empire continued to crumble. The Emperor Phocas reigned in Constantinople from 602 to 610 A.D. Boniface III, who became Pope in 607, had known him previously, for Boniface had been a legate to the Emperor Phocas before becoming pope. Boniface showed great skill in obtaining further official recognition from the Emperor.

"He [Boniface] sought and obtained a decree from Phocas which restated that 'the See of Blessed Peter the Apostle should be the head of all the Churches'. This ensured that the title of 'Universal Bishop' belonged exclusively to the Bishop of Rome, and effectively ended the attempt by Cyriacus, Bishop of Constantinople, to establish himself as 'Universal Bishop'". [16]

---

[15] Luke 22:25-26

[16] http://encyclopedia.thefreedictionary.com/Pope%20Boniface%20III 5/29/04
"[Emperor] Justinian...The recognition of the Roman see as the highest ecclesiastical authority (compare *Novellae*, cxxxi.) remained the cornerstone of his policy in relation to the West, although he thus grievously offended those of the East, and though he felt himself entirely free to show a despotic front toward the popes (witness his behavior toward Silverius and Vigilius)" http://encyclopedia.thefreedictionary.com/Justinian 5/29/04

Pope Boniface III shrewdly took hold of two measures to secure papal hegemony in the ecclesiastical domain of the failing empire. First, he made excellent use of the conjecture that Peter was the First Bishop in Rome.[17]   Second, his acquisition of the title of "Universal Bishop", granted to him by Emperor Phocas, accorded him dominion and power to reign in ecclesiastical supremacy from the central city of Rome to the utmost reaches of the Empire. This twofold stratagem has continued throughout history.

Fraudulent documents and the rise of the Papacy as a temporal power

It was not until the middle of the eighth century that the outlandish claim was made that the Emperor Constantine had transferred his power, authority, and palace to the Bishop of Rome. The fraudulent "Donation of Constantine" was purported to be the legal document in which the Emperor Constantine bestowed on Sylvester, the Bishop of Rome (314-335), much of his property and invested him with great spiritual power. The enormity and grandeur of the bequest allegedly given by Constantine to Sylvester in the spurious document is seen the following quotation from the manuscript,

> "We attribute to the See of Peter all the dignity, all the glory, all the authority of the imperial power. Furthermore, we give to Sylvester and to his successors our palace of the Lateran, which is incontestably the finest palace on the earth; we give him our crown, our miter, our diadem, and all our imperial vestments; we transfer to him the imperial dignity. We bestow on the holy Pontiff in free gift the city of Rome, and all the western cities of Italy. To cede precedence to him, we divest ourselves of our authority over all those provinces,

---

[17] The Scripture is utterly silent about the Apostle Peter going to Rome. The notion remains purely a conjecture. Nevertheless, according to Froom, "Innocent I (d. 417) had maintained that Christ had (a) delegated supreme power to Peter and (b) made him bishop of Rome, and that as Peter's successor he was entitled to exercise Peter's power and prerogatives..." The same was claimed by the legate of Pope Celestine at the Council of Ephesus in 431, which was allowed to stand unchallenged. Vol. I, p. 499

and we withdraw from Rome, transferring the seat of our empire to Byzantium; inasmuch as it is not proper that an earthly emperor should preserve the least authority, where God hath established the head of his religion."[18]

The "Donation of Constantine" was most likely forged a little before 754 A.D. Of it, the historian Wylie says, "In it Constantine is made to speak in the Latin of the eighth century, and to address Bishop Sylvester as 'Prince of the Apostles, Vicar of Christ'. During more than 600 years Rome impressively cited this deed of gift, inserted it in her codes, permitted none to question its genuineness, and burned those who refused to believe in it. The first dawn of light in the sixteenth century sufficed to discover the cheat."[19]

It was also in the eighth century that civil power came within the grasp of the Papacy. The kings of Lombardy, once barbarian and now believers in the Arian heresy, were intent on the conquest of all Italy, threatening even Rome itself. At the same time, the Muslims had overrun Africa, conquered some of Spain, and were also endangering Rome. Pope Stephen II looked to France for help. He called on Pepin the Short. Pepin, the son of Charles Martel (Charles the Hammer) and the father of Charlemagne, was the chief steward of the king's lands and army. Pepin had just usurped the throne from Childeric and needed approval for his new position. He therefore crossed the Alps with an army and was able to defeat the Lombards. The conquered towns he conceded to the Pope for his possession. Thus in 755 A.D. Pepin the

---

[18] Quoted from copy of the document in Pope Leo's letter in Hardouin's Collection, Epistola I., Leonis Papoe IX; *Acta Conciliorumet Epistoloe Decretales*, tom. 6, pp. 934; Parisiis, 1714. The English reader will find a copy of the pretended original document in full in *Historical Essay on the Power of the Popes*, Vol. II, Appendix, Tr. from French, London, 1838 in Wylie, Vol. I, Book First, Ch. 3, p.11.

[19] Wylie, Vol. I, Book First, Ch. 3, p. 11. See also reknown Roman Catholic historian Ignaz Von Döllinger [Janus, pseud.], *The Pope and the Council*, Auth. Tr. from German, 2nd ed. (London: Rivingtons, 1869) §7 "Forgeries", pp. 94-142.

Short made material the temporal power of the popes, and achieved papal approval for himself.[20]

Charlemagne, Pepin's son, continued to strengthen the temporal power of the Pope. The Lombards were again about to besiege Rome. The Pope again looked to France for help and this time to Charlemagne, who answered the call and defeated the Lombards. He confirmed and enlarged cities and lands given by his father, Pepin, to the Church of Rome. Later, on Christmas Eve 800, Charlemagne, as master of nearly all the Romano-Germanic nations, knelt before Pope Leo III. The Pope placed on his head the crown of the Western Empire. This act exhibited the Pope's growing power. In 538 the Emperor Justinian had given the Bishop of Rome the title of Pontifex Maximus. Two hundred sixty-two years later, it was the Pope who was crowning an emperor.[21]

---

[20] Wylie points out, "The Pope was nominally subject to the Emperor, but in many vital points, the *first* was *last*...The popes had not yet advanced a direct and formal claim to dispose of crowns and kingdoms, but the germ of such a claim was contained, *first*, in the acts which they now performed. They had already taken it upon them to sanction the transference of the crown of France from the Merovingian [Childeric] to the Carlovingian [Pepin the Short] family. And on what principle had they done so?...The principle on which he [the Pope] proceeded was plainly this—that in virtue of his spiritual character he was superior to earthly dignities, and had been vested in the power of controlling and disposing of such dignities....It was the usual manner of the Papacy to perform acts which, as they appeared to contain no principles hostile to the rights of society or the prerogatives of princes, were permitted to pass unchallenged at the time; but the Popes took care afterwards to improve them, by founding upon them the most extravagant and ambitious claims...." J. A. Wylie, *The Papacy: Its History, Dogmas, Genius, and Prospects*, (Edinburgh: Andrew Elliot, 1888) pp. 59-60.

[21] *Ibid.*, Wylie states, "The principle on which the whole system of the popes was founded virtually implied their supremacy over kings as well as over priests. They claimed to be the successors of Peter and the vicars of Christ....If their claim was a just one—if they were indeed the vicars of Christ and the vicegerents of God, as they affirmed—there were plainly no bounds to their authority, either in temporal or spiritual matters....According to their theory, there was strictly but one ruler on earth—the Pope....The pontiffs judged it premature to startle the world as yet by undisguised and open avowal of this claim: they accounted it sufficient, meanwhile, to embody its fundamental principles in the decrees of councils and in the pontifical acts, and allow them to lie dormant there, in hope that a better age would arrive, when it would be possible to avow in plain terms and enforce by direct acts, a claim which they had put forth only inferentially as yet." Wylie goes on to observe, "Hitherto the pontiff had been raised to his dignity by the suffrages of the bishops, accompanied by the acclamation of the Roman people and the ratification of the emperor. For till the imperial consent had been signified, the newly-elected pontiff could not be legally consecrated....When the Carlovingian line was decimated of strength, the Papacy shrewdly traded off their support to Charles the Bald in return for a grand purse and the surrender of all rights of the Emperor to interfere with the election to the pontifical throne. The trade off was quickly put into force. From mid tenth century on, the pontiffs ascended the pontifical throne without interference."

The fraudulent "Donation of Constantine", less than fifty years old, was already proving to be one of a number of very useful tools.[22] Pope Nicholas I in 865 drew from this and other forgeries a way to demand submission from bishops and princes and to amass tremendous riches to the Papacy. The arrogance of the popes grew from this time onward, as did their treasury. Popes became intoxicated with their own pride, some in their teens and twenties, losing their senses in nefarious practices. Infamous women of history, Theodora and Marozia, for many years governed the papal throne. As they desired they installed and deposed their lovers, sons, and grandsons as so-called masters of the Church. That unholy See, which pretended to rise above the majesty of kings and princes, descended into dregs of sin. For two centuries, the papacy was one wild arena of bedlam as the most powerful families of Italy disputed and fought over it like a possession. As Wylie recounts,

> "The candidate who was rich enough to offer the largest bribe, or powerful enough to appear with an army at the gates of Rome, was invariably crowned emperor in the Vatican….The popes did not trouble the world with any formal statement of their principles on the head of the supremacy; they were content to embody them in acts. They were wise enough to know that the speediest way of getting the world to acknowledge theoretic truth is to familiarize it with its practical applications—to ask approval of it, not as a theory, but as a fact. Thus the popes, by a bold course of dexterous management, and of audacious but successful aggression, laboured to weave the doctrine of the supremacy into the general policy of Europe."[23]

Lusts of the mind followed by murder and torture

The year 1073 was a turning point from the centuries of gross immorality.

---

[22] "In 774, Charlemagne confirmed the donation of his father, Pepin the Short; moreover, to give the papal claim to temporal power greater antiquity, the so-called Donation of Constantine to Pope Sylvester I was forged. On its basis later popes also claimed suzerainty over Naples, Sicily, and Sardinia." www.infoplease.com/ce6/history/A0860226.html 6/1/04

[23] Wylie, *The Papacy*, p. 63.

Rigorous discipline now became the norm of the Papacy. Reaching above the lusts of the flesh, the lusts of papal minds continued to clutch at total dominion, both ecclesiastical and civil. By this time, the line of Charlemagne had grown too weak to keep papal ambitions in check, and the Pope Gregory VII (also known as Hildebrand) was ambitious beyond all who had preceded him. He was convinced that the reign of the Pope was in fact the reign of God on earth and determined to subject materially all authority and power, both spiritual and temporal, to the "chair of Peter". It was Gregory VII who envisioned what was to become the vast structure of the Papacy. His goal was to be the supreme ruler and judge of all leaders both Church and state. Wylie summarizes,

> "Gregory rekindled, with all the ardour and vehemence characteristic of the man, the war between the throne and the mitre. The object at which Gregory VII aimed was twofold: 1. To render the election to the pontifical chair independent of the emperors; and, 2. To resume the empire as a fief of the Church, and to establish his dominion over the kings and kingdoms of the earth. His first step towards the accomplishment of these vast designs was…to enact clerical celibacy. His second was to forbid all ecclesiastics to receive investiture at the hands of the secular power."[24]

Gregory VII advocated the notion that the Pope is Christ's Vicar. This supremacy, which he claimed by divine right, demanded sure dominion over both emperors and kings.

> "The overthrow of the empire contributed most materially towards the elevation of the Bishop of Rome; for, *first,* it took the Caesars out of the way…*Second,* it compelled the bishops of Rome, now deprived of the imperial influence which had hitherto helped them so mightily in their struggles for pre-eminence, to fall back on another element…which consititutes the very essence of the papacy, and on which is founded the whole complex fabric of the spiritual and temporal domination of the popes…[the idea that] the

---

[24] Wylie, *The Papacy,* Book I, Chapter IV, p. 74.
http://www.wayoflife.org/papacy/01-04.htm#21 6/1/04

Bishop of Rome is the successor of Peter, the prince of the Apostles, and in virtue of being so, is Christ's Vicar on earth."[25]

This idea had been circulating for some time. "The primacy had been promulgated by synodical decrees, ratified by imperial edicts; but the pontiffs perceived that what synods and emperors had given, synods and emperors might take away. The enactments of both, therefore, were discarded, and the *Divine right* was put in their room, as the only basis of power which neither lapse of years nor change of circumstances could overthrow. Rome was henceforward indestructible."[26] The material supremacy of such a notion was not won in a day. But it was Gregory's astute grasp of the notion and his crushing ambition, coupled with the enormous wealth that the Roman Catholic Church by then possessed, that made its implementation possible. These shrewd enactments began to bear fruit even in Gregory's own rule from 1073-1085.

The pontiffs that followed him developed the structures he had established. They continued his projects and strove by deceit, by crusades, and by interdicts[27], to place the world under papal political control. For two centuries from the time of Gregory VII's reign, the papacy increased in power and glory, always at the price of thousands of destroyed lives, many deposed kings and princes, numerous ruined cities, and countless homesteads and farms utterly wasted, all in the name of the religion of Rome.

Popes Innocent III (1198-1216) and Boniface VIII (1294-1303) put the final touches to papal triumph of spiritual and temporal

---

[25] *Ibid.,* pp. 33-34. Emphasis in the original.

[26] *Ibid.,* p. 36. Emphasis in the original.

[27] An interdict was a papal decree whereby citizens were released from their oaths of allegiance to their prince or king, who had been placed under interdict. If the people did not obey the decree, all religious services were stopped including infant baptism and services for the dead. Only the Gospel could break such an iron grip on the lives of men.

power. Pope Innocent III proclaimed a crusade against the Albigenses[28] and offered to all who would engage in it the pardon of all sins to get to heaven without passing through purgatory. It was a war perpetrated with unimaginable cruelty. Whole villages and towns were indiscriminately butchered; thousands of others were burned alive at the stake, while others were subjected to the most hideous torture. The history of these horrendous deeds of cruelty and murder are established by numerous accounts.[29] Pope Boniface VIII "was stubborn, ambitious, intelligent,

---

[28] The Albigenses were a group of Christians, influential for their godly lives, who were condemned by the Church of Rome. George Stanley Faber, writing in 1838, provides an example of Papal work, "'According to the plan adopted by the Inquisitors of Languedoc, it was morally impossible for any of the accused Albigenses to escape [the charge of Manichèism]. By the twenty-second canon of the Council of Narbonne, which sat in the year 1244 for the purpose of aiding and abetting the recently-established Holy Office of Holy Dominic in its project of exterminating the reputed heretics of Southern France, Inquisitors…were forbidden to reveal the names of witnesses; by the twenty-fourth canon, it was enacted that the testimony of infamous persons, of criminals, and of those who confessed themselves to have been accomplices, should be received in the process of the Inquisition against the Albigenses; and by the twenty-sixth canon…it was decreed that he, who shall have been convicted by witnesses, or through any other proofs, shall henceforth be always reputed a heretic, even though he should deny the truth of the allegation. Hist. Gener. De Langued. Par un Benedictin. Livr. Xxv. §81. Vol iii p. 445' Deeply steeped in infamy as is the Pontifical Church, we can scarcely theorise a lower depth than this glaring and scandalous prostitution of justice. *One* benefit, however, may be said to result from it…No rational being can, by any conceivable possibility, believe a syllable of the tales of Manicheism related of the Albigenses, when those tales rest upon such a foundation as that which has been laid by the Council of Narbonne." *The History of the Ancient Vallenses and Albigenses,* pp. 107-108. Emphasis in original.

[29]Jean Paul Perrin [a Waldensian pastor], *History of the Ancient Christians* (1618); Sir Samuel Morland, *The History of the Evangelical Churches of the Valleys of Piemont,* (1658); J. A. Wylie, *The History of Protestantism* (1878); D'Aubigne, *History of the Great Reformation* (New York: Robt. Carter, 1842); Edward B. Elliot, *Horæ Apocalypticæ* (London, 1860); *Foxe's Book Of Martyrs* (Philadelphia: John C. Winston Company, 1926); John Knox, *The History of the Reformation of Religion within the Realm of Scotland,* orig. written between 1559 and 1571 (Edinburgh: The Banner of Truth Trust, 1898, 1982); Baron Thomas Babington Macaulay, *The History of England from the Ascension of James II* (New York: Harper & Bros., 1861); and elsewhere.

vain, and unscrupulous. He believed deeply that the pope was literally the Vicar of Christ on Earth and that he held extraordinary powers. Anyone who opposed him opposed God and therefore must certainly be wicked."[30] He is most famous for a statement in his papal bull *Unum Sanctum*, "We declare, say, define, and proclaim to every human creature that they by necessity for salvation are entirely subject to the Roman Pontiff."[31] Seventy-five popes, one after another, from Pope Innocent III to Pope Pius VII, approved of torture, murder, and burning at the stake, and the confiscation of the property of believers in the horrific centuries of the Inquisition. Many of those slain were true Bible believers.

More than 600 years of Papal Inquisition

The Inquisition is a term that historically applies specifically to the time when the Popes of Rome took the initiative in attempting to stamp out by torture, imprisonment, and death what they called "heresy". Before the popes began to decree such torture and death, a type of persecution involving incarceration and confiscation of property was practiced at the parish level and at the diocesan level in the Roman Catholic Church. The prophecies of Scripture had predicted what indeed happened, *"and it was given unto him to make war with the saints, and to over-come them."*[32] This text is fulfilled in the wars against the Waldenses, the Albigenses, and the other followers of the Lord at the time of the Papal persecutions. This prophecy is the same as what is found the book of Daniel, *"the same horn [that] made war with the saints, and prevailed against them."*[33]

During the Inquisition, "the most ghastly abomination of all was the system of torture. The accounts of its cold-blooded operations make one shudder at the capacity of human beings for cruelty. And it was decreed and regulated by the popes who claim to represent Christ

---

[30] http://history.boisestate.edu/westciv/babylon/04.htm 8/29/03

[31] Henry Denzinger, *The Sources of Catholic Dogma,* Tr. by Roy Deferrari from the Thirtieth Edition of *Enchiridion Symbolorum,* Revised by Karl Rahner, S. J. (St. Louis, MO: B. Herder Book Co., 1957), #469.

[32] Revelation 13:7

[33] Daniel 7:21

on earth. In 1252 Pope Innocent IV solemnly authorized it. Confirmatory or regulatory decrees about it were issued by Alexander IV, Clement IV, Urban IV and Clement V."[34]   The Papacy had become *"drunken with the blood of the saints, and with the blood of the martyrs of Jesus."*[35]   No other kingdom or power has ever drunk so deeply of this blood as has Papal Rome. The facts are undeniable.

"From the birth of Popery in 600, to the present time, it is estimated by careful and credible historians, that more than FIFTY MILLION of the human family, have been slaughtered for the crime of heresy by popish persecutors, an average of more than forty thousand religious murders for every year of the existence of Popery." [36]   The torture chambers of Inquisition, which lasted more than 600 years[37] , were all across the nations controlled by Rome. The instruments of torture were horrendous. If you are sensitive you ought to pray for courage to read on these in the account by Wylie:

"We pass on into the chamber, where more dreadful sights meet our gaze. It is hung round and round with instruments of torture, so numerous that it would take a long while even to name them, and so diverse that it would take a much longer time to describe them. We

---

[34] William Shaw Kerr, *A Handbook on the Papacy* (London: Marshall, Morgan & Scott Ltd., 1950) p. 239.

[35] Revelation 17:6

[36] "No computation can reach the numbers who have been put to death, in different ways, on account of their maintaining the profession of the Gospel, and opposing the corruption of the Church of Rome. A MILLION of poor Waldenses perished in France; NINE HUNDRED THOUSAND orthodox Christians were slain in less than thirty years after the institution of the order of the Jesuits. The Duke of Alva boasted of having put to death in the Netherlands, THIRTY-SIX THOUSAND by the hand of the common executioner during the space of a few years. The Inquisition destroyed, by various tortures, ONE HUNDRED AND FIFTY THOUSAND within thirty years. These are a few specimens, and but a few, of those which history has recorded; but the total amount will never be known till the earth shall disclose her blood, and no more cover her slain." (Scott's Church History) Quoted in John Dowling, *The History of Romanism* (Classic Reprints No. 57, Pensacola, FL: Vance Publications, 2002; originally publ. 1845) Book 8 Ch. 1, p. 542.

[37] From its inception under Pope Innocent III in 1203 A.D., until its final dissolution in Spain and Portugal in 1808, is 605 years.

must take them in groups, for it were hopeless to think of going over them one by one, and particularizing the mode in which each operated, and the ingenuity and art with which all of them have been adapted to their horrible end. There were instruments for compressing the fingers till the bones should be squeezed to splinters. There were instruments for probing below the finger-nails till an exquisite pain, like a burning fire, would run along the nerves. There were instruments for tearing out the tongue, for scooping out the eyes, for grubbing-up the ears. There were bunches if iron cords, with a spiked circle at the end of every whip, for tearing the flesh from the back till bone and sinew were laid bare. There were iron cases for the legs, which were tightened upon the limb placed in them by means of a screw, till flesh and bone were reduced to a jelly. There were cradles set full of sharp spikes, in which victims were laid and rolled from side to side, the wretched occupant being pierced at each movement of the machine with innumerable sharp points. There were iron ladles with long handles, for holding molten lead or boiling pitch, to be poured down the throat of the victim, and convert his body into a burning cauldron. There were frames with holes to admit the hands and feet, so contrived that the person put into them had his body bent into unnatural and painful positions, and the agony grew greater and greater by moments, and yet the man did not die. There were chestfuls of small but most ingeniously constructed instruments for pinching, probing, or tearing the more sensitive parts of the body, and continuing the pain up to the very verge where reason or life gives way. On the floor and walls of the apartment were the larger instruments for the same fearful end— lacerating, mangling, and agonizing living men; but these we shall meet in other dungeons we are yet to visit."[38]

Indictment on the Inquisition

The best summary statement on the papacy's Inquisition is that of the renowned Catholic historian Lord Acton. He declares,

"The Inquisition is peculiarly the weapon and peculiarly the work of the Popes. It stands out from all those things in which they

---

[38] Wylie, *The History of Protestantism*, Book 15, Chapter 11.

co-operated, followed or assented as the distinctive feature of papal Rome. It was set up, renewed and perfected by a long series of acts emanating from the supreme authority in the Church. No other institution, no doctrine, no ceremony is so distinctly the individual creation of the Papacy, except the dispensing power. It is the principal thing with which the Papacy is identified, and by which it must be judged. The principle of the Inquisition is the Pope's sovereign power over life and death. Whosoever disobeys him should be tried and tortured and burnt. If that cannot be done, formalities may be dispensed with, and the culprit may be killed like an outlaw. That is to say, the principle of the Inquisition is murderous, and a man's opinion of the Papacy is regulated and determined by his opinion of religious assassination.'"[39]

The Papacy inflicted excruciating torture and cruel death on true believers. It was like the sufferings recorded in the Old Testament, *"others had trial of cruel mockings and scourgings, yea, moreover of bonds and imprisonment: They were stoned, they were sawn asunder, were tempted, were slain with the sword: they wandered about in sheepskins and goatskins; being destitute, afflicted, tormented; of whom the world was not worthy."*[40] Arthur Pink comments, "Papists have exceeded pagans herein: witness their cruel massacres in France and other places: well may the Holy Spirit represent the whore Babylon as being *'drunk with the blood of the saints'* (Revelation 17:6)…*"Of whom the world was not worthy"*…the most merciless, conscienceless, cruel, and inveterate persecutors of God's elect have been *religious* people!"[41]

Characteristics of the Reformation and the Papacy compared
The Reformation period was full with historical figures and an enormous amount of theological debate. However in the midst of all the doctrinal issues and events there were five biblical principles accepted among

---

[39] "Letters to Mary Gladstone" by Lord Acton, in Kerr, p. 235.

[40] Hebrews 11:36-38

[41] Arthur Pink, *Exposition of Hebrews*, (Grand Rapids, MI: Baker Book House, 1954) commentary on Hebrews 11:37, 38, pp. 881-882.

the Reformers. In all matters of faith and morals, the final authority is the Bible alone. Before the all-holy God, an individual is saved by grace alone through faith alone, in Christ alone. Following on this, all glory and praise is to God alone.

For an overview of the distinctiveness of Reformation history, we have obtained an extended quotation,

"The Protestant Reformation possessed definite characteristics, many of which set it apart from any other revolution in history. One of the distinguishing features was its territorial scope. It began simultaneously and independently in various European countries. About the time that Martin Luther posted his ninety-five theses on the church door in Wittenberg in 1517, John Colet, dean of St. Paul's in England, was denouncing the abuses of the Catholic Church and upholding the supremacy of the Bible as the rule of faith. Lefevre in France and Zwingli in Switzerland were at the same time preaching against the evils of the church and pointing to Christ as the door of salvation. Although Luther is called the originator of the Reformation, the other Reformers discovered and preached the same message that he did, without having received knowledge of it from him.

"There was a power, however, that brought the Reformation into existence and made its progress possible—and that was the Holy Scriptures. The Greek New Testament prepared by Erasmus was a help to scholars all over Europe in learning the way of truth and life. After the Reformation once got under way, there existed a great friendship and fraternization among the Reformers. There was frequent interchange of ideas, and hospitality was freely extended. One of the surprising features of the Reformation was this extent of contact and cooperation among the Reformers as they encouraged each other in their efforts. The Reformation spread with great rapidity. Of course, consolidations, refinements, and extensions needed to be made; but that so tremendous a revolution, on such a vast scale, could be executed in so short a time, bringing with it a complete change in thought and habit, still remains one of the amazing events of history.

"The Protestant Reformation actually began in Europe's citadels of learning, her universities. There were scholars, such as Luther and Melanchthon at Wittenberg; Erasmus, Colet…at Oxford; Bilney, Latimer, and Cartwright at Cambridge; and Lefevre and Farel at Paris. Almost without exception the leaders of the Reformation were highly trained men of that generation. In some instances, as Beza and Tyndale, they ranked high as men of letters. Others, like Cranmer and Valdes carried responsibilities at court...

"Why was this so necessary at that time, when in other ages men of lesser abilities and education have been used effectively to preach the gospel with power? At least two answers can be given: Only the educated knew the Hebrew, Latin, and Greek necessary to read the Bible as it then existed. Then, too, it was essential that the Bible be translated into the vernacular of each country so that the common people could have the privilege of reading the Scriptures in their own tongue. This task demanded scholarship.

"All the preaching of many Luthers, Latimers, Zwinglis, Knoxes, and Wisharts would have failed to accomplish the Reformation if, at the same time, the Bible in the vernacular had not been provided for the common people. If at the moment Latimer was preaching at Cambridge it had not happened that Tyndale, who had fled to the Continent, was smuggling back thousands of copies of the English New Testament so that every Englishman could read the way of salvation for himself, there would have been no Reformation in England. A similar situation occurred in Germany, France, and other countries.

"With these two phases must be combined the indispensable third— the invention of printing, which had made possible the publication of the translations of the Bible and had brought the price within range of the common man's purse. Within a ten-year period many of the nations of Europe had received translations of the Bible in their own tongue. Luther had translated it for Germany in 1522, Lefevre for France in 1523, Tyndale for England in 1525, Bruccioli for Italy in 1532. Within the next ten years Francisco Enzinas had translated the Bible into Spanish, and Petri had translated it into Swedish. Shortly after, Karoli, one of the most energetic of Magyar preachers, had done the same in the Magyar tongue. Another noteworthy characteristic of the Reformers was the basic agreement on important doctrines. The tenet upon which all Reformers agreed was justification by faith. They believed that salvation is not obtained by works, fasting, money, or penance, but that it is God's free gift. This doctrine formed the cornerstone of the Reformation. Agreement also existed on the supreme and sufficient authority of the Scriptures, Communion in both kinds, and the disavowal of saint worship, images, relics, purgatory, mass, celibacy, and the pope as head of the church....

"The Reformation proper, the break with Roman Catholic authority, was accomplished in a relatively short time; but not all the papal teachings were abruptly terminated....The Reformation was a continuous, all-enveloping movement of action and reaction, accruing more glory by the addition of more light. It was a glorious spiritual awakening..."[42]

The Papacy and modern times

What had looked like a mortal wound to Papal power took place in 1798.[43] A general of Napoleon's army entered the Vatican, removing Pope Pius VI from his throne. With that, the Papacy lost its basis as a civil power. From the year 1846 Pope Pius IX, not having territorial or civil power, sought to re-establish the papacy to its former power and glory. An important part of his strategy was achieved by the declaration of papal infallibility. With remarkable ingenuity against not only the absurdity of the notion, but also in spite of the historical fact of heretical

---

[42] Gideon & Hilda Hagstotz, *Heroes of the Reformation* (Rapidan, VA: Hartland Publications, 1951) pp. 12-16, by permission

[43] "Edward King, insightful in 1800 wrote about this defeat as the mortal wound or end of Pontifical Power, "THIS IS THE YEAR 1798.—And just 1260 years ago, in the very beginning of the year 538, Belisarius put an end to the Empire, and Dominion of the Goths, at Rome…He had entered the City on the 10th of the preceding December, in triumph, in the name of Justinian, Emperor of the East: and had soon after made it tributary to him: leaving thenceforward from A.D. 538 NO POWER in Rome, that could be said to rule over the earth, excepting the ECCLESIASTICAL PONTIFICAL POWER." "Remarks on the Signs of the Times" (Philadelphia ed., 1800) pp. 18-19 in Froom, Vol. II, p. 767.

popes, papal infallibility was made a binding dogma of belief at Vatican Council I in 1870.[44] Further, the Papacy re-established itself internally by re-organizing Roman Catholic law into the 1917 *Code of Canon Law.*[45] In 1929 when Mussolini signed the Lateran Treaty with Pope Pius X1 officially conceding Vaticanus Mons (Vatican Hill) to the Pope, the wound that had been inflicted was healed; the Papacy once again became a sovereign civil state. The legal agreement with Mussolini was just the beginning of many civil concordats, one of the most infamous being that between Pope Pius XII and Adolf Hitler.[46] The Papacy had again consolidated its power from within by the 1917 *Code of Canon Law* and from without by legal concordats with the various nations.

---

[44] For Catholic sources, see Catholic historians August Hasler, *How the Pope Became Infallible: Pius IX and the Politics of Persuasion,* originally published in German under the title *Wie Der Papst Unferhlbar Wurde,*1979; English translation by Peter Heinegg (Garden City, NY: Doubleday, 1981) and Ignatius von Döllinger, *The Pope and the Council* (London: Rivingtons, 1869). A fascinating account of the arguments facing the Papacy at this point, including an extended history on the rise of the Papacy, is laid out by von Döllinger.

[45] Roman Catholic writer John Cornwell states, "At the turn of the century [1900], Pacelli [later Pope Pius XII]…collaborated in redrafting the Church's laws in such a way as to grant future popes unchallenged domination from the Roman center. These laws, separated from their ancient historical and social background, were packaged in a manual known as the Code of Canon Law, published and brought into force in 1917. The code, distributed to Catholic clergy throughout the world, created the means of establishing, imposing, and sustaining a remarkable new 'top-down' power relationship. As papal nuncio in Munich and Berlin during the 1920s, Pacelli sought to impose the new code, state by state, on Germany.…" *Hitler's Pope: The Secret History of Pius XII* (New York, 10014: Viking, 1999) p. 6-7.

[46] *Ibid.,* Cornwell also states, "In 1933 Pacelli found a successful negotiating partner for his Reich Concordat in the person of Adolf Hitler. Their treaty authorized the papacy to impose the new Church law on German Catholics and granted generous privileges to Catholic schools and the clergy. In exchange, the Catholic Church in Germany, its parliamentary political party, and its many hundreds of associations and newspapers 'voluntarily' withdrew, following Pacelli's initiative, from social and political action. The abdication of German political Catholicism in 1933, negotiated and imposed from the Vatican by Pacelli with the agreement of Pope Pius XI, ensured that Nazism could rise unopposed by the most powerful Catholic community in the world…" p. 7

Thus the Vatican, with its own citizens as part of a "fifth column" within sovereign nations across the world and with her civil agreements with the same nations, has a double cord of power. The individual Catholic, fearing for his salvation, and laden with his first allegiance being to "holy Mother Church", is a pliable pawn in the hand of the Papacy.

Modern cruelty through wars and intrigue

A partial list of Roman Catholic dictators with whom the Vatican had alliance in twentieth century is the following. Benito Mussolini in Italy, from 1922 to 1943; Adolf Hitler in Germany, 1933 to 1945; Francisco Franco in Spain, 1936 to 1975; Antonio Salazar in Portugal, 1932 to 1968; Engelbert Dollfuss and Kurt von Schuschnigg in Austria, 1932 to 1934; Juan Peron in Argentina, 1946 to 1955. Possibly the most brutal and bloodthirsty of all was Ante Pavelic in Croatia, 1941 to 1945.

The Papacy and Hitler's Germany

Adolf Hitler was baptized into the Catholic Church as an infant in Austria. He was both a communicant and an altar boy. To the day of his suicide, he remained a Catholic. His dealings with the Catholic Church show how far the Vatican will go with the powerful dictators. The alliance worked both ways. It established Catholicism more deeply in Germany while promoting the objectives of Nazi movement. Of it, John Robbins writes,

> "The fountainhead and stronghold of the Nazi movement in Germany was Bavaria in south Germany, Roman Catholic Germany, not Protestant north Germany. German Roman Catholics joined the Nazi Party en masse and enthusiastically supported the Hitler regime. Over half of Hitler's troops were Roman Catholic. At the height of his power in 1942, Hitler ruled over the largest Roman Catholic population in the world. They were accustomed to authoritarian government in their religious lives, which made them unquestioning and enthusiastic supporters of authoritarian civil governments as well. Of course, Roman Catholic laymen were simply following the example and the instructions of their religious leaders. Pius XI was the first head of state to recognize Hitler's government in 1933. Pius XI praised Hitler in public, even before

82

he extended official recognition to the Hitler regime. In 1933, Pius XI told Hitler's Vice Chancellor Fritz von Papen, also a Roman Catholic, 'how pleased he was that the German Government now had at its head a man uncompromisingly opposed to Communism....' Not only did Pius XI's 1931 encyclical *Quadragesimo Anno* influence Franklin Roosevelt's New Deal, it apparently persuaded German Chancellor Franz von Papen to bring Hitler to power in Germany."[47]

Regarding its involvement with Nazi Germany and other nations, the Vatican has repeatedly refused to open up its archives to scholars. Nevertheless, evidence outside the Vatican's archives shows that the Papacy encouraged, supported, and collaborated with both the Mussolini and Hitler regimes, and set up its own totalitarian state in Croatia during the Second World War. The Vatican's legal agreement with the Nazism of Germany and the Fascism of Italy, Spain, Portugal, Croatia, and Latin America are the consequences of the Papacy's economic and social teachings, and legal agreements between the Vatican and these nations.[48] The Crusades and the 605 years of the Inquisition have stopped, but the power of the Papacy to influence and to control governments, social, economic, political life and the destinies of peoples, has continued.

Power through concordats, laws, universities, welfare services and a Council

Jean-Guy Vaillancourt, associate professor of sociology at the University of Montreal, has written a book entitled *Papal Power: A Study of Vatican Control over Lay Catholic Elites.* After a perfunctory passing remark that the Inquisition's burning of heretics and the crusaders' holy wars were "but two more of the extreme forms of hierocratic

---

[47] John W. Robbins, *Ecclesiastical Megalomania: The Economic and Political Thought of the Roman Catholic Church* (Unicoi, TN 37692-0068: The Trinity Foundation,1999; ISBN: 0-940931-52-4) Ch. 16, pp. 163-4. For a similar estimation, see Roman Catholic historian August Bernard Hasler's *How the Pope Became Infallible: Pius IX and the Politics of Persausion,* pp. 255-261.
[48] For fuller documentation, see Robbins.

coercion during the late feudal period"[49], Vaillancourt makes some salient observations,

> "[After 1789 when the Roman Catholic Church was] no longer able to use the repressive power of the state, Church authorities became more and more interested in using the legal and ideological power of the state through the laws enshrined in the concordats, through education of youth in schools and universities and through welfare services such as hospitals and charity organizations. In fact, the [Catholic] Church increasingly became an ideological apparatus which fulfilled for the state and for the ruling class the functions necessary for their own growth and reproduction....Inside the Church, the bishops and priests became functionaries of the central organization, with little individual freedom of their own. An awakening laity was itself turned into a pawn in the papacy's frantic efforts to retain its position of absolute power in Europe and especially in Italy....The question of control of the laity became a key issue, because any initiative of the faithful at the grass-roots level which was not tightly controlled was seen by many Church officials as leading to the ideological and organizational breaking up of the Church."[50]

While the Papacy no longer has the military might by which to enforce its will, it has in no way renounced its sovereign control over men's minds and bodies, as Catholic law shows. Of necessity then, to reintroduce coercion of any consequence, there must first be enacted absolute law within the Catholic system. Second, it is necessary to ensnare the civil authorities in such a way that they are again subservient to Catholic purposes.[51]

---

[49] Jean-Guy Vaillancourt, *Papal Power: A Study of Vatican Control over Lay Catholic Elites* (Berkeley and Los Angeles, CA: University of California Press, 1980) p. 270.

[50] *Ibid.*, pp. 271-273. See also John Cornwell's *Hitler's Pope: The Secret History of Pius XII,* in which he speaks of the internal re-organization of Roman Catholic laws during the nineteenth century, culminating in the *Code of Canon Law* in 1917, and the consequences thereof.

[51] On September 12, 2005 FoxNews.com brought to light some of the tactics mentioned by Vaillaincourt in its article, "Ontario Rejects Use of Islamic Law". "Ontario, the most populous province in Canada, has allowed Catholic and Jewish

The Catholic Church made this major change of tactic visible in its Vatican Council II (1962-1965). That Council moved from a position of separation from other religions to their new program of false ecumenism, not only with the religions of the world, but more importantly with Bible believers in particular.[52] "Separated brethren" was the term coined for those who were always before considered heretics (and who in spite of the new terminology still remain on the books as heretics), while the pagan religions of Islam, Buddhism, and Hinduism now became to the Papacy accepted ways to God.[53] This new approach was established by the Roman Church to win the world to herself by many avenues, one main way being dialogue, the rules and goal of which she has carefully spelled out in her post-Conciliar Document No. 42 on ecumenism, which states that, "dialogue is not an end in itself...it is not just an academic discussion."[54] Rather, "ecumenical dialogue...serves to transform modes of thought and behavior and the daily life of those [non-Catholic] communities. In this way, it **aims at preparing the way for their unity of faith in the bosom of a Church one and visible.**"[55]

---

faith-based tribunals to settle family law matters on a voluntary basis since 1991. The practice got little attention until Muslim leaders demanded the same rights. Officials had to decide whether to exclude one religion, or whether to scrap the religious family courts altogether. McGuinty said such courts 'threaten our common ground,' and promised his Liberal government would introduce legistalion as soon as bossible to outlaw them in Ontario. 'Ontarians will always have the right to seek advice from anyone in matters of family law, including religious advice,' he said, 'But no longer will religious arbitration be deciding matters of family law.'" The Catholic Church's foothold into Canadian civil law has suffered a set-back for the moment by this decision of Premier McGuinty.

[52] Flannery, Vatican Council II Document No. 32, *Unitatis Redintegratio* (Decree on Ecumenism), 21 November 1964, Vol I., § 21, p. 468.

[53] Flannery, Vatican Council II Document No. 56, *Nostra Aetate*, 28 October 1965, Vol. I, p. 739. Through papal acceptance of Hinduism, Buddhism, and Islam, the influence of these pagan religions is being moved more effectively into the Western world via the respectability of Catholicism. Under the term New Age Movement, these old pagan religions have a home both outside of and now within the Roman Catholic Church.

[54] Flannery, Post Vatican Council II Document No. 42, "Reflections and Suggestions Concerning Ecumenical Dialogue", S.P.U.C., 15 August 1975, Vol. I, p. 549.

[55] *Ibid.,* p. 541.

Pope John Paul II consolidated the dictatorial powers afforded him by the 1917 *Code of Canon Law* and by purported infallibility bequeathed him by Vatican Council I. This he did by revising the 1917 *Code*, making it even more conservative than it had been. He had also been careful to appoint new cardinals and bishops in line with his centralized way of thinking.

Like another Pope Gregory VII, John Paul II was determined to build, with both Church and civil law, the structure by which the Papacy will again wield supreme might and power among the nations. The same Pope John Paul II was adamant in his efforts to update the laws of the Roman Catholic Church. Since the days of Gregory VII, the Papacy has seen the necessity of making iron and inflexible church laws before attempting to control both her subjects and those not Catholic by compulsion and coercion, if necessary. In 1983, John Paul II's revision of the 1917 *Code of Canon Law* added greater severity to the Roman Catholic laws. For example, it was decreed the following, "The Church has an innate and proper right to coerce offending members of the Christian faithful by means of penal sanctions." If one rejects submission of his intellect and will to the Pope's doctrine, there are also new decreed penalties. These are spelled out Canon 1371, Para. 1. "The following are to be punished with a just penalty: 1. a. person who...teaches a doctrine condemned by the Roman Pontiff..." Canon 1312 outlines specified penalties that are to be imposed, Para. 2. "The law can establish other expiatory penalties which deprive a believer of some spiritual or **temporal good** and are consistent with the supernatural end of the Church." The perverse vindictiveness of these laws contravenes the repeated scriptural commands that the leaders of the body of Christ are not to be despotic, as the rulers of this world are. Nonetheless even today—as it has been for the last 1,400 years—Catholic law, decrees and coercion supersede grace and the Gospel.

The outcome and the lesson
From its formal inception through the decrees of the Emperor Justinian I in the sixth century, the Papacy has grown enormously, nation by nation, in wealth and political influence by means of laws, intrigue, deception, and sacraments. The Papacy has always tried to cover

itself with a veneer of Christianity, yet this pagan ritual religion has ever repressed and persecuted true godliness and true believers. The history of the Papacy shows unequivocally that it is a power structure built on usurped authority both spiritual and temporal, forgeries, craft, persecution, a false gospel, church law, civil power, and concordats. Nonetheless, the Papacy for most of its history has succeeded in deluding millions. Present day Catholicism continues to insist that the Papacy represents God. The world, for the most part, while not necessarily believing this claim, certainly gives recognition to her shrine and to her Pontiff—for the Papacy is still a powerful force with which they must reckon.

Jesus Christ deposed the overbearing hierarchy of the Pharisees, and gave to His disciples an immediate relationship with the divine fountain of life. In the words Scripture believers are the "*elect according to the foreknowledge of God the Father, through sanctification of the Spirit, unto obedience and sprinkling of the blood of Jesus Christ*"[56], "*are sanctified in Christ Jesus*"[57] and are the "*assembly and church of the first-born, which are written in heaven.*"[58] The Vatican, however, presents the Church as a vast hierarchical empire. It consists of the pope, cardinals, patriarchs, major archbishops, archbishops, metropolitans, coadjutor archbishops, diocesan bishops, coadjutor bishops, episcopal vicar, eparchs (bishops of the Eastern Churches), apostolic vicars, apostolic prefects, apostolic administrators and vicars general.[59] The early bishops of Rome were subject to the Roman Emperors, and later to French and German emperors. The taste of power, however, brought with it addictiveness, and in time, she was able to recognize no authority other than her own. She still looks upon herself as Master of all, and boldly proclaims, "The First See is judged by no one."[60] Christ Jesus did not sanction any such absolute supremacy outside of Himself.

---

[56] I Peter 1:2

[57] I Corinthians 1:2

[58] Hebrews 12:23

[59] For more details, see *Our Sunday Visitor's Catholic Almanac* 2003, "Hierarchy of the Catholic Church" (Huntington, IN: Our Sunday Visitor, Inc) pp. 279-302.

[60] *Code of Canon Law,* Latin-English edition, New English Translation (Canon Law Society of America, 1983, 1999) Canon 1404

What has been so tragic in the history of the Papacy and still remains today is that this massive power system has substituted for the Gospel. Through this enormous structure men have imposed as divine their own decrees on the consciences of other men. In place of direct contact with the source of life in Christ Jesus, the hierarchical structure substitutes a sacramental system over which it has absolute control. The voice of the Church of Rome is said to be the voice of God Himself and as such, it holds influence and mastery over mind, will and soul—by tradition and by coercion, when necessary and possible.

The revealed Gospel teaches that salvation comes from God alone; that it is a gift from heaven; from the one and only Sovereign Ruler. *"And this is the record, that God hath given to us eternal life, and this life is in his Son."*[61] Christ Jesus the Son is life; eternal life is of His own essence. He is eternal life to the true believer, to whom He gives life. Eternal life and salvation are in Him **alone** and not in any system. The difference between the clarity of the Gospel and the Roman hierarchical structure is that of light and darkness. The key question before you now is this: where do you personally stand? Can you for your own part declare with the Apostle, *"I know whom I have believed, and am persuaded that He is able to keep that which I have committed unto Him against that day."*[62] Those who trust on Christ Jesus know in whom they trust. The salvation of their souls is entrusted to Him and to Him alone. An active obedient faith in Jesus Christ is the only surety that will keep a person all days of this life until that day of final reckoning. *"And you, that were sometime alienated and enemies in your mind by wicked works, yet now hath he reconciled in the body of his flesh through death, to present you holy and unblamable and unreprovable in his sight: if ye continue in the faith grounded and settled, and be not moved away from the hope of the Gospel, which ye have heard..."*[63]

The lesson from history that one learns concerns the very nature of the Papacy and its *modus operandi*. The mystery of iniquity

---

[61] I John 5:11

[62] II Timothy 1:12

[63] Colossians 1:21-23

spoken of in Scripture is not the evil lives of atheists, prostitutes, drunkards and the like, but rather the evil of false religion.[64] The Scripture reveals both a *"mystery of godliness"*[65] and a *"mystery of iniquity."*[66] The parallels between the two are both informative and frightening. Just as the Lord God sends His angels to seal His servants in their foreheads,[67] so also there is another who by his agents sets a mark in the foreheads of his devotees.[68] Christ Jesus performed miracles, so there is another who performs false signs.[69] The Savior is seated upon a throne in majesty, yet there is also a seat for one in opposition to Him.[70] Christ Jesus has His people, His Church; there is however another who also has his synagogue and his own false teachers.[71] Christ Jesus is truly the Light of the world; yet in opposition to Him there is one who is *"transformed into an angel of light."*[72]

Key feature of the Papacy and the assurance given in Christ

Deliberate unbelief is a refusal to submit to the righteousness of God and His authority. Often what follows is the establishment of a religion that has its own means of salvation. The self-importance of the Vatican is proverbial. It attempts to establish its own righteousness by devising the importance of merit, indulgences, purgatory and the observance of its sacraments. The folly is that Christ Jesus has come and has brought in an everlasting righteousness. He is the object of faith, and His followers belong to fellowships of believers, comprising His Church. No assembly of believers can ever substitute for the Lord, and no group

---

[64] Matthew 7:15, 24:24-25; II Thessalonians 2:3-12; I Timothy 4:1-2, Acts 20:29, II Peter 2:1

[65] I Timothy 3:16

[66] II Thessalonians 2:7 See J. A. Wylie, *The Papacy Is the Antichrist: A Demonstration* (Edinburgh: George M'Gibbon, no date) Photocopy of original produced by Still Waters Revival Books, Edmonton, AB, Canada.

[67] Revelation 7:3

[68] Revelation 13:16

[69] II Thessalonians 2:9

[70] Revelation 2:13

[71] Revelation 2:9, II Peter 2:1

[72] II Corinthians 11:14

of believers can assume onto themselves His authority. In history, this attempted replacement has been the key factor in the life of Catholicism and its hierarchy. It is the very same issue that negated the way of salvation to the Pharisees and their followers, *"for they being ignorant of God's righteousness, and going about to establish their own righteousness, have not submitted themselves unto the righteousness of God"*[73] This the Apostle calls a seeking for righteousness *"as it were by the works of the law"*[74], not directly, "but as it were" by the works of the law, substituting one thing for another.

As human creatures, each one of us has a supernatural and eternal end. We are therefore bound to answer to the Lord God in the total obedience that He requires. We soon discover, however, that all our efforts at achieving perfect obedience are fruitless, and that of ourselves it is impossible to meet the standards of divine perfection. This righteousness is found in the Lord Christ alone, who in the words of the Apostle, *"is made unto us wisdom, and righteousness, and sanctification, and redemption."*[75] Christ Jesus the Lord totally satisfied the justice of God so that we might be partakers of righteousness by faith, *"for he hath made him to be sin for us, who knew no sin; that we might be made the righteousness of God in him."*[76] It is insufficient to be not guilty; we must also be actually righteous in God's sight. Not only all sin must be forgiven, but also all righteousness must be fulfilled. All the perfection that God requires of us is found in Him on whom we trust. The actual obedience, which Christ lived in keeping whole law of God, is the righteousness whereby we are saved. If you are found in Him, not having your own righteousness but rather having the righteousness that is of God by faith, then indeed your life is hid with Christ in God and when Christ shall appear, you also shall appear with Him in glory.[77] ◆

---

[73] Romans 10:3
[74] Romans 9: 32
[75] I Corinthians 1:30
[76] II Corinthians 5:21
[77] Colossians 3:3-4 *"For ye are dead, and your life is hid with Christ in God. When Christ, who is our life, shall appear, then shall ye also appear with him in glory."*

Chapter 5

The Papal Claim to Have the Keys of the Apostle Peter

    For most Catholics, the authority of the Pope as derived from Peter is the main cornerstone of their faith. For the others, it is the lifesaver to fall back on when all else fails. In my own life, it was a presupposition that I did not question until the very end of my years as a priest. I did begin to investigate seriously the Pope's position when John Paul II came to visit Trinidad in 1985. I remember the loud and pompous ceremony of that day in the Port-of-Spain stadium. Vivid in my mind is the memory of the veneration given to the Pope by the crowds as he entered the stadium. The people rose and with one voice continued to shout, "JP, we love you", accompanied by the rhythmic beat of bongo drums. The Pope bowed in recognition to the adulation.

    Inside myself I was already debating the premise of whether or not he held the keys of the Apostle Peter. So painful was the evening to me that when it came to the end and each priest was to have a personal photograph taken together with the Pope, I quietly left. In driving home in the pouring tropical rain, it seemed as if dark clouds had come down on my presupposition. How could this man claim to have the authority and power of Peter since in most respects he was utterly different in manner and message from St. Peter? I thought of the account of Cornelius, *"Cornelius met him [Peter] and fell down at his feet, and worshiped him. But Peter took him up, saying, stand up; I myself also am a man."*[1] From that evening on, I knew that I had to begin analyzing in earnest the famous text in Matthew's gospel,

---

[1] Acts 10:25-26

blazoned in stone in Latin on St. Peter's basilica in Rome, "Tu est Petrus". I wish to share the thoughts I had then and now as I have continued to study the precious Word of the Lord.

The Petrine primacy of the Pope is an historic holdover from the false Decretals of Constantine and Isidore that we saw in Chapter Four. Nonetheless, the Papacy is the bulwark and foundation of the Church of Rome. It is also the pride and joy of devoted Catholics by giving them, they are assured, a direct link to Jesus Christ. And in these latter days, it appears that the world has rekindled its love of the Papacy. Against the voices of Scripture, history, and reason, the Papacy declares its Church to be founded on the Apostle Peter alone, stating that he was the first bishop of Rome thus bequeathing all of his authority to subsequent popes and bishops. This is the linchpin of Roman Catholicism. Officially the Church of Rome states,

> "The Lord made Simon alone, whom he named Peter, the 'rock' of his Church....This pastoral office of Peter and the other apostles belongs to the Church's very foundation and is continued by the bishops under the primacy of the Pope."[2]

This statement—in fact the whole Roman Catholic structure—is based on three presuppositions:

1. That the text of Matthew 16:16-20 means Peter was the foundation of the Church; that the Church was built on him;
2. That Peter went to Rome and was the first bishop in Rome;
3. That Peter's successors are the bishops of Rome under the primacy of the pope.

It is worth mentioning here that the list of Popes concocted by Rome is a fable. In its humble beginning, the church at Rome was guided by a plurality of elders rather than one single bishop. Then throughout its latter history, there was much intrigue with many of those claiming to be the successor of Peter, an overview of which I will include in the conclusion of this chapter. In this chapter, however, our main focus is not to recount the history of the Papacy but rather to analyze the premise of this notion that the Church of Rome takes for granted.

---

[2] *Catechism of the Catholic Church* (1994), Para. 881

Presupposition 1: The Lord made Simon alone, whom he named Peter, the "rock" of his Church, i.e. foundation of His Church.

"And Simon Peter answered and said, Thou art the Christ, the Son of the living God. And Jesus answered and said unto him, Blessed art thou, Simon Barjona: for flesh and blood hath not revealed it unto thee, but my Father which is in heaven. And I say also unto thee, That thou art Peter, and upon this rock I will build my church; and the gates of hell shall not prevail against it. And I will give unto thee the keys of the kingdom of heaven: and whatsoever thou shalt bind on earth shall be bound in heaven: and whatsoever thou shalt loose on earth shall be loosed in heaven. Then charged he his disciples that they should tell no man that he was Jesus the Christ." (Matthew 16:16-20).

Whatever his contemporaries apprehended Christ to be, this text of Scripture plainly shows that the disciples had a distinct knowledge of Him, expressed without hesitation by Peter on their behalf. The Lord attributes this intuitive knowledge that He was *"the Christ"* (Anointed-Messiah) and *"the Son of the Living God"* (co-eternal with the Father and therefore likewise God) to be a revelation from His Father in heaven. It is this revelation, the Lord declared, that would become the rock or foundation stone upon which He would build His Church. This cannot be argued against as it is the very concluding subject of the Lord's charge to the disciples, *"Then charged he his disciples that they should tell no man that he was Jesus the Christ."* To hold the view that Peter himself is the rock is to deliberately pervert the plain sense of the Lord's own words. To infer that the Church was built upon a mere man—and not upon God's revelation of Jesus as *the Christ, the Son of the living God*—is to insult Christ's doctrine and corrupt God's Word.

The Holy Spirit confirmed the true meaning of the verse by having it written in Greek. The word for Peter in Greek is *petros*. It is masculine in gender and signifies a piece of rock, larger than a stone. In contrast, the word for rock in Greek is *petra*. It is feminine in gender, describing bedrock, massive in size, and immovable. The Church was thus founded upon a massive bedrock, not a mere chip of granite. That bedrock is the God-given revelation by the Father in heaven. Congruent with this revelation is the distinct commission given to Peter in verse 19. "*Unto thee*", that is, to Peter personally, was given the "*keys of the kingdom of heaven.*" This prophetic declaration of the Lord was literally fulfilled when Peter was made the first instrument of opening the same revelation to the Jews, "*God hath made that same Jesus...both Lord and Christ*" (Acts 2:36), and to the Gentiles, (Acts 10:34-44). The power of the keys was concerning this same revelation of the Person of Christ, actuated by the initial proclamation of this revelation first to the Jews, and then to the Gentiles. The Apostle Peter alone fulfilled the initial proclamation. Succession to this prophetic commission is not possible since there was but one first opening of the kingdom for the Jews as for the Gentiles. The second part of verse 19 was a commission for the responsibility of binding and loosening. This is concerning church discipline and was given as well to the other Apostles, as is seen in Matthew 18:18. The whole focus, therefore, of the Matthew 16:16-20 text is on the divinity of Jesus as "*the Son of the living God,*" and His role as Messiah or Christ—this fact is the rock on which His Church is built.

The Catholic apologists argue that the gospel of Matthew was originally written in Aramaic. They claim that the original text of Matthew 16:18 used the word *Ke'pha* for both the name given to Simon Barjona and as the word for the rock upon which Christ promised to build His Church. The fallacy of these claims is that the New Testament was inspired in the Greek text, and that there is no Aramaic text in existence from which it is purported to have come. There are Aramaic and Syriac translations of the original Greek text; these, however, cannot be trusted to accurately represent any supposed original Aramaic text.

The Aramaic texts are merely uninspired translations of the original Greek text.[3]

Even without inventing a non-existing original Aramaic text, the Church of Rome has taken to their advantage the fact that the word Peter and the word "rock" closely resemble each other. As a result Rome has adeptly substituted the one for the other, and thus made the passage to read, "Thou art Peter; and upon thee, Peter, will I build my Church." However, the Lord said *upon this rock*", not "upon thee". "*This rock*" signified the truth that had just been enunciated in the words, "*the Christ, the Son of the living God*". This truth holds a place so fundamental and essential to the Church that it may be truly call "a rock".

Preposterous claims for a pontiff who substitutes for Christ

Jesus as the Christ has full, supreme, and universal power. This prerogative is His alone, and any pretension by another to hold this power is heinous and despicable. Yet the Church of Rome does not blush to claim Christ's power for her Pope. Thus she officially teaches,

> "For the Roman Pontiff, by reason of his office as Vicar of Christ, and as pastor of the entire Church has full, supreme, and universal power over the whole Church, a power which he can always exercise unhindered."[4]

Only Christ Jesus, being the very Son of God, can claim that every human creature is to be entirely subject to Him in faith and practice. The Church of Rome has ascribed to her Pontiff the offices that belong by nature to Christ alone. "Full, supreme, and universal power" solely and rightly belongs to "*the Son of the living God*".

---

[3] In in-depth study of this topic and its historical background (including a examination of the translations of the Greek New Testament which were made in the first five centuries of the Christian Church) is given by Pastor David Th. Stark at: http://www.gpcredding.org/petra.html 7/10/04

[4] *Catechism*, Para. 882

It delighted the Father that in Christ Jesus alone as Savior, all fullness should dwell, *"the fullness of him that filleth all in all."*[5] He alone abundantly gives to all that are His own people, *"grace for grace."*[6] The Church of Rome's lust for power is not satiated by attempting to usurp supreme and universal power over the whole Church, rather she alleges further that she has been allotted the very fullness of grace and truth, "…[T]he very fullness of grace and truth entrusted to the Catholic Church."[7] Thus the Roman Church has made herself into a substitute for Christ. She decrees therefore, "There is no offense, however serious, that the Church cannot forgive."[8] Outrageous and pretentious as these claims are, the Pontiff goes still further by declaring, "It is the right of the Roman Pontiff himself alone to judge…those who hold the highest civil office in a state."[9] The Roman Pontiff is presented as supreme, accountable to no one, and the sole judge of what is right and wrong.

The claim also speaks against the Holy Spirit, the True Vicar of Christ

In stating that "the Roman Pontiff, by reason of his office as Vicar of Christ, and as pastor of the entire Church has full, supreme, and universal power over the whole Church, a power which he can always exercise", the Church of Rome also speaks against the Holy Spirit. The Lord Jesus Christ entrusted the universal care of souls into the safekeeping of the Divine Person of the Holy Spirit. Concerning this third Person of the Trinity who was to be His substitute, the Lord promised that, *"when he is come, he will reprove the world of sin, and of righteousness, and of judgment."*[10] The Holy Spirit convicts of sin as He makes the sinner realize his lost condition and convicts him of his need of Christ's

---

[5] Ephesians 1:23

[6] John 1:16

[7] Declaration "Dominus Iesus", On the Unicity and Salvific Universality of Jesus Christ and the Church, Sect. 16, Sept. 5, 2000.

[8] *Catechism*, Para. 982

[9] *Code of Canon Law,* Latin-English Ed., New English Tr. (Canon Law Society of America, 1983) Canon 1405.

[10] John 16:8

righteousness. He it is who brings to life a soul dead in sin. This miracle of grace is spoken of in Scripture as, *"the exceeding greatness of His power to us-ward who believe, according to the working of His mighty power, which He wrought in Christ, when He raised Him from the dead."*[11] The majesty, greatness and indescribable power of the office of Vicar of Christ are such that a believer must stand in awe of His divine Person. That any human being should lay claim to the office of Vicar of Christ is totally absurd and blasphemous. Because there is a direct connection between the redemption of Christ and the ministry of the Holy Spirit, it is a soul-damning error to mistake the work of the Holy Spirit as Vicar of Christ with the position or work of any man. As Christ Jesus had been the Master, Counselor and Guide to the believers, He promised to send the Holy Spirit as His substitute so that He might abide with them for ever.[12] In believers' lives the Holy Spirit has full, immediate, and universal influence, as the Scripture so wonderfully teaches, *"Now the Lord is that Spirit: and where the Spirit of the Lord is, there is liberty. But we all, with open face beholding as in a glass the glory of the Lord, are changed into the same image from glory to glory, even as by the Spirit of the Lord."*[13] The work of the Spirit is transforming; the believers are changed from one degree of glorious grace unto another until by that same grace one day they will be perfect with Him in glory forever. How much therefore should Christians prize the full and complete ministry of the Holy Spirit!

In the face of these awesome truths concerning the role and ministry of the Holy Spirit of Jesus Christ, it is horrendous to learn that the Vatican proclaims, "The Pope enjoys, by divine institution, 'supreme, full, immediate, and universal power in the care of souls.'"[14] Persuading men and women that Christ the Lord left a mortal man to be His vicar on earth attempts to gainsay the very purpose of Christ Jesus.

---

[11] Ephesians 1:19-20

[12] John 14:16

[13] II Corinthians 3:17-18

[14] *Catechism*, Para 937

Historic devolution from the vicar of Caesar to Vicar of Christ

The outlandish assertion that the Pope is the Vicar of Christ came relatively late in the history of the Papacy. To begin with, the Bishop of Rome claimed to be the vicar of Caesar and his successors, the rightful heirs to the Caesars. The city that had been the seat of power for the Imperial Roman Empire became the city for the bishop of Rome to exercise his authority. Gradually other bishops and national monarchs accepted him as vicar and successor to Caesar with the same supreme title of "Pontifex Maximus". Next the bishops of Rome claimed to be "The vicar of the prince of the apostles"[15], that is, the vicar of Peter.[16] Thus in the early fifth century Bishop Innocent I (401-417AD) insisted that Christ had delegated supreme power to Peter and made him the Bishop of Rome. Following this, he held that the Bishop of Rome as Peter's successor was entitled to exercise Peter's power and prerogatives. Boniface III, who became Bishop of Rome in 607, established himself as "Universal Bishop", thus claiming to be vicar and master of all other bishops. It was not until the eighth century, however, that the particular title, "Vicar of the Son of God"[17], was found in the fraudulent document called "The Donation of Constantine".[18] Although this notorious document was proven false in the early sixteenth century, the Bishops of Rome have used the title "Vicar of Christ" since the eighth century. This title has been the Pope's supreme claim to spiritual and temporal supremacy. The taste of divine power, with which the title resonates, has proven to be addictive. The "Vicar of Christ" is able to recognize no authority other than his own. He looks upon himself as Master of all, and boldly proclaims, "The First See is judged by no one."[19]

---

[15] "Vicarius principis apostolorum" the official title in Latin.

[16] This has been a long-standing contention, since Scripture never mentions Peter as ever residing in Rome.

[17] "Vicarius Filii Dei" is the official title in Latin.

[18] "The Donation of Constantine" states "…as on earth he (Peter) is seen to have been constituted vicar of the Son of God, so the pontiffs, who are the representatives of that same chief of the apostles…" http://www.jmgainor.homestead.com/files/PU/PF/doco.htm 3/9/05

[19] *Code of Canon Law,* Canon 1404.

The end result of the Church of Rome's interpretation concerning what Christ said to Peter is the creation of a pontiff who claims inerrant infallible teaching authority and power over all creatures in both spiritual and temporal realms. The Apostle Paul foretold such an absurd office when he prophesied that there would come "*the son of perdition, who opposeth and exalteth himself above all that is called God, or that is worshiped; so that he as God sitteth in the temple of God, showing himself that he is God*"[20] in place of "*the Christ, the Son of the living God.*"[21] Indeed, there has been erected the Pontiff, the son of perdition. The Papacy at its core office and essence, professes to be an entire substitute for the true Christ and His work. This office must therefore be identified and denounced, as the Holy Scripture does, "*And the woman which thou sawest is that great city, which reigneth over the kings of the earth.*"[22]

Presupposition 2: That Peter went to Rome and was the first bishop in Rome

The Scripture is utterly silent about the Apostle Peter going to Rome. His visits to Samaria, Lydda, Joppa, Caesarea and Antioch were carefully recorded. But there is simply no mention made of his going to Rome, which is essential to establish the Roman Catholic position. Certainly the Holy Spirit would not have passed over an event so significant and essential. In his letter to the Romans, the Apostle Paul greets many in the Church at Rome but offers no salutation to Peter. The same Apostle Paul, being at Rome in the reign of Emperor Nero, never once mentions Peter in any of his letters written from Rome to the churches and to Timothy, although he does remember very many others who were with him in the city. Clearly this presupposition regarding Peter being in Rome as its first bishop is a supposed conjecture, a deception, pure and simple. It cannot be the rock solid foundation on which faith is based.

---

[20] II Thessalonians 2:3, 4

[21] Matthew 16:16

[22] Revelation 17:18

Presupposition 3: That Peter's successors are the bishops of Rome under the primacy of the Pope

This presupposition is officially stated in the following words,

> "Divine assistance is also given to the successors of the apostles, teaching in communion with the successor of Peter, and, in a particular way, to the bishop of Rome, pastor of the whole Church…"[23]

In Scripture there is no mention of successors to Peter or the Apostles. The criteria for apostleship are given in Acts 1:21-22. The position of the Apostles was unique to them and to Paul—all directly chosen by Christ Jesus with no hint of succession. In the New Testament, the Apostles appointed not other apostles but rather elders[24] and deacons. This false presupposition is of the essence of the Papacy. It is a huge system based on the concept of apostolic succession. But apostolic succession without apostolic doctrine is a fraud. The Lord God never entrusted His truth to a personal succession of any body of men. Such a foundation of its very nature is flawed. Visible apostolic succession throughout history was impossible. If one link failed, the whole sequence after it was invalid. Yet Catholicism hitched its star to the notion of apostolic succession.

The real roots of the Papacy are those of the Imperial Roman Emperor and not the Lord Christ Jesus. The Lord commanded, "*The kings of the Gentiles exercise lordship over them; and they that exercise authority upon them are called benefactors. But ye shall not be so: but he that is greatest among you, let him be as the younger; and he that is chief, as he that doth serve.*"[25] Christ absolutely proscribed all domination in his kingdom. The same condemnation of worldly ways was repeated by the Apostle Peter, "*Neither as being lords over God's heritage, but being examples to*

---

[23] *Catechism*, Para 892

[24] The terms overseer and elder/pastor are used interchangeably (Acts 20:17, 28; I Peter 5:1-4).

[25] Luke 22:25-26.

the flock."[26] The Roman Catholic Church is not the successor to the Apostle Peter but rather to the Imperial Roman Empire, as her hierarchical and totalitarian control so steadfastly demonstrates.

Early church leaders on the meaning of the Matthew 16 text

The early church leaders and theologians gave unanimous agreement, in writing, on the true meaning of the Matthew 16 text. The writings of forty-eight church leaders together with the "apostolical constitutions"[27] from the third to the eighth century are preserved. William Webster has compiled these writings in a scholarly article entitled "The Patristic Exegesis of the Rock of Matthew 16:18."[28] From this article we quote the testimony of Theodoret, the bishop of Cyrus, (393-457).

"Let no one then foolishly suppose that the Christ is any other than the only begotten Son. Let us not imagine ourselves wiser than the gift of the Spirit. Let us hear the words of the great Peter, 'Thou art the Christ, the Son of the living God.' Let us hear the Lord Christ confirming this confession, for 'On this rock,' He says, 'I will build my church and the gates of Hell shall not prevail against it.' Wherefore too the wise Paul, most excellent master builder of the churches, fixed no other foundation than this. 'I,' he says, 'as a wise master builder have laid the foundation, and another buildeth thereon. But let every man take heed how he buildeth thereon. For other foundation can no man lay than that is laid, which is Jesus Christ.' How then can they think of any other foundation, when they are bidden not to fix a foundation, but to build on that which is laid?

---

[26] I Peter 5:3.

[27] These were Augustine, Ambrose, Ambrosiaster, Aphraates, Apostolical Constitutions, Asterius, Athanasius, Basil the Great, Basil of Seleucia, Bede, Cassiodorus, John Cassian, John Chrysostom, Peter Chrysologus, Cyprian, Cyril of Alexandria, Cyril of Jerusalem, Didymus the Blind, Epiphanius, Ephrem Syrus, Eusebius, Firmicus Maternus, Firmilian, Fulgentius, Gaudentius of Brescia, Gregory the Great, Gregory Nazianzen, Gregory of Nyssa, Hilary of Poitiers, Ignatius, Isidore of Pelusium, Isidore of Seville, James of Nisbis, Jerome, John of Damascus, Maximus of Turin, Nilus of Ancyra, Origen, Pacian, Palladius of Helenopolis, Paschasius Radbertus, Paul of Emessa, Paul Orosius, Paulinus of Nola, Prosper of Aquitaine, Tertullian, and Theodoret.

[28] http://www.christiantruth.com/fathersmt16.html 8/24/04

The divine writer recognizes Christ as the foundation, and glories in this title.[29] Other foundation no man can lay but that which is laid, which is Christ Jesus (I Cor. iii.11). It is necessary to build upon, not to lay foundations. For it is impossible for him who wishes to build wisely to lay another foundation. The blessed Peter also laid this foundation, or rather the Lord Himself. For Peter having said, 'Thou art the Christ, the Son of the living God;' the Lord said, 'Upon this rock I will build My Church.' Therefore call not yourselves after men's names, for Christ is the foundation….[30]

"Surely he is calling pious faith and true confession a 'rock.' For when the Lord asked his disciples who the people said he was, blessed Peter spoke up, saying 'You are Christ, the Son of the living God.' To which the Lord answered: 'Truly, truly I say to you, you are Peter and upon this rock I shall build my Church, and the gates of hell shall not prevail against it.'[31]

"'Its foundations are on the holy mountains.' The 'foundations' of piety are divine precepts, while the 'holy mountains' upon which these foundations are laid are the apostles of our Saviour. Blessed Paul says concerning these foundations: 'You have been built upon the foundation of the apostles and prophets whose cornerstone is Christ Jesus.' And again he says: 'Peter, James and John who are perceived to be pillars.' And after Peter had made that true and divine confession, Christ said to him: 'You are Peter, and upon this rock I shall build my Church; and the gates of hell shall not prevail against it.' And elsewhere Christ says: 'You are the light of the world, and a city set on a hill cannot be hid.' Upon these holy mountains Christ the Lord laid the foundations of piety….[32]

"Let us inquire who is he that is called a stone; and at which appearing small, later became very great, and covered the earth.

---

[29] *Ibid.*, Philip Schaff, *Nicene and Post-Nicene Fathers* (Grand Rapids: Eerdmans, 1956), Volume III, Theodoret, Epistle 146, To John the Economus, p. 318.

[30] *Ibid.*, *Commentary on 1 Corinthians 1, 12*. Cited by J. Waterworth, *A Commentary* (London: Thomas Richardson, 1871), p. 149.

[31] *Ibid.*, *Commentary on Canticle of Canticles II.14*, M.P.G., Vol. 81, Col. 108

[32] *Ibid.*, *Commentary on Psalms 86.1*, M.P.G., Vol. 80, Col. 1561

Let us, therefore, hearken to God Himself saying by the prophet Isaias, 'Behold I lay in Sion a stone costly, a corner stone, precious, elect, into the foundations thereof, and everyone that believeth in it shall not be confounded' (Is. xxviii.16)...Let us also listen to the blessed David prophecying and crying out, 'The stone which the builders rejected, the same is become the head of the corner?' (Matt. xxi.42). And the blessed apostle Peter teaching among the Jews, and bringing before them the prophecy of the Lord, says, 'This is the stone which, rejected by you the builders, is become the head of the corner' (Acts iv.11). And the blessed apostle says, 'Built upon the foundation of the apostles and prophets, Jesus Christ Himself being the chief corner stone' (Eph. ii.20); and elsewhere he says, 'Other foundation no man can lay but that which is laid, which is Christ Jesus,' (1 Cor. iii.11); and again, 'They drank,' he says, 'of the spiritual rock which followed them, but the rock was Christ'(1 Cor. x.4). Wherefore we are taught by the Old and New Testament, that our Lord Jesus Christ is called a stone.[33]

"For if they say that these things happened before baptism, let them learn that the great foundation of the Church was shaken, and confirmed by divine grace. For the great Peter, having denied thrice, remained first; cured by his own tears. And the Lord commanded him to apply the same cure to the brethren, 'And thou,' He says, 'converted, confirm thy brethren' (Luke xxii.32)."[34]

Final word in conclusion

As we saw at the beginning of this chapter, the church at Rome was guided by a plurality of elders rather than by a single bishop. Throughout its latter history, there was much deceit, with many claiming to be the successor of Peter. What in fact these bishops demonstrated was that they were descendants of Adam and his sin. The concept of the bishop of Rome as a successor of Peter was not seriously held until the fourth

---

[33] *Ibid.*, *Commentary on Daniel ii.34*. Cited by J. Waterworth, *A Commentary* (London: Thomas Richardson, 1871), p. 153

[34] *Ibid.*, Haeret. Fab. Book 5, Chapter 28. Cited by J. Waterworth, *A Commentary* (London: Thomas Richardson, 1871), p. 152

century. It was first devised by Damasus, bishop of Rome (366-384), then Innocent I (401-417). It was more fully formulated in the teaching of bishop Leo I (440-461) in the fifth century. It took many centuries of intrigue and massive forgeries before the concept became dogma in the Roman church. The Hibernian Christians never accepted the teaching until the Norman Conquest in 1172. The Eastern Orthodox Churches have never accepted it.[35]

The desire to be the successor of Peter was the driving force of many men over the centuries so as to reign with power and majesty. Two, even three, concurrent popes were known to vie for the throne at the same time. Thus, for example, at one time three popes in their lust for power each claimed the authority of Peter amid the curses and excommunications with which they assailed one another. The Council of Constance in 1415 set out to settle the matter. The historian Wylie gives some of the details,

> "The way being thus prepared, the Council now proceeded to the trial of the Pope. Public criers at the door of the church summoned John XXIII to appear and answer to the charges to be brought against him.....The indictment contained seventy accusations, but only fifty were read in public Council; the rest were withheld from a regard to the honor of the Pontificate.....Thirty-seven witnesses were examined, and one of the points to which they bore testimony, but which the Council left under a veil, was the poisoning by John of his predecessor, Alexander V. The charges were held to be proven, and in the twelfth session (May 29th, 1415) the Council passed sentence, stripping John XXIII of the Pontificate, and releasing all Christians from their oath of obedience to him. When the blow fell, Pope John was as abject as he had before been arrogant. He acknowledged the justice of his sentence, bewailed the day he had mounted to the Popedom, and wrote cringingly to the emperor, if

---

[35] King Henry with a strong military carried out the designs of the Papacy in 1171. He received submission from Archbishop and Bishop at the Synod of Cashel in 1172. See our article "The Legacy of the True Historical Patrick" on our webpage: www.bereanbeacon.org

haply his miserable life might be spared[36]—which no one, by the way, thought of taking from him. The case of the other two Popes was simpler, and more easily disposed of. They had already been condemned by the Council of Pisa, which had put forth an earlier assertion than the Council of Constance of the supremacy of a Council, and its right to deal with heretical and simoniacal Popes. Angelus Corario, Gregory XII., voluntarily sent in his resignation; and Peter de Lune, Benedict XIII., was deposed; and Otta de Colonna, being unanimously elected by the cardinals, ruled the Church under the title of Martin V."[37]

Coming to reign on the chair of St. Peter was not done by election as it is commonly understood. Rather craft and intrigue of depraved men and women were the major part in deciding succession to the papal throne, as the historian Miller explains,

"For many years the papal tiara was disposed of by the infamous Theodora and her two daughters, Marozia and Theodora. Such was their power and evil influence, by means of their licentious lives, that they placed in the chair of St. Peter whom they would—men wicked like themselves. Our pages would be defiled by an account of their open unblushing immoralities. Such has been the papal succession. Surely Jezebel was truly represented by these women, and in the influence they obtained over the popes and the city of Rome. But, alas! alas! Jezebel, with all her associations, corruptions, tyrannies, idolatries, and uses of the civil sword, has been too faithfully represented by popery from its very foundation."[38]

Believing on Christ and believing on the pontiff are irreconcilable positions. As others in the past have noted, with the pontiff there is found an "altar" instead of a communion table, a "priest" instead of a preacher, ceremonies instead of sound doctrine, sacraments instead of

---

[36] Hardouin, *Acta Concil.*, tom. viii, pp. 361-362.

[37] J. A. Wylie, *History of Protestantism* (N. Ireland: Mourne Missionary Trust, 1878, 1985) Vol. I, Book 3, p. 153. See also Hartland Publications, Vol I, p. 242.

[38] Andrew Miller, *Miller's Church History* in *Books For The Ages* (Albany, OR USA: AGES Software) Ch. 16, p. 432

saving grace, traditions instead of the Written Word of God. This is not in the Church based on God's revelation of Jesus as *"the Christ, the Son of the living God"* but rather an institution based on the rule a pontiff. Therefore we voice the Lord's own exhortation, *"hearken unto me now therefore, o ye children, and attend to the words of my mouth. Let not thine heart decline to her ways, go not astray in her paths. For she hath cast down many wounded: yea, many strong men have been slain by her. Her house is the way to hell, going down to the chambers of death."*[39] Those persons or nations submitting themselves to her and her pontiff know neither life nor freedom. Only in the Lord Jesus Christ, the Son of the living God, is found freedom and eternal life! Believe on Him and Him alone *"and have no fellowship with the unfruitful works of darkness, but rather reprove them."*[40]

Scriptures proclaim that the one supreme sovereign head of the Church is the all holy, unchangeable, all-powerful, all knowing, all wise Lord Jesus Christ. The Roman Catholic Church proclaims "the Sovereign Pontiff John Paul II "[41], or the reigning Pontiff as head of the church of Jesus Christ. One cannot serve two sovereigns for the Lord's commands contradict those of the Pontiff. A man cannot be impartial between two masters who are incompatible. When the necessity of a choice arises, he is will despise the one he does not love supremely. So when the Lord Jesus Christ says, *"Thou shalt love the Lord thy God with all thy heart, and with all thy soul, and with all thy mind,"*[42] and the so-called Sovereign Pontiff demands, "a religious respect of intellect and will, even if not the assent of faith, is to be paid to the teaching which the Supreme Pontiff or the college of bishops enunciate...."[43], one must decide who it is that he loves and fears the most.

The Lord Christ Jesus died in place of the true believer. His life and finished sacrifice alone are the ransom for the believer. *"The Son*

---

[39] Proverbs 7:24-26

[40] Ephesians 5:11

[41] See "Dominus Iesus". http://www.vatican.va/roman_curia/congregations/cfaith/documents/rc_con_cfaith_doc_20000806_dominus-iesus_en.html 8/25/04

[42] Matthew 22:37

[43] *Code of Canon Law*, Canon 752

of man came not to be ministered unto, but to minister, and to give his life a ransom for many." This was the price demanded by the All Holy God in order that His justice might be satisfied in the forgiveness of sins. As a result of this payment the true believer on Christ Jesus alone is freed from sin and Satan. "*For the wages of sin is death; but the gift of God is eternal life through Jesus Christ our Lord.*" The Matthew 16:16-20 text is foundational to eternal life, as the role and the divinity of "*the Son of the living God*" is the rock on which His Church is built! ◆

Chapter 6

Baptism, Confirmation, and Anointing of the Sick

As a priest, I really believed that in bringing people to the sacraments, I was bringing them to Christ Himself. In all the parishes where I served, I always went door-to-door to encourage people to come to Church, to have their babies baptized, and in their last hours to call for the priest. If I could get people to the sacraments, I thought I was getting them to Christ. In this chapter, I will deal with three sacraments in particular: baptism, confirmation, and anointing of the sick. Baptism was for me the gateway to eternal life and the entrance into all the other sacraments. For those in the difficult teenage years, I believed and practiced the teaching that confirmation made the youth strong and perfect Christians. When I found people that lived a life of sin, it was a great consolation to me to be able to anoint such a dying person with the holy oils so that he might, indeed, in that way reach Christ after all. The presupposition at the back my mind was what is outlined in the *Catechism of the Catholic Church*,

"The Church affirms that for believers the sacraments of the New Covenant are *necessary for salvation.* 'Sacramental grace' is the grace of the Holy Spirit, given by Christ and proper to each sacrament."[1]

This is exactly what I believed and what I taught to the people. I believed that the grace of the Holy Spirit was what came out of the sacraments. Logically then, if people received the sacraments, they were receiving the grace of the Holy Spirit. In my mind, and in the hearts and minds of the people, the sacraments, the Holy Spirit, and Christ Jesus, were all tied together in a bundle.

---

[1] *Catechism of the Catholic Church* (1994), Para. 1129.

Reality, however, struck a cord in my being when after I had anointed people with the sacrament of the sick, I heard them die cursing God. When the teenagers, whom I had so carefully prepared for confirmation ended up in drugs, fornication, thefts, and despondency, the veracity of the facts spoke to me. When I saw that the babies I had baptized grew up no different from their Hindu or Buddhist neighbors, I wondered if indeed "Sacramental grace" was the grace of the Holy Spirit. As I discuss these three sacraments, I pray for the light and truth of the Holy Spirit that you may see what it took for me many years to understand. The Scriptures portray the glorious Christ Jesus in His work and sacrifice as the object of faith. Replacing Him by a ritual is disastrous to the soul. How do these rituals have such an attraction and continue to be in demand? This is what we must analyze in the truth and love of the Lord.

Rebirth by baptism

The idea that a person can be born again by baptism is quite attractive. If it were true, what parents are there who would not want the assurance that through this sacrament their baby would be reborn as a child of God? The official Catholic teaching that teaches rebirth by baptism, is given in the following words,

> "Baptism, the gate to the sacraments, necessary for salvation by actual reception or at least by desire, is validly conferred only by a washing of true water with the proper form of words. Through baptism men and women are freed from sin, are reborn as children of God, and, configured to Christ by an indelible character, are incorporated in the [Catholic] Church."[2]

For twenty-one years I baptized an average of thirty babies a month. I assured the mothers[3] and godparents that their children were now children of God. This is still what the priest is given to say, according to the required "proper form of words". Towards the end of the rite of the baptism of a child, the priest says, "Dearly beloved, this child has been

---

[2] *Code of Canon Law*, Latin-English Ed., New English Tr. (Canon Law Society of America, 1983) Canon 849.

[3] The fathers were for the most part were missing, as most of the children were illegitimate.

reborn in baptism. He (she) is now called a child of God, for so indeed he (she) is."[4] The appeal for adults is even greater. Not only is the new life of God promised, but also the assurance was given and still is given of the forgiveness of **all** sins. The words guaranteeing this are in the *Catechism,* "By Baptism *all sins* are forgiven, original sin and **all personal sins, as well as all punishment for sin**."[5]

"Spiritual streaking"

In the parishes in which I served, baby baptisms were common and adult baptisms were rare. Like many other priests, what I disliked most of all was baby baptism. I remember at the annual priests' conference one year, a few priests did what they called "spiritual streaking." They poured out their hearts concerning the depression with which they performed infant baptisms. Their greatest grief was the certainty that they would never see the mother or child again. Our job, one said, was that of "hatching, matching, and dispatching", in baptisms, marriages, and funerals. Of these, "hatching" was the most painful! Ten or twelve years into the life of a parish priest, there often arises the strong suspicion that all that happens is the howling and tears of the babies, some wetness on their heads, and the Certificate of Baptism in the mothers' hands. For those who performed baptisms year after year, the official words advertising infant baptism rang like a cracked gong,

"...The sheer gratuitousness of the grace of salvation is particularly manifest in infant Baptism. The Church and the parents would deny a child the priceless grace of becoming a child of God were they not to confer Baptism shortly after birth."[6]

Christ Jesus' command to believe and be baptized

In stark contrast to the statements of the Vatican, the words of the risen Christ in giving the Gospel are crystal clear. *"He that believeth and is baptized shall be saved; but he that believeth not shall be damned."*[7]

---

[4] *The Rites of the Catholic Church* as Revised by the Second Vatican Ecumenical Council, Study edition, 2 Vols. (Collegeville, MN: Pueblo Publishing Company, Inc., 1990) Vol. I, p. 405. Hereafter *The Rites.*

[5] *Catechism*, Para. 1263

[6] *Catechism*, Para. 1250

Faith is the key of saving grace, and unbelief is the chief damning sin. Faith is what is necessary for salvation and baptism is an ordinance that follows faith and simply testifies to it. Proof of this is found in the fact of the omission in the second half of the verse: it is not "he that is not baptized shall be damned," but rather "*he that believeth not.*" Faith is so indispensable that though one is baptized yet believes not, he shall be damned. The sinner is condemned because of his sin nature and his personal sin. God's divine justice is upon him; nothing can propitiate God's justice but saving faith in Christ. This faith, by God's grace, instantly brings God's act of justification.

The sacramental "power promises" of the Vatican only deceive people and mock both the justice and grace of the Lord God. According to the Bible, faith comes by hearing and hearing by the Word of God.[8] In the ministry of the Apostle Paul, the jail keeper in great agony of spirit asked, "*What must I do to be saved?*" The clear and direct answer of the Apostle Paul and Silas to the question was, "*believe on the Lord Jesus Christ, and thou shalt be saved, and thy house.*"[9] The jail keeper and his household heard the Word of the Lord first in order that they might believe. "*And they [Paul and Silas] spake unto him the word of the Lord, and to all that were in his house.*"[10] Clearly, the official teaching of the Vatican on baptism is a spurious counterfeit of true saving faith. Believing on Christ Jesus is life and salvation. In the words of the Apostle, baptism is important because the Lord commanded it. It testifies to saving faith and is a public declaration of the finished work of Christ applied to an individual soul. Faith is what is necessary for salvation; but baptism, while important, is not of the essence of salvation. In Christ Jesus' own words, "*he that heareth my word, and believeth on him that sent me, hath everlasting life, and shall not come into condemnation; but is passed from death unto life.*"[11]

---

[7] Mark 16:16

[8] Romans 10:17

[9] Acts 16:30-31

[10] Acts 16:32

Educational and medical attractions added on

My heart goes out to Catholics because baptism is the bait that leads into many other things Catholic. I had lived as a parish priest for twenty-one years and saw many young mothers who desired to have their children baptized in order to get the children into the Catholic education system. In Trinidad it was not just Catholics who came to have their babies baptized, but also Hindus, Buddhists, and even Muslims came presenting their babies for baptism. Some pretended to be Catholic; others said frankly that they wanted the Catholic baptism certificate so as to get their child into the Catholic primary school and later to the Catholic colleges. In this way, the Catholic education system works together with infant baptism to draw many families into the whole Catholic organization. The strategy of Rome is not simply to pour forth the sacraments; rather, the sacraments act as a gateway to attract many people into the Catholic education system and into the Catholic hospitals.

When Rome first set about winning Protestants to Catholicism in the United States of America, its documented plan was to entice them by education, medicine, and the sacraments. In 1810, Roman Catholic Bishop Bruté wrote of the strategy,

"Conversion of Protestants. It is necessary to consider the conversions: 1. by direct teachings, 2. by education among Catholics, 3. by mixed marriages, 4. by sojourns in the hospitals or otherwise, on the verge of death..."[12]

"...I observe first in brief that there have been a very strong proportion of Protestants converted in our United States since the American Revolution. Since 1810 when I arrived...Our schools, either of boys or of girls, all receive a great number of Protestant students. They follow all the religious exercises of the school and hear constantly the same instructions. Consequently the prejudices generally give way before these new lights. Many desire to become Catholics and obtain the consent of their parents."[13]

---

[11] John 5:24

[12] "Bishop Bruté's Report to Rome in 1836" in *Documentary Reports on Early American Catholicism* selected and introduced by Philip Gleason, a volume in the Arno Press Collection *The American Catholic Tradition*, Jay P. Dolan, Advisory Editor (New York: Arno Press, 1978) p. 229.

Sadly, these humanistic plans have been quite successful in augmenting the power of Rome and the numbers in its system. Such unbiblical schemes, however, are in total opposition to the means of establishing the kingdom of God as taught in the Scriptures. Christ Jesus declared, *"My kingdom is not of this world."*[14] His kingdom is not a political institution regulated by worldly policies. It is rather a spiritual regime regulated by the truth. The means He uses for its enlargement is His gracious Gospel.

The attraction of confirmation

In the late puberty years or early teens, the sacrament of Confirmation has a great magnetism to strengthen the hold of the Catholic system on children. Priest John O'Brien explains what confirmation is and how it is dispensed,

"Confirmation is administered by the bishop, and consists in the imposition of the hands and the anointing with chrism, a mixture of olive oil and balm, blessed by the bishop on Holy Thursdays. In anointing the forehead with chrism the bishop says: 'I sign thee with the sign of the cross, and I confirm thee with the chrism of salvation in the name of the Father, and of the Son, and of the Holy Spirit.

"The imposition of the hands symbolizes the descent of the Holy Spirit. Oil was used in ancient times to rub the muscles and limbs of wrestlers and athletes to render them more supple. Balm is used to preserve dead bodies from corruption. Thus the anointing with the chrism signifies that the persons confirmed receive the strength to fight as valiant soldiers of Christ and the grace to preserve the supernatural life of the soul from decay. After the anointing the bishop gives the person a slight blow on the cheek to remind him that now he must be ready to suffer persecution and even death itself for the faith of Christ."[15]

Rome officially teaches the claimed effects of Confirmation,

"Confirmation perfects Baptismal grace; it is the sacrament which gives the Holy Spirit in order to root us more deeply in the divine

---

[13] *Ibid.*, pp. 229, 230

[14] John 18:36

filiation, incorporate us more firmly into Christ, **strengthen our bond with the [Catholic] Church….**"[16]

"...For 'by the sacrament of Confirmation, [the baptized] **are more perfectly bound to the Church….**'"[17]

During Holy Week, the Bishop is responsible to make chrism that will be used in confirmation. Officially, "the bishop pours the balsam or perfume in the oil and mixes the chrism in silence….After this he sings or says the invitation: Let us pray that God our almighty Father will bless this oil so that all who are anointed with it may be inwardly transformed and come to share in eternal salvation."[18] Then he consecrates it with the astonishing words, "And so, Father, we ask you to bless this oil you have created. Fill it with the power of your Holy Spirit."[19] The Scripture, however, states that God seeks those who will worship Him *"in spirit and in truth"*.[20] In the light of the Scripture, one comes to understand that it is an ignorant and hopeless tradition to ask the divine Holy Spirit to fill a physical substance with His power. Against this sort of thing, two millennia ago Christ Jesus set forth the principle with utter clarity, *"It is the spirit that quickeneth; the flesh profiteth nothing: the words that I speak unto you, they are spirit, and they are life."*[21]

Follow-up investigation

In the journals that I kept over the years, there were many entries regarding Confirmation. Early in my seven years in the south of Trinidad, I had begun the practice of two years of preparation for this sacrament in the churches where I served. Towards the end of those seven years, I also introduced the practice of having follow-up meetings with the young people and their parents to see just how effective Confirmation

---

[15] John A. O'Brien, *The Faith of Millions: The Credentials of the Catholic Religion* (Huntington, IN: Our Sunday Visitor, Inc., 1963, 1974) p. 161

[16] *Catechism*, Para. 1316

[17] *Catechism*, Para. 1285. Square brackets are in the original text.

[18] *The Rites*, Vol. I, p. 710

[19] *The Rites*, "Consecratory Prayer", Vol. I, p 711

[20] John 4:23

[21] John 6:63

had been. The meetings were arranged at the church to which the parents and the young people were invited. I asked for testimonies from the young people to show that their lives had been changed by Confirmation. I was shocked first by the small attendance of those who had been confirmed, and then by how few of the parents, even of the mothers, bothered to come. I was encouraged, however, to hear a few of the young people tell me things that pleased me, but somehow deep down inside, I was beginning to realize even in those years in Pointe-a-Pierre, Gasparillo, Claxton Bay, and Marabella, that Confirmation did not deliver anything except a closer binding to the Church.

In my final seven years in the Sangre Grande Parish, the people there will testify that I spent over two years preparing the young people for Confirmation. There, however, as part of the instruction, each young person had to buy a Catholic *Jerusalem Bible*. The main group training I did myself, while volunteer teachers taught the subgroups. These subgroups were called by names of individual books of the Bible. The young people were told to study the Bible, and they were told to study especially the book in the New Testament after which their group was called. A toxic additive in those years was the fact that I also gave each young person the Catholic book entitled *The Message of Salvation*. That book does not give the biblical message of salvation, but rather gave the message of Catholic teachings. For example, Lesson Thirteen of this book begins the whole section on the Sacraments with the heading "Christ Comes to You in the Sacraments of the Catholic Church."[22] Lesson Sixteen has the heading "Christ Sends the Holy Spirit in the Sacraments of Confirmation." Then it states,

"In the Sacrament of Confirmation the Holy Spirit comes to your soul to make you strong in Christian belief and strong in the Christian life. In Confirmation the Holy Spirit fortifies, strengthens, completes, perfects and consolidates what He did in Baptism. Baptism is birth in the life of God and membership in Christ's family.

---

[22] Martin Farrell, *The Message of Salvation* Revised Edition 1978 (Des Plaines, IL: Fare, Inc., 1968, 1978) p. 85

Confirmation brings maturity to the Christian life. Confirmation is the Sacrament of Christian maturity."[23]

It was this sort of irrational mixture of Scripture and Catholic doctrine that I was teaching to the young people of my parish. The biblical message that I taught was for the most part wiped out by *The Message of Salvation* book and by the pageantry of what I did in performing the sacraments as a priest. For example, in the same book, the pomp of Confirmation is laid out,

"Confirmation is the occasion of big celebration in every parish church. The church is beautifully decorated and clergy from all the neighboring parishes are present to honor the bishop and the Sacrament he will give this day. The very solemnity of the occasion makes the Christian realize the new state to which he is being elevated and the obligation to spread the Faith that comes with Confirmation." (p. 103)

The Vatican's precise intention is that the drama and pomp that surrounds the so-called sacrament of Confirmation is calculated to spread not biblical faith, but rather the faith of the Catholic Church. I pray to God that the many hundreds of young people who I had led more deeply into Catholicism through Confirmation would now, *"hear the voice of the Son of God"* for *"they that hear shall live."*[24] As the Lord proclaimed, *"Verily, verily, I say unto you, He that heareth my word, and believeth on him that sent me, hath everlasting life, and shall not come into condemnation; but is passed from death unto life."*[25]

"Sealed with that Holy Spirit of promise"

The intent of Rome, as stated in her teaching, is to make people "more perfectly bound to the Church."[26] This, to some extent, she achieves at the price of deceiving millions. The idea of using a ritualistic physical sacrament, such as Confirmation, to complete Baptism and to seal the individual with the Holy Spirit is a deceitful tradition in conflict with the Scripture. It is through hearing, understanding, and responding to the Gospel that an individual is incorporated or sealed into Christ and

---

[23] *Ibid.*, p. 102

[24] John 5:25

[25] John 5:24

becomes a true Christian. Once the believer trusts on the Lord, he is sealed with the Holy Spirit, as the Scripture says, "*in whom [Christ] ye also trusted, after that ye heard the word of truth, the gospel of your salvation: in whom also, after that ye believed, ye were sealed with that Holy Spirit of promise.*"[27]   The simplicity of this truth is such that the Scripture also proclaims, "*Now if any man have not the Spirit of Christ, he is none of his.*"[28]

Anointing of the sick

The Roman Catholic teaching on the Anointing of the Sick is given in her *Catechism*. Rome officially declares,

"The special grace of the sacrament of the Anointing of the Sick has as its effects: the uniting of the sick person to the passion of Christ, for his own good and that of the whole Church; the strengthening, peace, and courage to endure in a Christian manner the sufferings of illness or old age; the forgiveness of sins, if the sick person was not able to obtain it through the sacrament of Penance; the restoration of health, if it is conducive to the salvation of his soul; the preparation for passing over to eternal life."[29]

"*Union with the passion of Christ.* By the grace of this sacrament the sick person receives the strength and the gift of uniting himself more closely to Christ's Passion...Suffering, a consequence of original sin, acquires a new meaning; it becomes **a participation in the saving work of Jesus**."[30]

By far the saddest memories of my days in the priesthood were the many times I was at the bedside of dying men and women. In the journals that I kept over my last fourteen years in the priesthood, I wrote the details of about two hundred of such cases in which I knelt at the bedside of those passing from life to death. The common theme of my counsel to those dying was that they should offer to God their sufferings with the sufferings of Jesus Christ, to participate in His redemption for the salvation of their own souls and of the souls of

---

[26] *Catechism,* Para 1285
[27] Ephesians 1:13
[28] Romans 8:9
[29] *Catechism*, Para. 1532
[30] *Catechism*, Para. 1521 Italic is in the original.

others. "Offer your pain with His pain, your agony with His agony. He has given us the ultimate example of laying down His life for others, now you lay down your life united with Him, your blood with His blood for the salvation of your own soul and the souls of others," I counseled them.

Such were my words in those days. That also had been my intention over those years as I had devoutly offered my own sufferings for the salvation of souls. I had remembered so well the words of Archbishop Finbar Ryan speaking to us when we were novices. In his most dramatic tones, he told us to imagine Christ Jesus presenting before us the cup with His blood poured out in it. Then the Archbishop said, "Put into this cup drop by drop, your own blood, in the sufferings that you offer, showing your life is offered with Him, so that the world may be saved." I was faithfully passing on to those on the threshold of eternity what I had learned from our official Catholic teaching, from such as Archbishop Finbar Ryan, and from the message as I was trying to live it.

In my Catholic charismatic days, I gave an added dimension to the Catholic message of participation in the sufferings of Christ by what I was learning from Pentecostalism. In my journal, I recorded cases where I would not simply tell the Catholic person to offer his or her sufferings with Christ, but I would say also, "Pray for sufficient faith to claim a healing for your cancer, have enough faith so that the Lord will be able heal you." In this way I was giving people a double guilt trip. Believing the basic assumption that the anointing of the sick was a participation in the sufferings of Christ, I added also the basic Pentecostal assumption, that if we had enough faith, all diseases and sickness could be healed. Today I truly thank God that my sins are all washed away in the precious blood of the Lamb, that I have forgiveness for teaching the damning messages that in all sincerity I gave to the dying. Now I pray that in the Lord, as He has forgiven me, He would use even these memories of the lies spoken into the ears of the dying to minister to those who are as yet bound by the traditions of Rome.

Prayer and anointing in the letter of James

The Lord Jesus Christ commanded two ordinances for His people. The essential ingredients of these are that they are from Him and that they testify to Him. The prayer and anointing recommended in the letter of James 5:14-16 is just that, "*the prayer of faith*". The conclusion in verse 16 summarizes the passage, "*the effectual fervent prayer of a righteous man availeth much.*" Rome takes this recommended prayer and weaves it into her sacrament to be performed by her sacrificial priest. She ends up by deceiving the elderly, those in great pain, and the dying. Her accursed message is that their suffering can have a union with the passion of Christ, as stated in Paragraph 1521 of her *Catechism*. This message of "a participation in the saving work of Jesus" is a damnable lie meant to be spoken into the ears of those who are sick and dying. Rather, Christ's redemptive work is His and His alone.

The doctrine of "a participation in the saving work of Jesus" is utterly perverse in that it holds out a false hope to trust in one's own suffering as adding something to that of the Lord. Such a concept is an utter lie as it denies the repeated statements of God's truth in Scripture. The work of redemption is "*by Himself,*"[31] "*without the deeds of the law,*"[32] "*not of yourselves, it is the gift of God: not of works, lest any man should boast,*"[33] "*not by works of righteousness which we have done, but according to His mercy He saved us....*"[34] To teach Satan's lie to those who are dying is truly an abomination.

A tragic curse on the dying

Rome claims also that her sacrament for the sick includes "the forgiveness of sins". In performing the ritual, the priest says, "May the Lord who

---

[31] Hebrews 1:3

[32] Romans 3:28

[33] Ephesians 2:8-9

[34] Titus 3:5

frees you from sin save you and raise you up."[35]   Forgiveness of sin, however, is the graciousness of God for those who look to Christ in faith and for the believer who directly confesses his sins unto the Lord. It is not bound up with any ritual. Christ Jesus is life and to Him alone belongs the power of the resurrection to the sick and dying. He alone is the object of one's faith. Instead of looking to a priest and his anointing at the hour of death, my prayer is that Catholics would *"look unto Jesus the author and finisher of our faith…and is set down at the right hand of the throne of God."*[36]   Since the Garden of Eden, Satan has always delighted in the twisting of God's Word. Praying for the sick is indeed something to be commended and upheld. However, Rome has taken the advice in the letter of James Chapter Five and turned it into a dramatized curse on the sick and the dying.

The deception is not only on those who are conscious of what is happening, but also it is recommended that the priest perform the rite even on those who are unconscious and may indeed be dead. Thus the ritual of the Church of Rome states,

"The sacrament of anointing is to be conferred on sick people who, although they have lost consciousness or the use of reason, would, as Christian believers, have at least implicitly asked for it when they were in control of their faculties.

"When a priest has been called to attend those who are already dead, he should not administer the sacrament of anointing.... But if the priest is doubtful whether the sick person is dead, he is to confer the sacrament, using the rite given in no. 269."[37]

The compassion of Christ is needed for those who dwell under the cruelty of this so-called sacrament. May the true Gospel, which is the power of God unto salvation, be delivered in the compassion of Christ to sick and elderly Catholics, for it is only by this means they will find the eternal life promised in the Scriptures. *"And this is the record, that God hath given to us eternal life, and this life is in his Son. He*

---

[35] *The Rites*, Vol. I, p 774

[36] Hebrews 12:2

[37] *The Rites*, Vol. I, p 781, # 14 & 15

that hath the Son hath life; and he that hath not the Son of God hath not life."[38]

The Gospel rather than trafficking with the souls of men

The merchandise of Rome in her sacramental system is a grave matter as *"our God is a consuming fire."*[39] The supreme enemy of Christ and His Gospel is not materialism and lust, but rather spiritual pride and apostasy of those that pretend to stand in His place. An individual's faith begins and ends in Christ Himself and not in the rituals of any church. As an individual believes on *"the only begotten of the Father, full of grace and truth,"*[40] he knows that *"of his fullness have all we received, and grace for grace."*[41]

The Catholic Church's teaching of sacraments as necessary for salvation is a futile and offensive exchange of her sacraments for the Lord and Giver of life. The merchandise involved in Baptism, Confirmation, and Anointing of the Sick is the souls of men.[42] Men, women, and children are made to believe that salvation begins in Baptism and is sealed in Confirmation. The souls of men crave for "holy oils" at the very gates of death. Cheating rituals are substituted for the simple act of faith in the Lord of glory. Satan's design is always to replace Christ and His Gospel with rituals and devotion, *"Having a form of godliness, but denying the power thereof: from such turn away."*[43] Looking to physical signs to give "sacramental grace" and calling that "the grace of the Holy Spirit" is literally a blasphemy against the all Holy God. It not only denigrates the Person and work of the Holy Spirit, but it presupposes that a priest dispenses His power in fixed and automatic ways. So momentous is this trafficking in the souls of men that the commandment and promise of the Lord must be

---

[38] I John 5:11-12

[39] Hebrews 12:29

[40] John 1:14

[41] John 1:16

[42] Revelation 18:12-13

[43] II Timothy 3:5

repeated, *"Wherefore come out from among them, and be ye separate, saith the Lord, and touch not the unclean thing; and I will receive you, and will be a Father unto you, and ye shall be my sons and daughters, saith the Lord Almighty."*[44]

God has promised to be a Father to true believers, that they shall be His sons and His daughters. This is the greatest honor possible to man. How ungrateful a thing, then, must it be if those to whom this dignity and privilege is explained should degrade themselves by attempting to replace Christ Jesus and eternal life with a form of godliness that does not deliver. Christ Jesus has promised that *"all that the Father giveth me shall come to me; and him that cometh to me I will in no wise cast out."*[45]   ◆

---

[44] II Corinthians 6:17-18
[45] John 6:37

Chapter 7

Encounters in the Confession Box

In my first year of ministry as a priest in Park Street Catholic Church, Port of Spain, Trinidad, I remember in vivid detail what a difficult time I had with the Saturday confessions. Each Saturday from 3:00 to 6:00 p.m., many Catholics queued up outside the confession box waiting their turn to enter to tell us their sins. I recall how profusely I sweated in those days, not just because I was living in the tropics, but rather it was the first time in my life that I was experiencing how horrific it is to have peoples' sins poured over oneself, sometimes in intimate detail, for three hours at a stretch. We had one final hour of this, after our evening meal, from 7:00 to 8:00 p.m. At 8:00 p.m. Carlton, the sexton of the Church, had to close the doors on people who still desired to come in to confess their sins to the priests. I used to feel how nervous people were in telling me of their sins, particularly young women explaining their sexual misconduct. I could see the perspiration just above the lips of many of those who confessed. The task became more difficult as, week after week, people returned confessing the same sins.

In that first year I did not at all doubt that I had power to say, "I absolve you from all your sins in the name of the Father and of the Son and of the Holy Spirit", which words we spoke in Latin. It was only in later years that serious doubts arose in my mind, although even in my first parish in Mayaro, in southeast Trinidad, I began to have some fleeting doubts. This happened particularly in the outstations where people came back week after week with the same plethora of sins, fornications, adulteries and thefts. To add to this difficulty, confessions had to be heard before the Mass, and each Sunday I had three different

Masses to say. Sometimes I had to go through the confessions quickly, giving very little counsel and advice to those who confessed because I had other Masses to do, and these were at set times. A growing problem was that after hearing confession, I felt as if I had been in a garbage pit where garbage had been thrown over me until I was nearly succumbing to the sheer weight of the knowledge of sin that had fallen on me. Encumbered as I was with this awful stuff and without any relief personally, I had then to go say Mass. The difficulty continued to grow, for I found the Mass to be of no help for my own increasingly burdened state.

Many years later in my final parish in Sangre Grande in northeastern Trinidad, I had real reservations about confession. From the Scripture, I had learned that forgiveness of sins came as one   believed on Christ Jesus. I knew also that the Scripture declared, "*Who can forgive sins but God only?*"[1] At that time, I stopped hearing confessions with the exception of elderly women who simply recited the list of sins they had memorized from their youth (I knew that they would be offended if I did not hear their confessions). In refusing to hear the confessions of the people generally, I was, of course, reported to the Archbishop. That was only one of the many problems that accrued as I began dealing with issues biblically in my last seven years as a parish priest. With this testimony in mind, perhaps one can more readily understand my plight as a priest who had studied the Catholic teaching, who had put it into practice as a parish priest, and who knew the frustration that the sacrament of Confession caused in the lives of the people as well as in my own.

Sins are only truly forgiven when people believe on the Lord Jesus Christ, "*Be it known unto you therefore, men and brethren, that through this man is preached unto you the forgiveness of sins.*"[2] In believing on the finished work of the Lord Christ Jesus, a soul has both the forgiveness of sins and perfect right standing with God

---

[1] Mark 2:7

[2] Acts 13:38-39

credited to him. *"But now the righteousness of God without the law is manifested."*[3] *"In whom we have redemption through his blood, the forgiveness of sins, according to the riches of his grace."*[4] Thus the Gospel is the power of God unto salvation, as the Apostle Paul proclaimed. When one does sin after salvation, it is a relationship problem with the Father in heaven to be resolved as one directly confesses his sin to God. *"If we confess our sins, he is faithful and just to forgive us our sins, and to cleanse us from all unrighteousness."*[5]

Catholic forgiveness

In stark contrast to the clear teaching of the Lord through Scripture, the Catholic is taught to look for forgiveness by confessing his sin not to God through the Lord Jesus Christ[6], but rather to an intermediary human priest. This is what devout Catholics practice. The thought behind the practice requires some explanation. In the *Catechism of the Catholic Church*, there are seven sacraments to be explained rather than the two scriptural sacraments of baptism and communion. "The Sacrament of Penance and Reconciliation" has five names[7], each name defining a particular element within the whole ritual. The first defining name is "the *sacrament of conversion*" while the second is "the *sacrament of Penance*", which is declared to be necessary for salvation. The official words of Rome are,

> "It is through the sacrament of Penance that the baptized can be reconciled with God and with the Church...This sacrament of Penance is necessary for salvation for those who have fallen after Baptism, just as Baptism is necessary for salvation for those who have not yet been reborn."[8]

The reason that the sacrament of Penance is "necessary for salvation" is given also,

---

[3] Romans 3:21

[4] Ephesians 1:7

[5] I John 1:9

[6] I Timothy 2:5

[7] *Catechism of the Catholic Church* (1994), Para. 1423, 1424

[8] *Ibid.*, Para. 980

"Christ instituted the sacrament of Penance [*sic*] for all sinful members of his Church: above all for those who, since Baptism, have fallen into grave sin, and have thus **lost their baptismal grace**…It is to them that the sacrament of Penance **offers a new possibility to convert and to recover the grace of justification**. The Fathers of the Church present this sacrament as 'the second plank [of salvation] after the shipwreck which is the loss of grace.'"[9]
Such teaching as this—that justification can be lost—flies directly in the face of Romans 8:29-39, I Peter 1:2-5, Romans 11:29, Numbers 23:19, etc. Thus Catholics have no assurance of their salvation.

The third name by which the sacrament of Penance is called is "the *sacrament of confession*, since the disclosure or confession of sins to a priest is an essential element of this sacrament…."[10] While the Catholic Church acknowledges that only God can forgive sins, confession to a priest is essential because her doctrine states that "by virtue of his divine authority he [Jesus] gives this power to men to exercise in his name."[11] The biblical reference cited here is John 20:21-23 when the Lord Jesus Christ in person was commissioning His Apostles.[12] The position of His Apostles was unique to them and to Paul—all directly chosen by Christ Jesus with no hint of succession. The judgment of sins (v. 23) was basically to be made through the preaching of the Gospel, as for example, when Peter preached to the men of Judah and Jerusalem[13], and when the Apostle Paul preached to the Thessalonians and to the Athenians of Mars Hill.[14]

Failing to understand apostleship biblically, the Catholic Church continued to expand on her own idea regarding the forgiveness of sins.

---

[9] *Ibid.*, Para. 1446. Square brackets are in the original. Para. 1447 states that the practice of penance originated in Eastern monastic tradition. Thus Para. 1447 contradicts Para. 1446, which states that Christ instituted the sacrament of Penance.

[10] *Ibid.*, Para. 1424

[11] *Ibid.*, Para. 1441

[12] The criteria for apostleship are given in Acts 1:21-22. In the New Testament the Apostles did not appoint other apostles. They appointed elders. (The terms overseer and elder/pastor are used interchangeably, Acts 20:17, 28; I Peter 5:1-4.)

[13] Acts, Ch. 2

[14] Acts, Ch. 17

She states, "But he [Christ] entrusted the exercise of the power of absolution to the apostolic ministry which he charged with the 'ministry of reconciliation' (2 Cor. 5:18)."[15] By this statement, it is clear that the Catholic Church has wrongly understood the priesthood of Christ because Hebrews 7:24 states that His priesthood is not transferrable.

Nevertheless, the next step in the Catholic Church's error is the development of the notion of apostolic succession. It is found in the section entitled "The Minister of This Sacrament",

"Since Christ entrusted to his apostles the ministry of reconciliation, bishops **who are their successors**, and priests, the bishops' collaborators, continue to exercise this ministry. Indeed bishops and priests, by virtue of the sacrament of Holy Orders, have the power to forgive all sins 'in the name of the Father, and of the Son, and of the Holy Spirit.'"[16]

Having seemingly wrested power from its rightful Owner, the bishops now use it according to their own ideas of penitence and forgiveness,

"Since ancient times the bishop, visible head of a particular Church, has thus rightfully been considered to be the one who principally has the power and ministry of reconciliation: He is the moderator of the penitential discipline. Priests, his collaborators, exercise it to the extent that they have received the commission either from their bishop (or religious superior) or the Pope, according to the law of the [Catholic] Church."[17]

Catholic thinking thus runs counter to the Scripture because their leaders, through their notion of apostolic succession, have taken to themselves the idea that they can forgive the sins of the people. From there, they claim the right to administer penance to all their people. This is an un-biblical idea.

---

[15] *Catechism*, Para. 1442 Although their proof text states, "*And all things are of God, who hath reconciled us to himself by Jesus Christ, and hath given to us the ministry of reconciliation*", they have overlooked the fact that in this epistle the Apostle Paul is not addressing the other Apostles. Rather he is writing to "*the church of God which is at Corinth, with all the saints which are in all Achaia.*"[15] In verse 19, which is not cited, the Apostle Paul explains very clearly the ministry of reconciliation entrusted to these believers, "*To wit, that God was in Christ, reconciling the world unto himself, not imputing their trespasses unto them; and hath committed unto us the **word** of reconciliation.*" This

Forgiveness, the fourth name in this sacrament, is defined as follows, "It is called the *sacrament of forgiveness*, since by the priest's sacramental absolution God grants the penitent 'pardon and peace.'"[18] The teaching on forgiveness goes much further than just stated. All offenses, no matter how grave are proclaimed to be in the power of the priests of the Church. In the Vatican's own words,

"There is no offense, however serious, that the Church cannot forgive. 'There is no one, however wicked and guilty, who may not confidently hope for forgiveness, provided his repentance is honest.'"[19]

The power of the priests is said to be greater than even the power given to angels and archangels. Rome states,

"Priests have received from God a power that he has given neither to angels nor to archangels...God above confirms what priests do here below. Were there no forgiveness of sins in the Church, there would be no hope of life to come or eternal liberation."[20]

It would be difficult to conjure up words of greater arrogance. It is blasphemy for any creature to undertake the pardon of sin because that is God's prerogative. "*I, even I, am he that blotteth out thy transgressions for mine own sake, and will not remember thy sins.*"[21] This Scripture passage is a gracious assurance that sins are blotted out for God's own name's sake. The pronoun is repeated to make it emphatic that He alone can forgive sins.

The last defining name by which this sacrament is called is "the *sacrament of Reconciliation*". Supposedly, it "imparts to the sinner

---

ministry does not state or carry with it the idea that there is any "exercise of the power of absolution" accompaning "*the word of reconciliation*" (i.e., the Gospel). Instead it explicitly denies that idea since the Apostle states that it is "*the word of reconciliation*" which has been entrusted to the believers.

[16] *Ibid.,* Para 1461
[17] *Ibid.,* Para. 1642
[18] *Ibid.*
[19] *Ibid.,* Para. 982
[20] *Ibid.,* Para. 983
[21] Isaiah 43:25

the love of God who reconciles"[22] , although no priest through this sacrament gives the Gospel, *"which is the power of God unto salvation"*.[23] The *"word of reconciliation"*[24] , which is the Gospel, has been left out of Catholic forgiveness and in its place has been put confession to a priest and the rituals of penance.

Obligation to confess

Rome's insistence that her people confess is seen in her laws. Samples of these rulings are the following,

> "One who desires to obtain reconciliation with God and with the Church, **must confess to a priest all the unconfessed grave sins** he remembers after having carefully examined his conscience."[25]

> "Individual and integral confession and absolution constitute the only ordinary way which the faithful person who is aware of serious sin is reconciled with God and the Church."[26]

> "A member of the Christian faithful is obliged to confess in kind and in number all serious sins committed after baptism and not yet directly remitted through the keys of the Church nor acknowledged in individual confession, of which one is conscious after diligent examination of conscience."[27]

The humiliating experience of the confessional is obligatory in Catholicism. This system of confession in the ear of a priest cannot but corrupt the Gospel by encouraging and promoting a ritual unknown in Scripture. A pure contrition of the heart as a requirement for forgiveness, minute detailing of "the kind and number all grave sins" to a priest is a degrading practice that often leads to sin.

---

[22] *Ibid.*, Para. 1424

[23] Romans 1:16

[24] II Corinthians 5:19

[25] *Catechism*, Para. 1493.

[26] *Code of Canon Law*, Latin-English Ed., New English Tr. (Canon Law Society of America, 1983) Canon 960.

[27] *Ibid.*, Canon 988 §1.

Forgiveness of sins as a judicial act of a priest

The rite of Confession in the Catholic Church has necessary words going with it that the priest must use. These are the following,

> "God, the Father of mercies, / through the death and the resurrection of his Son/ has reconciled the world to himself/ and sent the Holy Spirit among us/ for the forgiveness of sins;/ through the ministry of the Church/ may God give you pardon and peace, / and **I absolve you from your sins/ in the name of the Father, and of the Son, and of the Holy Spirit.**"[28]

The absolution that is necessary for the Catholic to obtain is not a declaration that God Himself has forgiven the person confessing, but it is rather a judicial act of the priest who says, "I absolve you from your sins." It is, therefore, the priest himself who acts as judge in forgiving the sins. In the words of the Council of Trent,

> "However, although the absolution of the priest is the dispensation of the benefaction of another, yet it is not a bare ministry only, either of an announcing the Gospel or declaring the forgiveness of sins, but it is equivalent to a judicial act, by which sentence is pronounced by him as a judge [can 9]."[29]

This "divine power" for priests judicially to forgive sins is also claimed in the *Catechism*,

> "Only God forgives sins. Since he is the Son of God, Jesus says of himself, 'The Son of man has authority on earth to forgive sins' and exercises this divine power: 'Your sins are forgiven.' Further, by virtue of his divine authority he gives this power to men to exercise in his name."[30]

It is mind-boggling arrogance to claim that divine judicial power is given to sinful men to forgive sins. It is made worse in that the basis for such a false claim is cited in Matthew 16:19, in the account of the Lord's personal commission to the Apostle Peter. But the *Catechism*

---

[28] *Catechism*, Para. 1449.

[29] Henry Denzinger, *The Sources of Catholic Dogma*, Tr. by Roy J Deferrari from *Enchiridion Symbolorum*, 30th ed. (St. Louis, MO: B. Herder Book Co., 1957) # 902. Because the Catholic Church claims that she is "irreformable" (Vatican Council II Document No. 28 *Lumen Gentium*, §25, p.380) and her popes infallible, the Council of Trent still officially stands and can in no way be abrogated by any official statements to the contrary.

[30] *Catechism*, Para. 1441

continues,

> "In imparting to his apostles his own power to forgive sins the Lord also gives them the authority to reconcile sinners with the Church. This ecclesial dimension of their task is expressed most notably in Christ's solemn words to Simon Peter: 'I will give you the keys of the kingdom of heaven, and whatever you bind on earth shall be bound in heaven, and whatever you loose on earth shall be loosed in heaven.' 'The office of binding and loosing which was given to Peter was also assigned to the college of the apostles united to its head.'"[31]

The Lord said to the Apostle Peter, *"And I will give unto thee the keys of the kingdom of heaven: and whatsoever thou shalt bind on earth shall be bound in heaven: and whatsoever thou shalt loose on earth shall be loosed in heaven"* (Matthew 16:19). *"Unto thee"* relates this promise to Peter alone. This declaration of the Lord was literally fulfilled to Peter, as he was made the first instrument of opening the kingdom of heaven by preaching the Gospel to the Jews (Acts 2:41) and to the Gentiles (Acts 10:44-47). The power of the keys was two-fold, to the Jews and to the Gentiles. It was fulfilled in the Apostle Peter and in him alone. There can be no successors to this prophetic commission, since there was but one first opening of the kingdom for the Jews as for the Gentiles. The binding and loosing of Matthew 16:19 and 18:18 has to do with the decisions of a church congregation in matters of discipline reached through prayer, the Word, and the Spirit, that will be ratified in heaven. It does not include the Lord's divine right to forgive sins. The concept of a sinful human being having been delegated divine authority to forgive judicially the sins of others is totally offensive to God and a denial of the truth of the Written Word of the Lord. Nonetheless this is exactly what the Church of Rome claims for her priests.

Church of Rome claims a biblical base for forgiveness through a priest

The scriptural backing claimed by Rome for the priest purportedly

---

[31] *Catechism*, Para. 1444

being able to absolve others of sin is found in Paragraph 1485 of her *Catechism*:

> "'On the evening of that day, the first day of the week,' Jesus showed himself to his apostles. 'He breathed on them, and said to them: 'Receive the Holy Spirit. If you forgive the sins of any, they are forgiven; if you retain the sins of any, they are retained.' (John 20:19, 22-23)."

The biblical response to this claim is found in the actual words of John 20:23, "*Whosesoever sins ye remit, they are remitted unto them; and whosesoever sins ye retain, they are retained.*" The Apostles were sent not to be priests but only witnesses to the truth. They were not mediators of the reconciliation, but rather preachers and publishers of it. Unquestionably the Lord Jesus Christ declared in a few words the sum of the Gospel. The Lord gave authority to His disciples to declare forgiveness to those whom God had already forgiven. The commission given in this passage in John is a parallel to similar passages such as Luke 24:47, Matthew 28:18-20, and Mark 16:15-16. This is the way the Apostles understood and obeyed the commission, as evidenced throughout the Acts of the Apostles, for Christ did not appoint confessors to probe intimately into each sin of people in whispers in a confession box. Rather He commissioned preachers of his Gospel and He caused their voice to be heard. Thus the Apostle Peter proclaimed, "*To him give all the prophets witness, that through his name whosoever believeth in him shall receive remission of sins.*"[32] If we believe in Him, He shall justify us. This is the great remission of sins that all need, without which each of us is still spiritually dead. The manner of forgiving sins in Scripture is the proclamation of the Gospel. It is not the whispering of sins committed into the ear of a mortal man in a confession box.

Dangers involved in confession

The real sadness that breaks my heart is the emptiness and wickedness that comes out of what is claimed to be the means to forgive sin. The engineered artifact of a confessional box, with two sinners inside, one

---

[32] Acts 10:43

claiming to be the overlord of conscience, is substituted for that personal and private spiritual communion with God by the one seeking His mercy and grace, made possible through the faithfulness of Christ Jesus. Souls have been trained to forsake the preciousness of true faith and grovel before another creature in a dangerous ritual. Salvation and forgiveness are no longer flowing to the sinner through the pure Word from the very heart of God, but rather men in their ignorance are attempting to siphon forgiveness into a processor, from which it is to be dispensed to the sinner through sacramental spigots by the mediation of priests.

In the Catholic system, therefore, intimate proximity to a man has been substituted for the work of the Holy Spirit and the joy of knowing forgiveness before the living God. The real vulnerability of boxed confession, however, is that it can be an occasion of sin and even of false accusations. These dangers are all admitted in the rules that go with the sacrament in Catholic system. In the Vatican laws on confession, Canon 977 declares,

"The absolution of an accomplice in a sin against the sixth commandment of the Decalogue is invalid except in danger of death." ["Thou shalt not commit adultery" is counted as the sixth commandment in the Catholic Church.]

This is such a problem that Pope John Paul II decided that some offenses by priests involving the sacrament of reconciliation and pedophilia are be judged exclusively by a Tribunal in Rome. The document addresses

"the grave offenses against the sacrament of reconciliation: 'To give absolution to someone who is an accomplice [of the priest] in a sin against the Sixth Commandment; to invite on the occasion, at the moment, or with the pretext of confession to sin against the Sixth Commandment; to violate directly the secret of confession.' Pederasty is the crime against customs. It is a 'sin against the Sixth Commandment committed between a minor younger than 18 years, and a priest.'"[33]

Such legislation may curb the dissemination of the scandals involving Confession on a local level, but it does nothing to curb inordinate desires of unregenerate men facing the abnormal situation of the close proximity of the confession box. To decree that men are so adorned with power that they by a judicial act absolve sins, and then to place them in an intimate and hazardous proximity with women and boys while expecting them to continually refrain from disgraceful sinful conduct is crass and supine arrogance on the part of the Church of Rome. In the ordinary business world, a company who thus treated its executives would be exposed immediately as criminal and citizens would be warned to cease to invest in its activities.

Further, Canon 984 §1 declares, "Even if every danger of revelation is excluded, a confessor is absolutely forbidden to use knowledge acquired from the confessional when it might harm the penitent." The law regarding secrecy that has been maintained as a priest's right to secrecy, can itself be another great occasion of sin for a priest. Particularly in small groups, such as hearing nuns' confessions, it is most difficult, if not impossible, to abstain from letting the information obtained in confessional influence one's actions afterwards when socializing with those whose confessions have been heard. Another of the general Vatican laws regarding confession is Canon 979, "The priest in posing questions is to proceed with prudence and discretion, with attention to the condition and age of the penitent, and he is to refrain from asking the name of an accomplice." This law shows the pitfalls that can await the posing questions in the confession box. The fact that the priest is forbidden to ask the name of a partner in crime shows also the propensity to sin that is encompassed in these confidential encounters in the confession box. These are just a sample of the grim laws designed to anticipate and limit the potential moral chaos arising from the practice of boxed private confession. If the ordinary rules of biblical counseling were observed, and the priest not left alone with someone to solicit or to be solicited, things would not be so hazardous. The Word of God teaches by precept and example that the knowledge of evil is always a source of pollution to a creature who possesses it.

---

[33] www.mgr.org/PedoVat.html 7/26/03

One of the principal joys of heaven toward which true believers yearn in the depths of their being is to be finally free from the presence, power, and knowledge of sin. The very reason why the Lord God reserved the knowledge of good and evil to Himself in the Garden of Eden was because only an All-Holy, Infinite Being of unlimited power and goodness can retain that knowledge without contracting pollution from it. It is, therefore, the height of spiritual stupidity and silly presumption to devise and mandate a private ritual wherein the depths of human depravity and weakness are explored under a cloak of seeking forgiveness and grace. Nevertheless, it is even a law in the Church of Rome that confessions are to be heard in the confessional box, and not in another place.[34]

It is a tremendous burden to see that under the pretense of forgiving sins, there is the undermining of the unique office of Christ Jesus that can end up as a serious occasion for sin. Sincere priests doing their duty, and devout Catholics seeking to alleviate guilt, can find themselves prey to sin in the very rite through which it is purported they may be delivered from sin. The scandals that have resulted from the confessional and other close encounters within the Catholic system have reached such horrendous proportions that it is difficult to keep up with the documented evidence.[35] Our hearts ought to grieve in anguish and our desire increase to give the pure Gospel to Catholics so that they can come to the Lord Himself, and know the freedom and joy it is to be His very own. *"If the Son therefore shall make you free, ye shall be free indeed."*[36]

It is a gracious promise of the Lord to all who continue in His Word that they shall know the truth and that truth will set them free. The Gospel truth frees one from the yoke of the ceremonial rites that routinely deceive and ensnare but do nothing to free a man's conscience

---

[34] *Code of Canon Law,* Canon 964 §3: "Confessions are not to be heard outside a confessional without a just cause."

[35] See the summary report of Massachusetts Attorney General p 2 www.ago.state.ma.us 7/23/03. Many Roman Catholic WebPages show the bad fruit that arises from wrong doctrine and practice.

[36] John 8:36

before God. The soul trusting on the Lord alone for salvation, and for His mercy day by day for forgiveness, beholds the glory of the Lord, and is changed into the same image from glory to glory, even as by the Spirit of the Lord. Our prayer is that God, who commanded the light to shine out of darkness, would shine forth into the hearts of those sitting in the gloomy darkness of man-made traditions to give *"the light of the knowledge of the glory of God in the face of Jesus Christ."*[37]

Biblical forgiveness
In Scripture, forgiveness is mediated through Jesus Christ alone, the only Mediator between God and man.[38] The instrument of forgiveness is not a church, but rather faith in the Lord Jesus Christ, *"Believe on the Lord Jesus Christ, and thou shalt be saved, and thy house."*[39] *"But to him that worketh not, but believeth on him that justifieth the ungodly, his faith is counted for righteousness."*[40]

The forgiveness of all sins is of God and not that of any church. This is so in order that we come to understand that it is He, God, Who is *"just and the justifier of him which believeth in Jesus."*[41] To attempt to bring the Catholic priest and the sacrament of Confession into the nature of the saving work of the Godhead, indeed to attempt to make the priest and the sacrament the fount of forgiveness is gross blasphemy. In Scripture, forgiveness and acceptance are in Christ Jesus alone.

The God of all grace
In spite of clear biblical teaching, the Catholic Church claims that a mere man, with the right formula of words, is an effective means of grace in a judicial act of forgiveness. The rite of Confession, in particular, claiming that, "by virtue of his [Christ's] divine authority he gives this

---

[37] II Corinthians 4:6

[38] John 14:6; Acts 4:12, I Timothy 2:5

[39] Acts 16:31.

[40] Romans 4:5.

power to men to exercise in his name"[42] is sufficiently serious to merit the full wrath of God for those who have invented and practice this evil parody on the forgiveness of the Lord. In Scripture *"the God of all grace"*[43] by means of His Word directly seeks, finds, and saves His people. Forgiveness is God's gift to the believer. It is granted to the believer based on Christ's finished work on the cross.[44] God's action in Christ Jesus shows His graciousness to believers so that their eyes of faith are fixed on Him alone. *"For if by one man's offence death reigned by one; much more they which receive abundance of grace and of the gift of righteousness shall reign in life by one, Jesus Christ."*[45] ◆

---

[41] Romans 3:26.

[42] *Catechism*, Para 1441

[43] I Peter 5:10.

[44] Romans 4:5-8; II Corinthians 5:19-21; Romans 3:21-28; Titus 3:5-7; Ephesians 1:7; Jeremiah 23:5-6; I Corinthians 1:30-31; Romans 5:17-19.

[45] Romans 5.17.

Chapter 8

The Mass as a Sacrifice

This topic is a very sensitive one. Soon after I left the priest-hood, people would ask me what I thought of the Mass. I would say that the topic is too excruciating for me to begin to analyze and I did not deal with it. And so the issue remained for more than two years. I dealt with other topics, but it was only during my fourth year after leaving the priesthood, that I began to analyze the Catholic teachings on Holy Communion and the Mass.

Popular Catholic authors exult in the power and the prestige of the priest to bring Christ down from heaven to the altar at Mass. They explain that the priest offers up again the same sacrifice that Christ offered on Calvary. An example is the words of the Catholic priest John O'Brien,
> "When a priest pronounces the tremendous words of consecration, he reaches up into the heavens, brings Christ down from His throne, and places Him upon our altar to be offered up again as the Victim for the sins of man. It is a power greater than that of monarchs and emperors: it is greater than that of saints and angels, greater than that of Seraphim and Cherubim.
> "Indeed it is greater even than the power of the Virgin Mary. While the Blessed Virgin was the human agency by which Christ became incarnate a single time, the priest brings Christ down from heaven, and renders Him present on our altar as the eternal Victim for the sins of man—not once, but a thousand times! The priest speaks

---

[1] John A. O'Brien, *The Faith of Millions: The Credentials of the Catholic Religion* (Huntington, IN: Our Sunday Visitor, Inc., 1963, 1974) pp. 255-256. Italic is in the original.

and lo! Christ, the eternal and omnipotent God, bows his head in humble obedience to the priest's command.

"Of what sublime dignity is the office of the Christian priest who is thus privileged to act as the ambassador and the vice-regent of Christ on earth! He continues the essential ministry of Christ: he teaches the faithful with the authority of Christ, he pardons the penitent sinner with the power of Christ, he offers up again the same sacrifice of adoration and atonement which Christ offered on Calvary. No wonder that the name which spiritual writers are especially fond of applying to the priest is that of *'alter Christus'*. For the priest is and should be *another Christ*."[1]

Many of us who were priests had great difficulty with such teaching even while we still celebrated the Mass. Alexander Carson in his testimony explained his own struggle,

"On a Sunday night in July 1972... I began to read the book of Hebrews in the New Testament. This letter exalts Jesus, His priesthood, and His sacrifice over all the Old Covenant or Testament. This is some of what I read: *"Who needeth not daily, as those high priests, to offer up sacrifice, first for his own sins, and then for the people's: for this he did once, when he offered up himself..."* (Hebrews 7:27). This startled me, and I began to feel very uneasy. I understood for the first time that Jesus' sacrifice was a one-time sacrificial offering at Calvary, in itself effectual to reconcile me and believing penitents of all ages to God. I saw at this time that the 'Holy Sacrifice of the Mass' offered by me and thousands of other Roman Catholic priests daily throughout the world was a fallacy and completely irrelevant. If the 'sacrifice' I daily offered as a priest was meaningless, then my 'priesthood' which existed for the purpose of offering that 'sacrifice' was likewise without meaning."[2]

---

[2] Alexander Carson, "Free Indeed", in *Far from Rome, Near to God: The Testimonies of Fifty Former Roman Catholic Priests*, Richard Bennett and Martin Buckingham, eds., Second Edition (Carlisle, PA: The Banner of Truth Trust, 1997) p. 53.

The accomplishment of the Cross

Before detailing the exact teaching of the Catholic Church on the Mass, it is important to grasp at least an outline of the culminating achievement of God in the sacrifice of Christ. The absolute perfection of the sacrifice of Christ is because of the dignity of His person. It was the God-man who obeyed, suffered and died. Nothing equal could again be offered. The sacrifice itself portrayed the gracious work of Christ Jesus. Aptness and excellence could never be surpassed, as it was the work of Him who *"thought it not robbery to be equal with God."*[3] Christ's readiness and willingness to complete the sacrifice is seen in His words, *"Lo, I come to do thy will, O God."*[4] The Father's will centered and terminates in Christ's sacrifice; it was both an act of His will, and most profitable for His people. The priceless double empowerment of Christ's perfect sacrifice is proclaimed by the Holy Spirit, *"by the which will we are sanctified through the offering of the body of Jesus Christ once for all."*[5] Christ's sacrifice originated in the will of God the Father. It was essential that the Father should be willing to call His Son to this work, for He was the person to whom the satisfaction was to be made. The sacrifice was the Father's plan and purpose, *"Him [Christ Jesus] being delivered by the determinate counsel and foreknowledge of God."*[6] *"But this man, after He had offered one sacrifice for sins for ever, sat down on the right hand of God....For by one offering He hath perfected for ever them that are sanctified."*[7]

The one offering of Christ, willed by the Father, was once offered. The Divine perfection is seen in the fact that it was one sacrifice once offered. To propose a reenactment of the one offering once offered is to attempt to denigrate the very will and purpose of the Father. The majesty, power and absolute perfection of Christ Jesus the

---

[3] Philippians 2:6

[4] Hebrews 10:9

[5] Hebrews 10:10

[6] Acts 2:23

[7] Hebrews 10:12,14

Lord is seen in His one offering, once offered. He manifested also the effect of His sacrifice, which was the sanctification of His people. The contrast between the all-sufficient offering of Christ and the ineffectual offerings under the law is described thus, "*And every priest standeth daily ministering and offering oftentimes the same sacrifices, which can never take away sins: But this man, after He had offered one sacrifice for sins for ever, sat down on the right hand of God.*"[8]

Christ Jesus has triumphed in His sacrifice, and to all those that come to Him, He will perfectly give freedom from the guilt, power, and punishment of sin. He will put them into sure possession of perfect holiness and joy of fellowship with Himself and the Father. "*And their sins and iniquities will I remember no more. Now where remission of these is, there is no more offering for sin.*"[9] The true believer's sins and iniquities the Father will remember no more! This shows the riches of Divine grace, and the sufficiency of Christ's satisfaction on the cross, "*where remission of these is, there is no more offering for sin.*" There shall be no more remembrance of sin against true believers, either to shame them now or to condemn them hereafter. The sacrifice of Christ was once for all time. Its power is eternal. "*There is therefore now no condemnation to them which are in Christ Jesus.*"[10] Nothing can ever separate His people from the love of God. "*Wherefore he is able also to save them to the uttermost that come unto God by him, seeing he ever liveth to make intercession for them.*"[11] Christ procured a perfect eternal salvation for His own!

The Catholic victim

Many times as a priest, I looked down on the bread and the wine after the words of consecration and thought that I had just offered Christ Jesus' sacrifice. The exact words I said were, "Look with favor on your Church's offering, and see the Victim whose death has reconciled

---

[8] Hebrews 10:11-12

[9] Hebrews 10:17-18

[10] Romans 8:1

[11] Hebrews 7:25

us to yourself."[12] I was praying to the Father in Heaven to accept Christ, as a "sacred victim". I did not realize at that time that what I was doing did not match the Scriptures. Amy Bentley, a former Catholic nun, explains it this way, "Our Church leaders taught a daily sacrifice, yet according to Hebrews 10:10 we are sanctified through the offering of Jesus '*once for all*'. It never occurred to me to question how the 'true Church' could be filled with leaders who teach that the sacrifice of Calvary was incomplete."[13]

This is the terrain of Catholic worship that now must be addressed with utter reverence before the All Holy God. The truth of the matter is that Christ's one perfect offering was accepted because He is now risen from the dead, ascended into heaven, and seated at the right hand of the Majesty on High. His one sacrifice, perfect and complete, has been accepted by the Father to the eternal glory of His name and the glory of Christ Jesus Himself. Although this truth is a hard one for sincere and devout Catholics, nevertheless there is no way around it.

The Catholic claim that Christ is immolated in the Mass
Vatican Council II documents teach,

> "For in the sacrifice of the Mass **Our Lord is immolated** when 'he begins to be present sacramentally as the spiritual food of the faithful under the appearances of bread and wine.' It was **for this purpose that Christ entrusted this sacrifice to the [Catholic] Church**…Participation in the Lord's Supper is always communion with Christ **offering himself for us as a sacrifice** to the Father."[14]

---

[12] "Eucharistic Prayer No. 3", *New Saint Joseph People's Prayer Book,* Rev. Francis Evans, General Editor (New York, NY: Catholic Book Publishing Co., 1980) p. 120.

[13] Amy Bentley, "The Conversion of a Catholic Nun" in *The Truth Set Us Free: Twenty Former Nuns Tell Their Stories*, Richard Bennett, Editor (Mukilteo, WA: WinePress Publishing, 1997) p. 77. Available from www.bereanbeacon.org.

[14] *Vatican Council II: The Conciliar and Post Conciliar Documents,* No. 9, *Eucharisticum Mysterium*, 25 May 1967, Austin Flannery, O. P., Gen. Ed., 1981 ed., 2 vols., (Northport, NY: Costello Publ. Co., 1975) Vol. I, §3, pp. 102-103

The present day Catholic Church, which has officially ratified the Council of Trent, continues to curse all who do not hold that her Mass is indeed a propitiatory sacrifice. To propitiate is defined as to appease one offended and render him favorable. What the Catholic Church presently ratifies is the following,

"If anyone says that the sacrifice of the Mass is one only of praise and thanksgiving, or that it is a mere commemoration of the sacrifice consummated on the Cross but not one of propitiation; or that it is of profit to him alone who receives; or that it ought not to be offered for the living and the dead, for sins, punishments, satisfactions, and other necessities: let him be anathema."[15]

The clarity of Christ's command stands diametrically opposed to all such teaching. Christ's words, "*Take and eat*", were addressed not to His Father in heaven—but rather to the Apostles. He did not command them to "offer and propitiate", but simply to "*Take and eat*". His sacrifice that followed was His and His alone, as the Scripture declares, "*when he had by himself purged our sins, sat down on the right hand of the Majesty on high.*"[16]

The Catholic "the sacred victim"

The center of Catholic worship and life is the Mass. The Church teaches her faithful that they are to offer themselves with "the sacred victim", Jesus Christ, and to receive the same "sacred victim". Thus she declares,

"Consequently the **eucharistic sacrifice is the source and the summit of the whole of the [Catholic] Church's worship and of the Christian life**. The faithful participate more fully in this sacrament of thanksgiving, propitiation, petition and praise, not only when **they whole-heartedly offer the sacred victim, and in it themselves, to the Father** with the priest, but also when they receive this same victim sacramentally."[17]

---

[15] Henry Denzinger, *The Sources of Catholic Dogma*, Tr. by Roy J Deferrari from *Enchiridion Symbolorum*, 30th ed. (St. Louis, MO: B. Herder Book Co., 1957) Council of Trent, Session XXII (Sept. 17, 1562) Canon 3.

[16] Hebrews 1:3

[17] Flannery, No. 9, *Eucharisticum Mysterium*, p. 104

Christ was never a victim and the idea of His being victimized is nowhere in Scripture. Rather it was of His own free will that He chose to fulfill His Father's will. He declared, *"Therefore doth my Father love me, because I lay down my life, that I might take it again. No man taketh it from me, but I lay it down of myself. I have power to lay it down, and I have power to take it again. This commandment have I received of my Father."*[18] The erroneous concept of Rome focuses the mind on a tragic Christ as victim, and not Christ as victor, Lord of Lords and King of Kings. The Catholic Church repeats her command that the faithful ought to offer the divine victim to God when she states,

> "Therefore the **eucharistic celebration is the center of the assembly of the faithful over which the priest presides**. Hence priests teach the faithful to offer **the divine victim** [Jesus Christ] to God the Father in the sacrifice of the Mass and **with the victim to make an offering of their whole life**..."[19]

The priest is told to instruct his people "to make with the victim an offering of their whole life". They are to make satisfaction to God for their sins by offering "the divine victim" and with the victim to make an offering of their whole life. This is how Jacqueline Kassar lived her life. She begins her testimony by saying, **"Forty-five years of my life were spent as a Roman Catholic, twenty-two of them as a nun in an enclosed convent dedicated to adoration, reparation and suffering. I believed it was a nun's calling to be a miniature savior of the world, like Jesus Christ."**[20] She did not realize that offering reparation as "a miniature savior" belittled the one perfect sacrifice once offered, insinuating that it could be perfected.

---

[18] John 10:17-18

[19] Flannery, Vatican Council II Documents No. 63, *Presbyterorum Ordinis*, 7 Dec. 1965, Vol. I, Sec 5, p. 871

[20] Jacqueline Kassar, "From a Nuns' Convent to Biblical Conversion" in *The Truth Set Us Free: Twenty Former Nuns Tell Their Stories*. p. 11.

The Cross and the Mass claimed as one single sacrifice

While purporting that the Church is doing what the Lord commanded, the Vatican further claims that the sacrifice of Calvary and the Mass are the same, "one single sacrifice". Thus she teaches,

> "The sacrifice of Christ and the sacrifice of the Eucharist are *one single sacrifice:* 'The victim is one and the same: the same now offers through the ministry of priests, who then offered himself on the cross; only the manner of offering is different.' 'And since in this divine sacrifice which is celebrated in the Mass, the same Christ who offered himself once in a bloody manner on the altar of the cross is contained and **offered in an unbloody manner**...this sacrifice is truly propitiatory.'"[21]

Thus clearly the Catholic Church alleges that Christ is offered in her Mass, in an unbloody mode. The Holy Spirit's teaching, however, is that Christ's sacrifice was once offered, in contrast to the daily offering of sacrifices of the Old Testament, *"nor yet that he should offer himself often...for then must he often have suffered since the foundation of the world: but now once in the end of the world hath he appeared to put away sin by the sacrifice of himself."*[22] Divine perfection is seen in the fact that it was one sacrifice, once offered. To put forward a reenactment of the one offering, once offered, is to attempt to degrade the will and propose of God.

Second, for anyone to deem himself fit to offer the immortal Christ Jesus in His perfect sacrifice is arrogance of the highest order. Christ Jesus alone was qualified to offer Himself. He alone had the absolutely unique qualifications as the Holy Spirit teaches, *"For such an high priest became us, who is holy, harmless, undefiled, separate from sinners, and made higher than the heavens."*[23] Third, Rome's claim is that Christ "is offered in an unbloody manner". Scripture equates offering and suffering. In a propitiatory sacrifice, to offer and to suffer are the same thing. This truth is so important that it is given as an

---

[21] *Catechism*, Second Ed., Para. 1367

[22] Hebrews 9:25-26

[23] Hebrews 7:26

absolute principle, *"without shedding of blood is no remission."*[24] Hence in this context to propose a bloodless sacrifice is a contradiction in terms. A bloodless sacrifice is a senseless inconsistency that can have no purpose other than to deceive.

The unique oneness of Christ's sacrifice is in this very fact, that it was one offering once made. The concept "once" is deemed so important that it is asserted seven times by the Holy Spirit in the New Testament. The perfection of Christ's sacrifice is contrasted with the repeated daily sacrifices of the Old Testament. The truth of the excellence of Christ's sacrifice is highlighted by the word "once". For example, the Apostle Paul teaches, *"For in that he died, he died unto sin once: but in that he liveth, he liveth unto God."*[25] The Apostle Peter likewise declares, *"For Christ also hath once suffered for sins, the just for the unjust, that he might bring us to God."*[26] The same truth is taught in the book of Hebrews five times with the conclusion, *"So Christ was once offered to bear the sins of many; and unto them that look for him shall he appear the second time without sin unto salvation."*[27] The majestic truth is found in the Lord's declaration from the Cross, *"It is finished."*[28]

Satisfaction is what Christ alone has done

In Scripture satisfaction is what Christ—and Christ alone—has done. Christ has suffered as the substitute for His people to satisfy for them the demands of the law and to procure for them everlasting righteousness. The whole nature of His work is that of representative head of His people, that He has legally borne their sins and has legally fulfilled all righteousness. He is literally in the words of the prophet Jeremiah *"THE LORD OUR RIGHTEOUSNESS."*[29] Christ has legally fulfilled all righteousness; He has procured full satisfaction for the sins of His people.

---

[24] Hebrews 9:22
[25] Romans 6:10
[26] I Peter 3:18
[27] Hebrews 9:28
[28] John 19:30
[29] Jeremiah 23:6

Christ was alone the perfect One that could make satisfaction. This is the glory of Christ. It shows forth the radiance of the person of Christ, the wonder of who He is as mediator and substitute for His people. In Christ's sacrifice is the purging of the believers' sins to bring them close to God, as the Holy Spirit tells us, *"how much more shall the blood of Christ who through the eternal Spirit offered himself without spot to God, purge your conscience from dead works to serve the living God?"*[30] It was He who was without spot. Christ alone was worthy to offer sacrifice. He alone was worthy to pay satisfaction. This is the splendor of Christ.

Real affectionate communication

In analyzing the exact words of Scripture, the Word of God is clear cut in its teaching that the Lord's table is not a sacrifice, it is equally clear that the Lord's supper is not a bare and naked sign of a past event. Just as Moses in the Old Covenant declared, *"This is the blood of the testament which God hath enjoined unto you,"*[31] so the Lord Christ Jesus declared, *"This cup is the new testament in my blood: this do ye, as oft as ye drink it, in remembrance of me."*[32] Christ's command in the institution of the His Supper is not simply "'in memory of' but in an affectionate calling to mind of His Person."[33] The root meaning of the word "remembrance"[34] entails the concept of personal interaction with the Lord Himself. Such fellowship in the New Testament times was foretold in the Old Testament, *"I will put my law in their inward parts, and write it in their hearts; and will be their God, and they shall be my people. And they shall teach no more every man his neighbour, and every man his brother, saying, Know the Lord: for they shall all know me, from the least of them unto*

---

[30] Hebrews 9:14

[31] Hebrews 9:20

[32] I Corinthians 11:25

[33] W. E. Vine, *And Expository Dictionary of New Testament Words* (Old Tappan, NJ: Fleming H. Revell Co., 1940) #1. anamnesis, pp. 274-275

[34] *Thayer's Greek Lexicon*, # 364 anamneesis, "a remembering, recollection to call me (affectionately) to remembrance". PC Study Bible for Windows V3.1

the greatest of them, saith the LORD...."[35]   Such communion is the essential quality of the New Covenant. The Lord Christ Jesus is the mediator of this legacy, as declared, *"and for this cause he is the mediator of the new testament, that by means of death, for the redemption of the transgressions that were under the first testament, they which are called might receive the promise of eternal inheritance."*[36]   The inheritance is the intimate knowledge of the Father and the Son. *"And this is life eternal, that they might know thee the only true God, and Jesus Christ, whom thou hast sent."*[37]

Who may partake of the Lord's Supper?

Only those who have been saved according to the Bible's standard are those who are to partake of the Lord's communion table. True believers are those who adhere to the all-Holy God in His authority alone as shown in the Bible, who are saved by grace alone through faith alone, and in Christ alone. Besides this the true believer must *"examine himself, and so let him eat of that bread, and drink of that cup."*[38] As the same passage of Scripture declares, *"wherefore whosoever shall eat this bread, and drink this cup of the Lord, unworthily, shall be guilty of the body and blood of the Lord."*[39]   Notice that the Word of God says "unworthily," and not "whoever is unworthy". None is ever worthy in himself to receive of the Lord's Table, that is, each true believer comes taking shelter in Christ Jesus' righteousness alone. Such a true believer must examine his own conscience in the sight of God to see if he is approaching the Lord's Table with respect and reverence, having confessed and repented to the Lord any sin of which he is conscious.[40]   Whatever the believer's consciousness of personal unworthiness may be he must not let that detain him from partaking,

---

[35] Jeremiah 31:33-34

[36] Hebrews 9:15

[37] John 17:3

[38] I Corinthians 11:28

[39] I Corinthians 11:27

[40] *"If we confess our sins, he is faithful and just to forgive us our sins, and to cleanse us from all unrighteousness."* I John 1:9

once he has come clean with the Lord in genuine repentance, and desires to draw to Him at His table.

Togetherness with the Lord in His Supper

The Apostle Paul puts stress on the key idea of togetherness with the Lord in His supper when he states, *"The cup of blessing which we bless, is it not the communion of the blood of Christ? The bread which we break, is it not the communion of the body of Christ?"*[41] The essential identity in the Lord's Table cannot be literally the physical presence of the Lord for reasons given in the scriptural accounts themselves, which will be addressed in the next chapter. The oneness taught is that of spiritual communion with God and with His people and is celebrated in the Lord's Table. In the New Jerusalem this communion will be face to face as outlined by the Apostle John, *"Beloved, now are we the sons of God, and it doth not yet appear what we shall be: but we know that, when he shall appear, we shall be like him; for we shall see him as he is."*[42] But for now in the New Covenant, the reality of our togetherness with the Lord is celebrated in signs, and not face to face. *"This cup is the new testament in my blood, which is shed for you."*[43] His New Covenant observance is intimate spiritual communion with Him.

Basis for confidence as being the Lord's own people

The truth of the Lord's Word is that He desires believers to have full assurance regarding what He has done and said. The authentication and pledge of His work is confirmed by an oath that they might have full assurance and consolation.[44] *"This cup is the new testament in my blood, which is shed for you."* This is the legal declaration of Christ Himself, to believers, that they belong to Him. Just as ordinary human life has its legal declarations in marriage vows, title deeds for houses and cars, etc., here also in these words of the Lord is the strict legal

---

[41] I Corinthians 10:16

[42] I John 3:2

[43] Luke 22:20.

[44] Hebrews 6:17 *"Wherein God, willing more abundantly to show unto the heirs of promise the immutability of his counsel, confirmed it by an oath..."*

declaration regarding what belongs to believers. In Scripture what had been foretold in the Old Testament took place in the New Testament. Christ has given believers possession of Himself in His blood and in His body. He has given them the formal legal declaration of the New Covenant in which they have His absolute promise and His assurance.

Believers have in this New Testament ordinance the title to all the blessings of Christ confirmed to them by His blood. As His words declare, "*This cup is the new testament in my blood: this do ye, as oft as ye drink it, in remembrance of me. For as often as ye eat this bread, and drink this cup, ye do shew the Lord's death till he come.*" The purpose is clearly given. It is to show forth Christ's death, to proclaim and publish it. It is not merely a remembrance of Christ, of what He has done and suffered, but rather for believers to participate in His glorious giving of Himself to them. They are to declare His death to be their life, the cause of their comfort and hope. They show forth His death and participate in its fruits before God the Father. The New Covenant has to do with His being their God and they being His people. His decrees focus on the desire and the contentment of their minds and hearts, in a word, divine fellowship with Him. "*For this is the covenant that I will make with the house of Israel after those days, saith the Lord; I will put my laws into their mind, and write them in their hearts: and I will be to them a God, and they shall be to me a people.*"[45]

Spiritual communion taught by contrast

The Apostle Paul very forcefully teaches fellowship with the Lord by using stark contrast to the well know occult practice of spiritual contact with devils. The strong teaching has the purpose of outlawing the intolerable sacrilege of fellowship with idols. Such communication is real, highly dangerous and forbidden. "*I would not that ye should have fellowship with devils.*"[46] The dissimilarity of spiritual contact is clearly seen in the command, "*Ye cannot drink the cup of the Lord,*

---

[45] Hebrews 8:10

[46] I Corinthians 10:20

and the cup of devils: ye cannot be partakers of the Lord's table, and of the table of devils."[47]

It is most important to see that the Apostle is insisting on an awareness of a real fellowship, a spiritual union between Christ and believers. What is being stressed is not mere memorial, since the contrast as such would not make sense. The direct contrast is between spiritual intimacy with devils and the Lord. From this passage, therefore, it may be concluded that *"the communion of the blood of Christ"*[48] is that real togetherness that the believers have with the Lord in the celebration of His Supper. The Lord introduced the meal with His longing expressed as follows; *"with desire I have desired to eat this passover with you...This cup is the new testament in my blood, which is shed for you."*[49] Likewise with desire ought believers desire to share this meal with Him. This communion with Him comes from the essence of the New Covenant. His declaration is that it is literally the New Testament in His blood. In this context of true and false worship the Lord reveals the true spirit of worship, *"to this man will I look, even to him that is poor and of a contrite spirit, and trembleth at my word."*[50] To worship Him worthily believers ought to thirst for His communion at His table. When they do they will by grace realize ever more deeply the words of the Lord, *"blessed are they which do hunger and thirst after righteousness: for they shall be filled."*[51]

My prayer to the Father for each believer in the celebration of the Lord's supper is, *"that he would grant you, according to the riches of his glory, to be strengthened with might by his Spirit in the inner man; that Christ may dwell in your hearts by faith; that ye, being rooted and grounded in love, may be able to comprehend with all saints what is the breadth, and length, and depth, and*

---

[47] I Corinthians 10:21

[48] I Corinthians 10:16

[49] Luke 22:15, 20

[50] Isaiah 66:2

[51] Matthew 5:6

height; and to know the love of Christ, which passeth knowledge, that ye might be filled with all the fulness of God. Now unto him that is able to do exceeding abundantly above all that we ask or think, according to the power that worketh in us, unto him be glory in the church by Christ Jesus throughout all ages, world without end. Amen."[52] ◆

---

[52] Ephesians 3:16-21

Chapter 9

Holy Communion

I remember many of the events of my own First Communion day and the ardor that I had as I approached the altar rail. I recall the reverence with which I had gone to Mass as a young boy and received Holy Communion. In my late teens I began to go to Mass daily. In my years in training for the priesthood, we had Mass every single day and we prepared for it for half an hour with mental prayer and the singing of the Divine Office. It was with great devotion that I took the host in Holy Communion and we spent about four to five minutes in personal prayer after we had received it. All who have been devoutly Catholic will understand these feelings and emotions associated with Holy Communion.

Anibal Pereira Dos Reis of Brazil explains his own first Communion day. He says,

"I was moved with the purest feelings. One incident, though, has obscured the solemn atmosphere of that hour. One of our companions, as soon as the priest placed the wafer on his tongue, began to shout, 'The wafer is stuck, Father.' The priest very quickly approached the nervous boy and advised him to keep quiet and not to take the wafer out of the 'heaven of mouth' with his fingers. Touching the wafer with his finger was sacrilege. After leaving the church, the boys and girls turned to the intervening boy with loud recriminations, saying he had shown a lack of due respect to the sacred Lord."[1]

---

[1] Anibal Pereira Dos Reis, "If I Had Stayed In Roman Catholicism I Would Not Have Found Jesus" in *Far from Rome, Near to God*, Second Ed. (Banner of Truth Trust, 1997) p. 97

This account shows the premise upon which we believed: it was the conviction that the wafer was indeed the sacred Lord. Former nun Sophia Tekien says, "From my early years, it was also impressed upon me that Jesus founded the Roman Catholic Church, that only in the Catholic Church was He actually present (body and blood) in Holy Communion and that 'outside the Roman Church there was no salvation'."[2] Then later in her story she states, "in due time, despite my staunch Roman Catholic belief in the Real Presence in Holy Communion, I began to wonder if in fact one did get to know Jesus better through frequent reception of the sacraments. Year after year I saw no change in myself, in the sisters I lived with, nor in the children we taught in CCD classes."[3] This was also my own experience over the years as I began to be honest enough to admit it. As Catholics begin to search for a deeper significance in their religion, the topic of Holy Communion must be clearly examined because this is the centerpiece of Catholic sacraments on which they depend.

Catholic teaching of how the bread becomes the body of Christ
The Catholic Church teaches that in the round white wafer, the host, is contained the physical Christ, His soul and divinity. This is explained by the Catholic Church as the transubstantiation of the bread and wine into the body and blood of Christ. The official teaching reads as follows,

> "By the consecration the transubstantiation of the bread and wine into the Body and Blood of Christ is brought about. Under the consecrated species of bread and wine Christ himself, living and glorious, is present in a true, real, and substantial manner: his Body and his Blood, with his soul and his divinity."[4]

Historical origins of the doctrine
In 831 A.D., a Benedictine monk named Paschasius Radbert published a treatise, "Concerning the Body and Blood of Christ". He

---

[2] Sophia Tekien, "And the Truth Made Me Free" in *The Truth Set Us Free* (www.bereanbeacon.org, 1997) p. 107

[3] *Ibid.*, p. 110.

[4] *Catechism of the Catholic Church* (1994), Para 1413

held that the bread and wine used in the Lord's Supper were by consecration converted into the body and blood of the Lord Jesus Christ, and were actually the same body and blood as was born of the Virgin Mary. This new doctrine caused astonishment in the minds of many and yet was opposed by Rabanus, Heribald, and the famous Irishman, Johannes Scotus. Nonetheless the new doctrine fermented and grew in the Church of Rome. Finally the notion of "transubstantiation" was officially proclaimed as a dogma of faith, necessary for salvation, at the Lateran Council under Pope Innocent III in 1215 AD.[5] Present day Rome continues to teach this medieval tradition in the following words,

> "'...this holy Council [Council of Trent] now declares again, that by the consecration of the bread and wine there takes place a change of the whole substance of the bread into the substance of the body of Christ our Lord and of the whole substance of the wine into the substance of his blood. This change the holy Catholic Church has fittingly and properly called transubstantiation.'"[6]

The implications involved in the teaching has led the Catholic priest John O'Brien to express his thoughts as Christ Jesus becoming incarnate in the communion bread,

> "While the Blessed Virgin was the human agency by which Christ became incarnate a single time, the priest brings Christ down from heaven, and renders Him present on our altar as the eternal Victim for the sins of man—not once, but a thousand times! The priest speaks and lo! Christ, the eternal and omnipotent God, bows his head in humble obedience to the priest's command."[7]

Such heretical teaching denies the eternal nature of the Incarnation. Christ Jesus became incarnate a single time and forever and it is never to be repeated. If what the priest John O'Brien wrote were true, then in the same the Mass, "Christ" would be de-incarnated once the communicant has absorbed the elements and they no longer contained

---

[5] More details concerning the teaching of Paschasius Radbert are found in John Dowling's *The History of Romanism*, Classic Reprints No. 57 (Pensacola, FL 32524: Vance Publications, 2002) Book 4, Ch. 2, p. 194.

[6] *Catechism*, Para. 1376

[7] O'Brien, *The Faith of Millions: The Credentials of the Catholic Religion* (Huntington, IN: Our Sunday Visitor, 1963, 1974) p. 256

"Christ". What a horrific insult this notion is, for it both assails the Lord and deceives people.

The meaning of transubstantiation

The Catholic Church maintains that transubstantiation consists in the transmutation of the bread and wine into the soul and divinity of Christ Jesus the Lord. The whole substance of the sacramental elements is, according to the claim, changed into the true and real body and blood of the Lord. The host, therefore it is claimed, under the form of bread, contains the Lord's identical body, soul, and Deity. Nothing of the substance of bread and wine remains after consecration. All of it, except the appearances, is transformed into Christ in His Godhead with all its perfections, and in His manhood with all its component parts, soul, body, blood, bones, flesh, nerves, muscles, veins and sinews. Thus, for example, the Church of Rome states,

> "The mode of Christ's presence under the Eucharistic species is unique. It raises the Eucharist above all the sacraments as 'the perfection of the spiritual life and the end to which all the sacraments tend.' In the most blessed sacrament of the Eucharist 'the body and blood, together with the soul and divinity, of our Lord Jesus Christ and, therefore, *the whole Christ is truly, really, and substantially* contained.'"[8]

The Lord, according to the claim of this dogma, is not only in the whole substance of what appears to be bread, but He is also complete in every part of the bread as it is broken. The whole Divinity of the Lord and His whole manhood is contained in every crumb of the bread and in every drop of the wine. Thus the official teaching of Catholicism is,

> "The Eucharistic presence of Christ begins at the moment of the consecration and endures as long as the Eucharistic species subsist. Christ is present whole and entire in each of the species and whole and entire in each of their parts, in such a way that the breaking of the bread does not divide Christ."[9]

In face of this, the simple warning given by the Lord pertains, "*if any man shall say to you, lo, here is Christ; or, lo, he is there; believe*

---

[8] *Catechism*, Para. 1374

[9] *Catechism*, Para. 1377

him not."[10] We respect and believe in the one body of Christ Jesus the Lord, *"who is gone into heaven, and is on the right hand of God; angels and authorities and powers being made subject unto him."*[11] When the physical Christ Jesus the Lord does come down again to earth it will not be according to the machinations of man, but rather *"as the lightning, that lighteneth out of the one part under heaven, shineth unto the other part under heaven; so shall also the Son of man be in his day."*[12]

According to the decrees of Rome, Christ Jesus the Lord is whole and complete in the bread, and His entirety is in the wine also. It is held that the Lord is in every particle of each element. It is asserted that Christ Jesus the Lord is entire without division, in countess hosts on numberless altars. This belief requires irrational absurdity that the whole of Christ is equal to a part of Him, and a part of Him is equal to the whole Christ. If one were to believe this tradition, he would have to accept that by transubstantiation there is given to man the power to create the Creator. Christ Jesus is held to be in the bread and this Creator and Lord becomes yet another Creator and Lord when the bread is broken, down to one more Creator and Lord in each crumb. This illogicality reaches the zenith of the bizarre. In contrast to this, the truth is declared in the Scriptures, *"this same Jesus, which is taken up from you into heaven, shall so come in like manner as ye have seen him go into heaven."*[13] There is a day appointed in which the Lord will physically come in like manner to His ascension. One must not expect Him back until that appointed day when, *"he will descend from heaven with a shout, with the voice of the archangel, and with the trump of God."*[14]

To propose that Christ has come back to earth not appearing in His flesh but rather in the inanimate form of bread and wine is a

---

[10] Mark 13:21

[11] I Peter 3:22

[12] Luke 17:24

[13] Acts 1:11

[14] I Thessalonians 4:16.

studied opposition to Him. It is, therefore, *"that spirit of antichrist"*.[15] This dreadful antichristian spirit sets itself against the Son of God and all the testimony that the Holy Spirit has given concerning Him in Scripture. To use such a "bread and wine christ" is an attempt to usurp Christ's glorified position in majesty in heaven and put in His place a controllable "eucharistic christ". The Papacy's teaching is against the Lord Jesus Christ because they presume to be in possession and control of elements that contain Him. The Vatican law goes so far as to say that their "Eucharistic Christ" is to be "locked in" the tabernacle.[16]

In Scripture the Holy Spirit proclaims that Christ's relationship to the Father in heaven is that He (Christ) is *"the brightness of his glory, and the express image of his person, and upholding all things by the word of his power, when he had by himself purged our sins, sat down on the right hand of the Majesty on high."*[17] Thus, the Holy Spirit gives testimony to Jesus Christ, who was in the world in a fleshly body like ours, with the clear witness that He is now in heaven. One may be assured that any teaching that contradicts this revelation is far from both God and heaven. The Lord of glory is now exalted *"far above all principality, and power."*[18] The glorious Lord is now seated on high. To propose a "bread and wine christ" that in the words of the Vatican is in "danger of decomposition"[19] is to put forward a christ that could be put to open shame. As mediator and redeemer, the Lord Christ Jesus is endowed with the highest honor, authority, and activity

---

[15] *"And every spirit that confesseth not that Jesus Christ is come in the flesh is not of God: and this is that spirit of antichrist."* I John 4:3

[16] *Code of Canon Law*, Canon 938 §3. "The tabernacle in which the Most Holy Eucharist is reserved habitually is to be immovable, made of solid and opaque material, and **locked in** such a way that the danger of profanation is avoided as much as possible."

[17] Hebrews 1:3

[18] Ephesians 1:21

[19] "The bread used in the celebration of the Most Holy Eucharistic Sacrifice must be unleavened, purely of wheat, and recently made so that there is no danger of decomposition." *"Redemptionis Sacramentum"* Para 48 www.vatican.va/ r o m a n _ c u r i a / c o n g r e g a t i o n s / c c d d s / d o c u m e n t s / rc_con_ccdds_doc_20040423_redemptionis-sacramentum_en.html 5/12/04

for the good of His people. Having assumed human nature and suffered in it on earth, He ascended to heaven and has highest honor. He is now beyond the dominion of suffering and shame. When the Lord again comes to earth, it will be at the Second Coming. True believers whose lives are now hid with Christ in God shall then appear with Christ in that glory which He now enjoys in heaven, *"When Christ, who is our life, shall appear, then shall ye also appear with him in glory."*[20]

Consequences of the doctrine

As we have seen, the whole and entire Christ, the Vatican declares, is in the Host or bread, and the whole and entire Christ is in the wine. The Council of Trent states,

> "To begin with, the holy Council teaches and openly and straight-forwardly professes that in the blessed sacrament of the holy Eucharist, after the consecration of the bread and wine, our Lord Jesus Christ, true God and man, is truly, really and substantially contained under the appearances of those perceptible realities."[21]

To appear not as man but as bread attempts to subject Christ Jesus to humiliation that is utterly degrading. The form Christ Jesus the Lord takes, according to Rome, is that of bread and wine, and in neither appearance can He walk or talk. He is debased to a form of lower existence than the animals, to that of inanimate bread and wine. To imagine the Lord present in human form that is not His own glorified flesh is to engage in idolatry. The teaching of Rome in fact endeavors to pour the greatest contempt upon the Son of God, and therefore upon the Almighty Father, who commands all people to reverence His Son. They that so misrepresent Christ leave Him open to public shame and reproach, as the official teaching of Rome admits of "the danger of profanation".[22]

---

[20] Colossians 3:4

[21] *The Christian Faith in the Doctrinal Documents of the Catholic Church*, Neuner, SJ., and Dupuis, SJ., eds., Revised ed. (New York, NY: Alba House, 1982) # 1513

[22] *Code of Canon Law,* Latin-English Ed., New English Tr. (Canon Law Society of Washington, 1983) Canon 938, §3. "The tabernacle in which the Most Holy Eucharist is reserved habitually is to be immovable, made of solid and opaque material, and locked in such a way that **the danger of profanation** is avoided as much as possible."

The charge against Rome and her priests can be expressed in the words of the Prophet Isaiah, *"they that make a graven image are all of them vanity; and their delectable things shall not profit; and they are their own witnesses; they see not, nor know; that they may be ashamed."*[23] The priests of Rome are witnesses against themselves. If they would but follow their own consciences in the light of the Scriptures, they would see how ridiculous it is to hold and practice the teaching of forming Christ Jesus into an inanimate piece of bread. If what these priests do at Mass did form Christ, God and man, then they have in their hands a diminution of Him that can neither see nor know and could be "in the danger of profanation". They themselves shall be put to shame, for God will not be mocked.

Calculating how transubstantiation works

The word "transubstantiation" means change or transfer of one substance into another while only the externals or "accidents" look the same. Thomas Aquinas, the most eminent Catholic theologian in the thirteenth century, wrestled with the contradictions built into the doctrine. He used the physics and metaphysics of the pagan philosopher Aristotle to justify the acceptance of transubstantiation. Thus he rationalized,

> "I answer that, It is necessary to say that the other accidents which remain in this sacrament are subjected in the dimensive quantity of the bread and wine that remains: first of all, because something having quantity and color and affected by other accidents is perceived by the senses; nor is sense deceived in such. Secondly, because the first disposition of matter is dimensive quantity, hence Plato also assigned 'great' and 'small' as the first differences of matter (Aristotle, Metaph. iv). And because the first subject is matter, the consequence is that all other accidents are related to their subject through the medium of dimensive quantity; just as the first subject of color is said to be the surface, on which account some have maintained that dimensions are the substances of bodies, as is said in Metaph. iii. And since, when the subject is withdrawn, the accidents remain according to the being which they had before, it follows that all accidents remain founded upon dimensive quantity."[24]

---

[23] Isaiah 44:9

[24] Thomas Aquinas, *Summa Theologica*, Tertia Pars Question 77 article: www.newadvent.org/summa/407702.htm 5/10/04

Then in words difficult to understand, he philosophizes the following on the thesis "Whether this proposition is false: 'The body of Christ is made out of bread'?" he said,

"I answer that, This conversion of bread into the body of Christ has something in common with creation, and with natural transmutation, and in some respect differs from both. For the order of the terms is common to these three; that is, that after one thing there is another (for, in creation there is being after non-being; in this sacrament, Christ's body after the substance of bread; in natural transmutation white after black, or fire after air); and that the aforesaid terms are not coexistent.

"Now the conversion, of which we are speaking, has this in common with creation, that in neither of them is there any common subject belonging to either of the extremes; the contrary of which appears in every natural transmutation.

Again, this conversion has something in common with natural transmutation in two respects, although not in the same fashion. First of all because in both, one of the extremes passes into the other, as bread into Christ's body, and air into fire; whereas non-being is not converted into being. But this comes to pass differently on the one side and on the other; for in this sacrament the whole substance of the bread passes into the whole body of Christ; whereas in natural transmutation the matter of the one receives the form of the other, the previous form being laid aside. Secondly, they have this in common, that on both sides something remains the same; whereas this does not happen in creation: yet differently; for the same matter or subject remains in natural transmutation; whereas in this sacrament the same accidents remain.

"From these observations we can gather the various ways of speaking in such matters. For, because in no one of the aforesaid three things are the extremes coexistent, therefore in none of them can one extreme be predicated of the other by the substantive verb of the present tense: for we do not say, 'Non-being is being' or, 'Bread is the body of Christ,' or, 'Air is fire,' or, 'White is black.' Yet because of the relationship of the extremes in all of them we can use the preposition 'ex' [out of, which denotes order; for we can truly and properly say that 'being is made out of non-being,' and 'out of bread, the body of Christ,' and 'out of air, fire,' and 'out of white, black.' But because in creation one of the extremes does not pass into the other, we cannot use the word 'conversion' in creation, so as to say that 'non-being is converted into being': we can, however, use the word in this sacrament, just as in natural transmutation. But since in this sacrament the whole substance is converted into the whole substance, on that account this conversion is properly termed transubstantiation."[25]

Aquinas' way out of the absurdities involved in transubstantiation was by means of a philosophy that sets up the wisdom of man in opposition to the wisdom of God as revealed in Scripture. The Lord's own words, *"It is the spirit that quickeneth; the flesh profiteth nothing: the words that I speak unto you, they are spirit, and they are life."*[26] The doctrine of Christ Jesus being the literal substance that is contained under the externals of bread and wine, profits nothing, but rather leads one into monumental deceit and gross idolatry. Thus the Holy Spirit through the Apostle Paul warns believers, *"Beware lest any man spoil you through philosophy and vain deceit, after the tradition of men, after the rudiments of the world, and not after Christ."*[27] The command of the Lord stands firm; *"your faith should not stand in the wisdom of men, but in the power of God."*[28]

Obligation to worship

The teaching of Rome on transubstantiation defies the truth of Scripture, the evidence of the senses, and reason itself. Nonetheless Rome persists in holding the doctrine because the Mass—with the claimed real body of Christ present—is central to Catholicism. She summarizes her teaching with the words, "It is by the conversion of the bread and wine into Christ's body and blood that Christ becomes present in this

---

[25] *Summa Theologica* Tertia Pars Question 75 Article 8 www.newadvent.org/summa/407508.htm 12/13/02 Emphasis added.

[26] John 6:63

[27] Colossians 2:8

[28] I Corinthians 2:5

sacrament...."[29] Biblically this is a denial words of institution as given in Scripture, *"For as often as ye eat **this bread**," "...whosoever shall eat **this bread**', "But let a man examine himself, and so let him eat of **that bread**."*[30] The demonstrative adjectives, "this" and "that", limit the element spoken of to refer only to bread. No other explanation is possible.

The Church of Rome, however, does not stop when she has claimed that after the words of consecration by the priest, the element on her altars is indeed the true substance of the body of Jesus. Rome strongly commands that the element is to receive the worship that is due to the true God. Thus she declares,

"There should be no doubt in anyone's mind 'that all the faithful ought to show **to this most holy sacrament the worship which is due to the true God**, as has always been the custom of the Catholic Church. **Nor is it to be adored any the less because it was instituted by Christ to be eaten**.'"[31]

This is one of many official teachings in the Catholic Church—claiming that the element is due the worship which truly belongs to God—and people are to offer to the communion bread the worship that is due to God alone. There are in the Catholic Church convents of nuns devoted to worshipping the host on a rotation system day and night. There are devout Catholics who spend hours kneeling before the element worshipping it and praying to it and getting solace, they say, from being in the presence of Christ Jesus. The horrifying fact is that such people professing that they are worshipping Christ in a religious and holy way, are literally practicing gross idolatry.

True worship of God and the consequences of idolatry
True worship of God must be in spirit and truth, and it brings true peace and true Christian living. The Lord's words spoken at the Last Supper

---

[29] *Catechism*, Para. 1375

[30] I Corinthians 11:26, 27, 28

[31] *Vatican Council II: The Conciliar and Post Conciliar Documents*, No. 9, *Eucharisticum Mysterium*, Austin Flannery, Gen. Ed., Vol. I, §3, p. 104.

are precise and clear, *"take, eat: this is*[32] *my body, which is broken for you."*[33] *"Take, eat"* is not "worship and adore." Worship of the element brings about the wrath of God as promised in His Word. Idolatry is spiritual adultery. God looks upon those who practice idolatry as haters of Himself, though they pretend love to Him. The Scripture plainly states that He will visit the iniquity *"of the fathers upon the children unto the third and fourth generation of them that hate me; and showing mercy unto thousands of them that love me, and keep my commandments."*[34]

Believers must truly worship Him in spirit and truth, as the Lord proclaimed, *"God is a Spirit: and they that worship him must worship him in spirit and in truth."*[35] To command worship of the communion element is idolatry. It is an absurd and impious doctrine that by necessity imposes worship of something that is eaten and carried into the stomach. Not without the dreadful crime of idolatry can the worship due to God alone be transferred to the communion bread.

The claim that power flows from the elements

In face of the clarity of Scripture, Rome nevertheless insists that the elements are actually the body and the blood of Christ. Additionally, Rome claims that power effectively flows from the elements themselves. Thus the Church of Rome declares, *"Holy Communion separates us from sin.* The body of Christ we receive in Holy Communion is 'given up for us', and the blood we drink 'shed for the many for the forgiveness of sins.'"*[36] This is what priests constantly preach. This was what I

---

[32] The Greek word used by the Holy Spirit in this context is "eimi" as a copula, indicates that the subject is to be compared to the thing expressed by the predicate. It is not "ginomai" meaning to become, i.e. "to come into existence", "to begin to be", "to receive being", as was the meaning when the Lord changed water into wine in John 2:9 "the water that was made wine".

[33] I Corinthians 11:24

[34] Exodus 20:5-6

[35] John 4:24

[36] *Catechism*, Para. 1393.

heard as a young boy and later in my teenage years. Many of those accused and found guilty of pedophilia, homosexuality and other forms of immorality have been those who would be termed "devout Catholic priests". This shows readily that Holy Communion does not separate anyone from sin; rather it leads people into a horrendous false security in which they think themselves to be spiritual, while in fact they become more immersed in the sins of the flesh and of the mind. To attempt to claim a causative effect for that which was given to testify to the Lord is divination. It is setting one's hope on a physical form of bread, rather than on Christ Jesus Himself as He is at the right hand of the Father in glory and majesty.

Likewise, concerning the same "Eucharist", the Church of Rome teaches, "By the same charity that it enkindles in us, the Eucharist *preserves us from future mortal sins*."[37] Rome here teaches her people to look to a physical thing as a means of conveying God's grace, to look to a physical element as if it had supernatural power. Such a teaching comes under the eternal curse of perverting the Gospel of Christ.[38] To propose an oral ingesting of Christ's flesh is bad enough, however, what is taught is much worse. The Vatican declares that it "preserves us from future mortal sins". These enticing words of human philosophy teach the age-old practice of looking to a physical substance in order to procure life. What makes the doctrine even more repulsive is that this very teaching, which speaks of preserving from serious sin, is itself blasphemous.

The Lord God gives us the means of perseverance from sin as we look to the Person of Christ Jesus and keep His commandments. Believers are reminded of their position in Christ, "*ye are dead, and your life is hid with Christ in God…Mortify therefore your members which are upon the earth; fornication, uncleanness, inordinate affection, evil concupiscence, and covetousness, which is idolatry.*"[39]

---

[37] *Catechism*, Para. 1395, emphasis in the original.
[38] "*If any man preach any other gospel unto you than that ye have received, let him be accursed.*" Galatians 1:9
[39] Colossians 3:3, 5

In addition, believers *"are kept by the power of God through faith unto salvation ready to be revealed in the last time."*[40] This power of God to preserve believers from sin is clearly laid out by the Apostle Peter. It is not by any ritual but by perseverance in the power of God amidst the realities of life.

> *"According as his divine power hath given unto us all things that pertain unto life and godliness, through the knowledge of him that hath called us to glory and virtue: ...And beside this, giving all diligence, add to your faith virtue; and to virtue knowledge; And to knowledge temperance; and to temperance patience; and to patience godliness; And to godliness brotherly kindness; and to brotherly kindness charity. For if these things be in you, and abound, they make you that ye shall neither be barren nor unfruitful in the knowledge of our Lord Jesus Christ....Wherefore the rather, brethren, give diligence to make your calling and election sure: for if ye do these things, ye shall never fall."*[41]

True believers are protected from sin, through the power of God as they look to the Person of Christ Jesus through Scripture.

Chapter Six of the Gospel of John

The sixth chapter of the Gospel of John is a very important part of Scripture for Catholics. While we did not read the Scriptures as such we knew John chapter six had verses that were vital to prove the Catholic teaching on Holy Communion. I remember in Trinidad in the very first parish where I was an assistant priest, the teacher who was preparing children for First Communion drilled them hour after hour on the fact that they were to eat the body of Christ. All of this I heard outside my office where she had her open-air class. I knew what she taught was in accord with the Catholic meaning of John, chapter six. Now I see clearly that the theme of the sixth chapter is apprehending Christ by faith. Since this chapter of the Gospel of John is of great consequence to many Catholics, we should let words of the Lord speak for themselves.

---

[40] I Peter 1:5

[41] II Peter 1:3-10

Christ Jesus: meat and drink to believers

According to the teaching of the Lord Jesus Christ Himself, the spiritual desire of the believer is not, *"for the meat which perisheth"* but rather *"for that meat which endureth unto everlasting life."*[42] When the Jews asked the Lord, *"what shall we do, that we might work the works of God?"*[43], He answered, *"This is the work of God, that ye believe on him whom he hath sent."*[44] This answer sets the stage for what was to come. Believing on Him whom the Father has sent is central to what He proclaimed. Christ Jesus also explained the standard by which His teaching was to be understood. He said, *"it is the spirit that quickeneth; the flesh profiteth nothing: the words that I speak unto you, they are spirit, and they are life."*[45] His words are to be understood spiritually, and not after a physical and literal manner. This is so clear that He equates spiritual thirst with believing on Him, *"he that believeth on me shall never thirst."*[46] *"And this is the will of him that sent me, that every one which seeth the Son, and believeth on him, may have everlasting life."*[47]

Then the Lord explains that He is going to give His flesh for the life of the world. *"The bread that I will give is my flesh, which I will give for the life of the world."*[48] Here, Christ Jesus presents Himself not only as the One who came down from Heaven, but also as the One who had come here to die. To give His flesh was to offer Himself as a sacrifice, to voluntarily lay down His life. In these words, we have the heart of the Gospel. His flesh He gave willingly in His sacrifice *"for the life of the world."*

"Then Jesus said unto them, verily, verily I say unto you, except ye eat the flesh of the Son of man, and drink his blood, ye

---

[42] John 6:27

[43] John 6:28

[44] John 6:29

[45] John 6:63

[46] John 6:35

[47] John 6:40

[48] John 6:51

have no life in you."[49]   This speaks of the essential requirement of faith in Christ Jesus the Lord. It is so serious that if one does not trust in the Lord's sacrifice on the cross, he will not have eternal life. Eating the flesh and drinking the blood of the Son of man signifies trusting on the Lord in His sacrifice. Christ Jesus accomplished all the benefits of redemption: pardon from sin, acceptance with God, the adoption as children of God, access to the throne of grace, and eternal life. Receiving this by faith is aptly called eating His flesh and drinking His blood. Eating His flesh and drinking His blood is being by faith totally identified with Him. His sacrificial death must be appropriated by faith if men are to be saved. "Eating" is equivalent to "believing" and confirms the central theme of what He proclaimed which He summarized as, *"He that believeth on me hath everlasting life."*[50]

Christ Jesus is meat and drink to the souls of believers. Physically eating flesh with blood in it was prohibited in Scripture. The pagan custom of the eating of slaughtered animals from which the blood has not been properly drained was forbidden. Thus the Word of God commanded, *"flesh with the life thereof, which is the blood thereof, shall ye not eat"*[51] and *"only be sure that thou eat not the blood: for the blood is the life; and thou mayest not eat the life with the flesh."*[52]   As we saw above, the literal eating of flesh and drinking of blood cannot be understood in accordance with Scripture; rather it is the privileges of the Gospel that are as flesh and blood to true believers. In Christ and His Gospel, there is a real provision and a solid contentment that is indeed meat and drink, filling and satisfying our spirit. The Lord can truly say that in Him there is real supply and solid satisfaction; this is the meat and drink that indeed fills and replenishes the soul. By faith we must eat the flesh of the Son of man and drink His blood.

Again, Christ Jesus says, *"he that eateth my flesh, and drinketh my blood, dwelleth in me, and I in him. As the living*

---

[49] John 6:53

[50] John 6:47

[51] Genesis 9:4

[52] Deuteronomy 12:23

Father hath sent me, and I live by the Father; so he that eateth me, even he shall live by me."[53]   In this discourse, the grace to the believer's soul is represented by bodily actions. This figurative language makes the truths of Christ more intelligible. Yet some have misconstrued the words of the Lord. The Jews, to whom the discourse was first addressed, misunderstood it. They strove among themselves and said, *"How can this man give us his flesh to eat?"*[54]   The Jews had seen and heard Him and yet they did not believe in Him. Like the Jews, Catholics understand Christ's message as a corporal and carnal eating of Christ's body. His words have been misread to support their doctrine of transubstantiation. This doctrine, as we have seen, contradicts the Lord's essential message of the need to believe solely in Him for salvation.

Divinely simple and yet wonderfully significant is the figure of speech "eating". Eating is an extremely personal act. It is something that no one else can do for you. If you are to be nourished, you must eat. No one can believe in Christ Jesus for you. Unless you eat personally the Bread of life, He has profited you nothing. On the contrary, *"if any man eat of this bread, he shall live for ever."*[55]   Once a sinner is convicted that he is dead in trespasses and sin and knows that without Christ he will eternally perish, he will promptly and gladly   believe on Christ alone for salvation.

We have seen that "to eat" is "to believe," and His flesh for the life of the world was His sacrifice on the cross. Nothing could be clearer than the criterion for understanding His words than what He himself said, *"It is the spirit that quickeneth; the flesh profiteth nothing: the words that I speak unto you, they are spirit, and they are life."*[56]   The doctrine of eating Christ's flesh and drinking His blood, if it were understood literally, profits nothing but rather leads one into

---

[53] John 6:56-57

[54] John 6:52

[55] John 6:51

[56] John 6:63

deception and increasing spiritual impoverishment. In contrast, through a God-given sense of personal faith in Christ atoning sacrifice, a person is born again to eternal life. The words that He spoke are indeed spirit, and they are life.

Believers reviled and persecuted

Many have suffered death at the stake and violent persecution at the hands of the Church of Rome because they held to the truths of Scripture and would neither attend the Roman Catholic Mass nor bow down nor worship the communion bread. One of these was James Bainham of Gloucestershire, England, in 1529. He delighted in the study of the Scriptures, and began to exhibit in his life in eminent degree the evangelical virtues. He was arrested and finally sentenced to burn at the stake.

> "Standing on the pitch-barrel, he addressed the people, telling them that 'it was lawful for every man and woman to have God's Book in their mother tongue,' and warning them against the errors in which they and their fathers had lived. 'Thou liest, thou heretic,' said Master Pane, town-clerk of London. 'Thou deniest the blessed Sacrament of the altar.' 'I do not deny the Sacrament of Christ's body and blood, as it was instituted by Christ, but I deny your transubstantiation, and your idolatry of the bread, and that Christ, God and man, should dwell in a piece of bread; but that he is in heaven, sitting on the right hand of God the Father.'"[57]

Like so many others, James Bainham joyfully gave his life for the sake of personal faith in Christ Jesus alone and for his refusal to accept transubstantiation and the idolatry of the bread.

Pope Innocent VIII in 1487 planned the persecution of the Vaudois who had remained faithful to biblical faith since apostolic times. The choice given to these Vaudois believers was to go to attend Mass or to be butchered as sheep. In 1488-1489 that threatened butchery was perpetrated on these Christians. If they had wished to accept the Mass and the worship of the bread, they would have been allowed to

---

[57] J.A. Wylie, *History of Protestantism*, Vol. 4, Book 23, Ch. 6, p. 1830.

live and possess theirs home and land in peace. They, however, chose Christ Jesus and personal faith in Him. Under orders from Pope Innocent VIII, Albert Cataneo, who was a papal legate, pursued the fleeing Vaudois believers until they found refuge in a cavern in the mountains near Angrogna in the French Alps. La Palu, a commander of Cataneo's troops,

> "saw the danger of permitting his men to follow them into the depths of their hiding place. He adopted the easier and safer method of piling up at its entrance all the wood he could collect and setting fire to it. A huge volume of black smoke began to roll into the cave, leaving to the unhappy inmates the miserable alternative of rushing out and falling by the sword that waited for them, or of remaining in the interior to be stifled by the murky vapor. Some rushed out, and were massacred; but the greater part remained till death slowly approached them by suffocation. 'When the cavern was afterwards examined,' says Muston, 'there were found in it 400 infants, suffocated in their cradles, or in the arms of their dead mothers. Altogether there perished in this cavern more than 3,000 Vaudois, including the entire population of Val Loyse. Cataneo distributed the property of these unfortunates among the vagabonds who accompanied him, and never again did the Vaudois Church raise its head in these bloodstained valleys.'"[58]

In the course of history, the biblical truth of Christ Jesus has meant so much to true believers that they have sacrificed all they had for it, including their lives. In our own day, however, so-called leading Evangelicals have formally accepted Catholics as "brothers and sisters in Christ" and then as a mere remaining rubric at the end of "Evangelicals and Catholics Together II", they state, "we recognize that there are necessarily interrelated questions that require further and urgent exploration. Among such questions are these: the meaning of baptismal regeneration, the Eucharist..."[59] Men, professing themsleves to be

---

[58] Wylie, *History of Protestantism*, Vol. 3, Book 16, Ch 2, p. 1162. See fuller account of the testimony of Vaudois Christians on our Webpage, www.bereanbeacon.org, under History. See also Samuel Moreland's account in *The History of the Evangelical Churches of the Valleys of Piemont* (1658) Reprinted by The Baptist Standard Bearer, Inc., #1 Iron Oaks Drive, Paris, AR 72855; ISBN #1-57978-541-7.

[59] "The Gift of Salvation", *Christianity Today*, December 8, 1997

Evangelical, have seldom so flagrantly denied biblical truth in the past. To sidestep the issue of the Eucharist [Mass] as if it were just an adjunct to the faith—rather than its being the heart and center of the Catholic denial of faith in Christ alone—is not only a grave offense to the Lord Himself, but also to those millions who have died to uphold His Gospel.

Closing summons

It was necessary in this chapter to show the horrendous distortions that have been made of precious words of Christ Jesus. While this was crucial we must not close without again seeing the positive side of that which Christ Jesus emphasized so strongly: the need to be identified with Him in true faith. *"Verily, verily I say unto you, except ye eat the flesh of the Son of man, and drink his blood, ye have no life in you."*[60] He is indeed the "Son of man", the "new Adam", the "Messiah". He is the one who has fulfilled all righteousness, and died for sinners, such as you and I. The need to consume Him, as it were, to become totally identified with Him in His perfect life as the "Son of man", the need to partake of His blood sacrifice, and to be legally acknowledged as being in Him, this is truly partaking of Him with the greatest hunger and desire! It is a hunger to know and realize that His life is your life, His perfection your perfection, His finished work your finished work, where He lived you live, where He died you die. Indeed may His Word be true for you, *"Blessed are they who hunger and thirst after righteousness, for they shall be filled."*

Our Lord's message was given with an urgency that faith is not simply a suggestion. It is meat and drink. It is life and righteousness. It is the revelation of the perfection of Christ Jesus within the scope of the life of the believer. We eat the flesh of the Son of man and drink His blood by believing on Him. How does one do that? One does it first by personally realizing the truth of what the Apostle says concerning oneself, *"there is none righteous, no, not one: there is none that understandeth, there is none that seeketh after God."*[61] The Lord's

---

[60] John 6:53

[61] Romans 3:10-11

promise regarding the Holy Spirit is that *"when he is come, he will reprove the world of sin, and of righteousness, and of judgment."*[62] As one is convicted of sin, he realizes his lost condition before the All Holy God; then he is ready by God's grace to believe on the Lord Christ Jesus as his Savior—for he knows he needs One who really can save. He realizes that he is spiritually dead in trespasses and sins and therefore without any hope of salvation. His receiving from Christ and in Christ is all summed up in one word: grace. *"Of his fulness have all we received, and grace for grace."*[63] Salvation is gratuitously given that no flesh may glory in God's presence. It is God and God alone who grants salvation, *"no man can come to me, except the Father which hath sent me draw him: and I will raise him up at the last day. It is written in the prophets, and they shall be all taught of God."*[64] As the Holy Spirit teaches you express your heartfelt belief directly to God, then as you trust on Christ alone you will indeed know that you have partaken of the One who is eternal life! *"Now unto him that is able to keep you from falling, and to present you faultless before the presence of his glory with exceeding joy, to the only wise God our Saviour, be glory and majesty, dominion and power, both now and ever. Amen."*[65] ◆

---

[62] John 16:8

[63] John 1:16

[64] John 6:44-45

[65] Jude 24-25

Chapter 10

The Mystic Plague

I have vivid memories of Voodoo in my days as a priest. Voodoo in Trinidad was called Shango, as it is called Santería in such places as Cuba, and Candomble Jege-Nago in Brazil. Whatever name is used, it is basically the same pagan practice with a veneer of Catholicism that has been handed down by tradition in such places as Haiti, the Caribbean, and many nations of South America. The witch doctors I met in the parishes where I served knew how to call down the evil spirits upon a person. One method they used was via the famous Black Candle in order to put "light on somebody's head". This meant to bring evil upon an enemy, even to death. The person who asked for "a light" to be put on his or her enemy meant that a curse was to be put upon him or her in the name of some of the pagan gods of Africa, together with names of some Catholic saints. The witch doctors also called down evil spirits upon people by using a small male or female doll to represent the enemy that one wanted to damage or curse. The witch doctor would put needles into the doll and at that same time, call down the spirits to torment and bring suffering on the one whose name was inscribed on the forehead of the doll. All this was fairly common practice in the rural parishes where I worked.

Overt occult practices

When I learned how these curses worked, I became apprehensive regarding the people in my own parish. When I was parish priest in Gasparillo, South Trinidad, I found out that some of the members of the choir were also part of the Shango group. I spoke with them, telling them of my apprehensions. They told me not to worry, that this was part of their Catholicism and that previous priests had not had any objection to it. I let things go, though I still made inquiries as to what happened at the Shango meetings and at the individual encounters that the witch doctors had with their clients. I found out that the effects of the Shango gatherings were quite effective and destructive. Then, when a young man came to me to ask for permission to attend one of the Shango meeting on Bonne Aventure Road in Gasparillo, I told him that I was fearful for his well being and I told him not to attend. He gave me the address of the house where the feast was to be held.

At the appointed time, I went to the address and I saw people enter the house. First of all, they dipped their hand into a large glass bowl of goat's blood. Some just dipped their hand in the blood; others dipped their hand and made a sign of the cross in the same way they did with the holy water when they came into the church. Then, they proceeded through the house into the backyard. From the vantage point I had outside the house, I could see right into the backyard. The people assembled in a circle. About six bongo drummers began to play prior to the witch doctors beginning their incantations. The bongo drums became louder and louder, and as the darkness came over the yard, lanterns and candles were lit, so I continued to see what was happening. The incantations became more high-pitched, and then some of the people arose and began to dance in frenzy. I was frightened when I saw some men and women fall on the ground and squirm like they were snakes, shrieking and crying out. At that stage I left, not realizing that the young man whom I had told not to go was in fact present.

Two days later, the young man's mother came to see me. She told me that he had been diagnosed as totally insane and taken to the mad asylum in Saint Anne's in Port-of-Spain. I went to see him at the asylum and was shocked because the young man was completely out of his mind. As I tried to speak to him, he seemed to be hallucinating. Finally, the wardens came and removed him. My second visit was even worse than the first. The young man ranted and raved in words that made no sense. I could communicate nothing to him and left in desperation.

Cultural cover for the occult

It was only after this incident that I began to have serious misgivings about the infiltration of Shango into the life of our rural parishes. I brought the matter up with one of the professors of the Catholic seminary. When I told him of this incident and of the other horrors in Shango, he told me that I was misinformed and that I did not understand the culture of Trinidad. I told him that he had lived most of his life in Port-of-Spain and had not lived in the countryside and that it was he who was ignorant of Trinidad culture. Even though I tried forcefully to make my case with this local priest, he would not listen to me. I continued to make a stand against Shango but all I met with in fellow priests was ignorance, indifference, and a general acceptance of all practices that were considered cultural.

The occult, the United States, and Europe

The occult power behind Shango or Voodoo, which I had apprehended in my years as a priest, continues today in Catholicism in the developing nations. It is necessary to study what is behind these practices because more and more of these things are coming into the United States and Europe. While the overt forms of the occult in United States and Europe are not well known, the same spirit of blending the occult into so-called ordinary life is thriving in the West. The Catholic Church in the Western world, as in the developing world, is persistent in her quest to draw all to herself. One of her major strategies is the marketing of mysticism under various guises. This is because, as different world religions begin to adopt the idea that they must work together for the well being of civilization, Rome truly believes that "well-being" can only come through unity with herself as "the mother of all believers."[1] Through crises such as famine, war, racism, human rights, ecological problems, and poverty, Rome is appealing for togetherness at the level of faith.

Her attempted appropriation of Evangelicalism and her false ecumenism with Christian churches to promote her gospel, we will document in a later chapter. But very dangerous, and for the most part unnoticed,

---

[1] *Catechism of the Catholic Church* (1994), Para. 181

is her effort to bond with the pagan religions of the world. The common ground among them all is mysticism, which easily puts within her grasp the religions of Hinduism, Buddhism, and Islam. From both Catholic mysticism and these pagan religions come the tide of secular mysticism flowing through the Western world into health programs, education, and entertainment. Public programs and private services now openly promote a mystic agenda all around us, the consequences of which are becoming apparent in our society. Mysticism has always been the highway into the occult as many seek to find their identity in various kinds of god-consciousness. Mystical god-consciousness is an attempt to circumvent Christ Jesus' redemption and salvation.

Infiltration through Catholic mysticism

Mysticism is an attempt to gain ultimate knowledge of God by a direct experience that by-passes the mind. The strong influence of Catholic mysticism has helped immensely to transform the New Age Movement from being merely a counter-culture sub-culture to becoming a new source of spiritual vision for the world. Catholic mysticism has very effectively and subtly invaded many facets of life without being recognized or critically examined. This has been actively promoted through self-help medical, educational and psychological programs that employ methods such as meditation, philosophical programming, and self-hypnotic contemplation. In melding Eastern subjective spirituality with Western self-assurance, Catholic mysticism has done much to effectively invert the core beliefs and values of the West.

Catholicism married to pagan religions and pantheism

For centuries the Roman Catholic Church has assimilated into herself the mystery elements of pagan religions. Subjective religious experience, or mysticism, continues to be the meeting point of pagan religions and Catholicism, particularly so since Vatican Council II when Rome changed her major strategy in an attempt to bring Protestants back under the papal fold. The marriage between Romanism and paganism is documented in official statements from Rome. For example, in Vatican Council II documents she states,

"... In Hinduism men explore the divine mystery and express it both in the limitless riches of myth and the accurately defined insights of philosophy. They seek release from the trials of the present life by ascetical practices, profound meditation and recourse to God in confidence and love. Buddhism in its various forms testifies to the essential inadequacy of this changing world. It proposes a way of life by which man can, with confidence and trust, attain a state of perfect liberation and reach supreme illumination either through their own efforts or by the aid of divine help... The Catholic Church rejects nothing of what is true and holy in these religions. "[2]

Jesuit priest William Johnston explains how it happened,

"Then came the Second Vatican Council (1962-1965). Overnight the Catholic Church which had been a Western institution exporting its wares to the East became a world community. Asian and African bishops and theologians assembled in Rome and, with their European and American confreres, acknowledged that the Spirit of God is at work in all peoples and in all religions. Since then, most theologians recognize non-Christian religions as 'valid ways'."[3]

It is on such a quagmire that Catholicism stands hand-in-hand with Buddhism and Hinduism, out of which well-known Catholic mystics such as Johnston and Thomas Keating have emerged. For example, Johnston describes the effect of enlightenment, "Self-realization lies at the very heart of Buddhism... In self-realization I become one with God just as the object is one with the mirror and just as Jesus is one with his Father."[4] The famous mystical monk, Thomas Merton, developed this pantheistic identification with God, as does his present day devotee, William Shannon. Merton states,

"...now I realize what we all are. And if only everyone could

---

[2] *Vatican Council II: The Conciliar and Post Conciliar Documents*, No. 56, *Nostra Aetate*, "Declaration on the Relation of the Church to Non-Christian Religions," 28 Oct. 1965, Austin Flannery, Gen. Ed., Vol. I, Para. 2, p. 739.

[3] William Johnston, *The Mirror Mind* (New York: Fordham University Press, 1990) p. 7. For a better understanding of the Hindu roots and methods of the New Age Movement, the general category under which both Merton and Johnston must be catalogued, see Christian writer Tal Brooke, *Riders of the Cosmic Circuit* (Batavia, IL: Lion Publ. Corp., 1986; ISBN 0 7459 1217 6). Although Brooke does not distinguish between Christian and Catholic, he shows the goals of the present manifestation of "enlightened masters" and traces their methods back to Babylon.

[4] *Ibid.*, p. 33, 39

realize this!…I suddenly saw all the secret beauty of their hearts, the depths of their hearts where neither sin nor desire nor self-knowledge can reach, the core of their reality, the person that each one is in God's eyes. If only they could all see themselves as they really *are*. If only we could see each other that way all the time. There would be no more war, no more hatred, no more cruelty, no more greed….I suppose the big problem would be that we would fall down and worship each other."[5]

Shannon endorses this idolatrous self-identification with God and cites his mentor, Merton,

"A person of true faith travels, not without difficulty, towards the heart of mystery. Such a person, as Merton puts it, works 'his way through the darkness of his own mystery until he discovers that his own mystery and the mystery of God merge into one reality, which is the only reality.' *DQ* 180"[6]

These quotations are standard descriptions of the pantheistic myth that we are all in God. In their own minds, Merton and Shannon have literally transmuted God Himself into their own image, for have they not, in the words of Romans 1:23, "*changed the glory of the incorruptible God into an image made like to corruptible man…*"?

Leading Buddhists acknowledge soul unity with Catholicism

Leading Buddhists recognize the marriage of Rome and paganism. Thich Nhat Hanh states,

"Buddhists and Christians know the nirvana, or the Kingdom of God, is within their hearts. The Gospels speak of the Kingdom of God as a mustard seed planted in the soil of consciousness. Buddhist sutras speak of Buddha nature as the seed of enlightenment that is already in every one's consciousness. The practices of prayer and meditation help us touch the most valuable seeds that are within us, and they put us in contact with the ground of our being."[7]

---

[5] Thomas Merton, *Conjectures of a Guilty Bystander*, Image edition Dec. 1989 (Garden City, New York: Doubleday, 1966) pp. 157, 158. This book has official Roman Catholic approval.

[6] William Shannon, *Seeds of Peace: Contemplation and Non-Violence* (New York: Crossroad Publ. Co, 1996) p. 73

The Buddhist Dalai Lama, on visiting the grave of Thomas Merton at Gethsemane Abbey, prayed, "Now our spirits are one...."[8] It is an appalling blasphemy to affirm of the thrice-Holy God that the Kingdom of God is "as a mustard seed planted in the soil of consciousness," that "meditation help[s] us touch the most valuable seeds that are in us," and that it "put[s] us in contact with the ground of our being." Rather, the message of the Redeemer is crystal clear, *"Except a man be born again, he cannot see the kingdom of God."*[9] The Holy Spirit's unique office is to lead true believers into all truth by convicting them of *"sin, and of righteousness, and of judgment."*[10] It is not by the darkness of meditation on "the ground of our being" that leads us to the kingdom of Christ; rather according to Scripture, it is the Father *"which hath made us meet to be partakers of the inheritance of the saints in light: who hath delivered us from the power of darkness, and hath translated us into the kingdom of his dear Son."*[11]

Evangelical endorsement of pantheism

A leading Evangelical, Richard Foster, lauds this pantheistic identification with God. Foster states, "Contemplative Prayer immerses us into the silence of God. How desperately we in the modern world need this wordless baptism!...Progress in intimacy with God means progress toward silence."[12] Foster asks rhetorically, "What is the goal of Contemplative Prayer?" And he answers, "To this question the old writers answer with one voice: union with God....Bonaventure, a follower of Saint Francis, says that our final goal is 'union with God,' which is a pure relationship where we see 'nothing'."[13] Seeing "nothing"

---

[7] Thich Nhat Hanh, Introduction, in *Contemplative Prayer* by Thomas Merton, Image Book Edition (New York, NY: Doubleday, 1996) p. 5

[8] http://www.americancatholic.org/Messenger/Jan1997/feature1.asp 10/8/2002 The website also states that Merton died in Bangkok, Thailand, in 1968, apparently electrocuted by a faulty room fan.

[9] John 3:3

[10] John 16:8

[11] Colossians 1:12-13

[12] Foster, Richard J., *Prayer: Finding the Heart's True Home* (San Francisco: Harper, 1992) p. 155

and "wordless baptism" are just an Evangelical rehashing of Catholic irrational superstitious myth. Rather, as II Corinthians 4:3 states,

> "But if our gospel be hid, it is hid to them that are lost: in whom the god of this world hath blinded the minds of them which believe not, lest the light of the glorious gospel of Christ, who is the image of God, should shine unto them. For we preach not ourselves, but Christ Jesus the Lord...For God, who commanded the light to shine out of darkness, hath shined in our hearts, to give the light of the knowledge of the glory of God in the face of Jesus Christ."

Thomas Keating, a Catholic priest, agrees with Foster as he writes, "Contemplative Prayer is the opening of mind and heart—our whole being—to God, the Ultimate Mystery, beyond thoughts, words and emotions."[14] Thus, Keating depersonalizes God, making Him a nameless "Ultimate Mystery". This impersonal, "Ultimate Mystery" is a non-speaking, non-judging "god". Is Keating in the twenty-first century any better off than the men on Mars Hill to whom Paul spoke regarding their "altar with this inscription, TO THE UNKNOWN GOD, whom therefore ye ignorantly worship"?[15] Is any morality derived from Keating's "Ultimate Mystery"? Thus, Keating, Merton, and Shannon, in their pantheistic identification of God, have attempted to destroy God's self-sufficiency as Creator and the Lord God Almighty. They have endeavored to clone God into the image of humans. According to Romans 1:25, have they not "changed the truth of God into a lie, and worshipped and served the creature more than the Creator, who is blessed for ever"? No wonder Merton admits, "If only they could see themselves as they really are...I suppose the big problem would be that we would fall down and worship each other." In the place of the true worship of God, they have set about to establish pantheistic idolatry.

---

[13] *Ibid.*, p 159

[14] Thomas Keating, "The Method of Centering Prayer" http://www.thecentering.org/centering 10/22/02

[15] Acts 17:23

Dramatized mysticism

The Pentecostal Word of Faith movement is simply a dramatized form of mysticism. In a sermon tape, Kenneth Copeland states, "You don't have a god in you, you are one."[16] In a 1987 crusade, Copeland is documented as saying, "I say this and repeat it so it don't upset you too bad. [*sic*] When I read in the Bible where He (Jesus) says, I AM, I say, Yes, I am too!"[17] Kenneth Hagin in Word of Faith states, "You are as much the incarnation of God as Jesus Christ was. Every man who has been born again is an incarnation and Christianity is a miracle. The believer is as much an incarnation as was Jesus of Nazareth."[18] Casey Treat, known for the infamous quote, "When God looks into the mirror, He sees me! When I look into the mirror I see God!"[19], proclaims on his WebPage, "God dwells in you. God walks in you. When you walk, God walks. When you show up, God shows up. When you show up, a winner shows up. You won't lose."[20]

Paul Crouch, Benny Hinn, Charles Capps, Robert Tilton, Paul Yonggi Cho, Marilyn Hickey, Morris Cerullo, T.L. Osborn, and Jerry Savelle are just a few of the well-known names that promote stage-managed mysticism. As one might suspect, many of the gurus of dramatized mysticism promote fellowship with Catholicism. The Trinity Broadcasting Network, one of the largest radio and TV networks in the world today, through its founders, Paul and Jan Crouch, fosters fellowship with Roman Catholics amid mysticism presented in all the whirling garments of emotionalism.

Catholic Charismatics draw from many sources: the traditional mysticism of the sacraments, the Word of Faith movement, and both Catholic and Zen mystics. In biblical terms they are thrice dead in

---

[16] Kenneth Copeland, "The Force of Love" (Fort Worth, TX: Kenneth Copeland Ministries, 1987), audiotape # 02-0028

[17] www.watchman.org/reltop/unbiblcl.htm 11/11/02

[18] www.watchman.org/reltop/unbiblcl.htm 11/11/02

[19] Michael Horton, *The Agony of Deceit* (Chicago: Moody Press, 1990) p. 91

[20] www.caseytreat.org/godsword Being_In_Christ 11/11/02

deceit, for what has been quoted here are pieces of insolence, blasphemy, and falsehood. The Copelands, the Crouches, Hinn, Hagin, and others like them would have you rejoice in the light within by claiming that you are a god within. The Lord God Almighty proclaims, *"I am the Lord; that is my name: and my glory will I not give to another, neither my praise to graven images."*[21] The Word of the Lord still stands, *"To the law and to the testimony: if they speak not according to this word, it is because there is no light in them."*[22]

Pope's official approval of mystical tradition

In an official "Apostolic Letter", Pope John Paul II endorsed Rome's own mystical tradition and the "great mystical tradition of the Church both East and West." His official teaching is,

"…we are greatly helped not only by theological investigation but also by that great heritage which is the 'lived theology' of the saints. The saints offer us precious insights…through their personal experience of those terrible states of trial which the mystical tradition describes as the 'dark night'. Not infrequently the saints have undergone something akin to Jesus' experience on the Cross in the paradoxical blending of bliss and pain. In the Dialogue of Divine Providence, God the Father shows Catherine of Siena how joy and suffering can be present together in holy souls: 'Thus the soul is blissful and afflicted: afflicted on account of the sins of its neighbour, blissful on account of the union and the affection of charity which it has inwardly received. These souls imitate the spotless Lamb, my Only-begotten Son, who on the Cross was both blissful and afflicted'….What an illuminating testimony!…Is it not one of the 'signs of the times' that in today's world, despite widespread secularization, there is a widespread demand for spirituality, a demand which expresses itself in large part as a renewed need for prayer? **Other religions, which are now widely present in ancient Christian lands, offer their own responses to this need, and sometimes they do so in appealing ways**….The great

---

[21] Isaiah 42:8

[22] Isaiah 8:20

mystical tradition of the Church of both East and West has much to say in this regard. **It shows how prayer can progress, as a genuine dialogue of love, to the point of rendering the person wholly possessed by the divine Beloved...**"[23]
This is a brilliant piece of political bridge building on the Pope's part. By citing experiences of "saints", he attempts to make these experiences universal standards of deep and authentic spirituality. Then he grants approval to other religions by stating that they meet the "renewed need for prayer" in ways which are "appealing", affirming the idea that the process of prayer can become so consuming that it "render[s] the person wholly possessed by the divine Beloved." If "a progress, as a genuine dialogue of love, to the point of rendering the person wholly possessed by the divine Beloved" were true, there would have been no need of salvation by the Redeemer. Scripture declares the reality and truth, *"not by works of righteousness which we have done, but according to his mercy he saved us."*[24]

Truth contrasted to crafted mythology
True Christianity is unique among the religions of the world in that it is a rational-historical faith. For the Christian, salvation is based on something entirely outside of man. Salvation is found in the faithfulness and perfect sacrifice of the Christ of history. Catholic and Eastern mystics claim to discover God in the depths of their being. The true Christian looks away from himself to the righteousness of Christ Jesus. Before God, Christ's satisfaction for sin is a reality that is all sufficient. It does not need to be supplemented. God's verdict of justification is not grounded on any state of being within the believing sinner, rather it is established on Christ Jesus alone. The principle that man can save himself by his experience and by his own life has been the foundation of every pagan religion, as it is of Catholicism. What is so sinister about

---

[23] OFFICIAL APOSTOLIC LETTER OF POPE JOHN PAUL II "NOVO MILLENNIO INEUNTE"
www.vatican.va/holy_fa ther/john_paul_ii/apost_letters/documents/hf_jp-ii_apl_20010106_novo-mill ennio-ineunte_en.html+Novo+Millennio+Ineunte
Para 27, 33 Bolding in any quotation indicates emphasis added by this author.
[24] Titus 3:5

the present communion of Rome with paganism is that it is contaminating our entire society.

The deadly deceptions of mysticism arrogantly advertise a way of direct access to the All Holy God and thereby repudiate any need of the Lord Jesus Christ, the One Mediator between God and men. The believer's worship and approach to God is in the Lord's own words to be with "*all thy heart, and with all thy soul, and with all thy mind.*"[25] In the words of the Apostle Paul, "*I will pray with the spirit, and I will pray with the understanding also.*"[26] The same Apostle warned believers, "*Let no man beguile you of your reward ...intruding into those things which he hath not seen, vainly puffed up by his fleshly mind.*"[27] The censure of the Lord God remains on those who have issued lies, "*Woe unto the foolish prophets, that follow their own spirit, and have seen nothing!*"[28] Because of this debasement of Christ and His Gospel we again outline the essentials of historical faith.

Objective salvation in the Lord of glory

As Mediator, Christ Jesus is the only means of union between God and man, "*that in the dispensation of the fullness of times he might gather together in one all things in Christ, both which are in heaven, and which are on earth; even in him.*"[29] Christ Jesus is exalted to "*the right hand of the Majesty on high*"[30] as the One Savior. He and His Gospel are objective and real. This Gospel is not an idle tale, nor a piece of incomprehensible mysticism; rather it is the proclamation of the awesome historical work of redemption accomplished by God Himself. The Father appointed Christ Jesus as the guarantor of real salvation. Christ Jesus was glorified in finishing the Father's mightiest work. In Christ's own words, "*I have glorified thee on earth; I have*

---

[25] Matthew 22:37

[26] I Corinthians 14:15

[27] Colossians 2:18

[28] Ezekiel 13:3

[29] Ephesians 1:10

[30] Hebrews 1:3

finished the work which thou gavest me to do."[31] He had fulfilled all the Father's will and so gloriously honored the Father. As Savior He is exalted high above "*all principality, and power, and might, and dominion, and every name that is named, not only in this world, but also in that which is to come.*"[32] He alone—not some mystic charm of Rome or Buddha—has been given all authority in heaven and in earth. He has been given power over all flesh that He should, in His own words, "*give eternal life to as many as thou hast given him.*"[33] He alone has been given a name, which is above every name, "*that at the name of Jesus every knee should bow, of things in heaven, and things in earth, and things under the earth; and that every tongue should confess that Jesus Christ is Lord, to the glory of God the Father.*"[34] It is God's commandment that we trust on Christ, "*This is his command, that we should believe on the name of his Son Jesus Christ.*"[35]

True faith involves a repudiation of the self-deceit of experiential mystical means of reaching God, "*for there is one God, and one mediator between God and men, the man Christ Jesus.*"[36] The Lord Jesus stands ready to receive every sinner who will throw away his rebellion and pride and trust in Him alone for salvation. Preaching the real historical Christ and His Gospel is the answer to the mindless adumbrations of Rome and the ecumenical mystics. Thus alone can the true Church, God's People go "*forth fair as the moon, clear as the sun, and terrible as an army with banners.*"[37] The Gospel is a mighty deliverance from the groveling religious subjectivism of Rome and her pagan mistresses. To know God is life itself to a Christian. In the words of the Lord Himself, "*this is life eternal, that they might*

---

[31] John 17:4

[32] Ephesians 1:21

[33] John 17:2

[34] Philippians 2:10-11

[35] I John 3:23

[36] I Timothy 2:5

[37] Song of Solomon 6:10

know thee the only true God, and Jesus Christ, whom thou hast sent."[38]   Knowledge of God, and faith in Him, are the means whereby all spiritual supports and comforts are conveyed to the true believers. *"According as his divine power hath given unto us all things that pertain unto life and godliness, through the knowledge of him that hath called us to glory and virtue."*[39]

Fulfillment of the New Age aspiration?
The goal of the New Age Movement consistently has been to bring in the Age of Aquarius when all will recognize "the god within themselves". A major step towards this, in the words of the New Age prophetess, Alice Bailey, is "the regeneration of the churches."[40]   Her vision was that "The Christian church in its many branches can serve as a St. John the Baptist, as a voice crying in the wilderness, and as a nucleus through which world illumination may be accomplished."[41]   In a word, she desired the time when the "Christian churches" would embrace the New Age concepts of illumination and self-realization. The New Age plan to bring in world peace cannot fully establish the Golden Age of Aquarius until biblical Christianity is outlawed or destroyed.

Now that the Church of Rome has entered into liaison with paganism, she has again concocted another successful work of syncretism. In terms of sheer numbers, organization, and influence, Catholicism is the religion of the European Union. The desires of New Age leaders appear to be coming true. Even at the local parish level according to William Shannon "contemplative spirituality" has now widely replaced old-style Catholicism.[42]   With New Age convictions being voiced by leading Catholics and Evangelicals, it appears that the desired goal is closer to being achieved. The New Age aspiration to establish a one-world order lead by "a Christ Leader" is being met by the Pope

---

[38] John 17:3

[39] II Peter 1:3

[40] Alice Bailey, *Problems of Humanity* (New York, NY: Lucis Publ. Co., 1964) p. 152
[41] Alice Bailey, *The Externalization of the Hierarchy* (New York, NY: Lucis Pub. Co., 1957) p. 510.
[42] Shannon, *Seeds of Peace,* p 25.

and his Church. All of this ought not to surprise any believer because the Bible has persistently warned believers of the enormity, growth and prevalence of the apostate church system and her daughters.

Gospel Power and final destruction of the apostate kingdom
The ruin of the Antichrist's kingdom is declared by the Apostle Paul, *"Because they received not the love of the truth, that they might be saved. And for this cause God shall send them strong delusion, that they should believe a lie: that they all might be damned who believed not the truth, but had pleasure in unrighteousness."*[43]   I have written an article, "The Antichrist Unveiled"[44], in which much about the signs and lying wonders of the Papal system was pointed out. Its machinations, however, will have come to completion only when it has rejected the Christ of history, and has received "the christ of Satan", which "christ" is "enlightenment", "Ultimate Mystery" and "self realization". The Lord foretold the destruction of Antichrist's reign as *"...that Wicked... whom the Lord shall consume with the spirit of his mouth, and shall destroy with the brightness of his coming."*[45]   In the meantime, the victory of the Gospel is present for those who wait on Him. His power has always been greatest in the day of utmost need. The character of God in His gracious Gospel is *"the spirit of his mouth"*. This has been understood and lived out as *"the power of God unto salvation to every one that believeth."*[46]   We see His power as we boldly proclaim His graciousness, every individual who is saved *"being justified freely by his grace through the redemption that is in Christ Jesus."*[47]

Conclusion and application
What has been shown in this chapter regarding the outright invasion of Evangelicalism by Catholic mysticism and its commandeering of New

---

[43] II Thessalonians 2:10b-12

[44] www.bereanbeacon.org/Articles

[45] II Thessalonians 2:8

[46] Romans 1:16.

[47] Romans 3:24

Age verbiage and paraphernalia, should cause serious individuals to examine carefully the foundation upon which their hopes are built. A mere "I hope I am saved" is not enough. Nothing short of the full assurance of faith on the solid Rock, the Lord Christ Jesus, will suffice. It is in God's light, and in it only, that *"we see light."*[48] True Christians are to interpret all religious experience by the revelation of God recorded for them in the Holy Bible. The wicked love darkness, but God's people love the Light! Mystics have unscrupulously equated the true God with "the god within". They have thought to divest themselves of God Himself by turning to inward self-realization and enlightenment. Rather, the values that they set are based on personal inner feelings that are often incapable of reasoned explanation, nor are they likely to have assessed truthfully the depths of their own wickedness.[49] The Gospel is the exact opposite; it is the historical message of the cross of Christ for a lost world. The Gospel proclaims Christ Himself, and the God and Father of our Lord and Savior Jesus Christ, who in His love gave His Son to die for sinners.

There is no valid excuse for true believers to be deceived by "false apostles", who transform themselves into the "apostles of Christ", *"for Satan himself is transformed into an angel of light."*[50] There are many false prophets gone out into the world, but if we diligently study these things which God has recorded for our safeguard against the subtle deceptions of Satan, we need not mislead nor be misled. True believers in Christ must take to heart solemn warnings of the Apostle Paul, *"Be not unequally yoked together with unbelievers: for what fellowship hath righteousness with unrighteousness? and what communion hath light with darkness? And what concord hath Christ with Belial? ...be ye separate, saith the Lord, and touch not the unclean thing; and I will receive you."*[51] *"And have no fellowship with the unfruitful works of darkness, but rather reprove them."*[52]

---

[48] Psalm 36:9

[49] Jeremiah 17:9-10

[50] II Corinthians 11:13-14

"Choose you this day whom ye will serve"

In 1986, Pope John Paul II seized the inter-faith initiative by gathering one hundred sixty of the world's religious leaders for a prayer summit at Assisi, Italy. They flew in from around the globe, Islamic Mullahs from nine nations, the Dalai Lama (traditionally regarded by Buddhists as a living deity), native American shamans and Indian cultists, African animists, Hindus, Zoroastrians, Catholics and, of course, Protestants. "We will stand side by side asking God to give us peace," declared the Pope.[53] The grand encore to this initial dramatization of Luciferian unity occurred in January 2002, as Pope John Paul II led two hundred leaders of different religions once again at Assisi, Italy. By public demonstration, by official sanction, in countless books and seminars, as well as WebPages with broad ecumenical support, the Papacy has set a mystical agenda that the world loves and accepts. Any believer or confessing fellowship group that remains silent in the face of such bald-faced blasphemy inevitably lends credence to the Pope's deceit. Rome still assumes her ancient legal principle to stand: "He who is silent is understood to consent."[54] *"The lusts of our flesh, fulfilling the desires of the flesh and of the mind"*[55] are Satan's strongholds in the souls of many, for these proud conceits exalt themselves against the knowledge of God. The Lord God Almighty commands each one of us to cast *"down imaginations, and every high thing that exalteth itself against the knowledge of God, and bringing into captivity every thought to the obedience of Christ."*[56] ◆

---

[51] II Corinthians 6:14,15,17

[52] Ephesians 5:11

[53] *L'Osservatore Romano*, English version of the official Vatican newspaper, Oct. 27, 1986, p. 1

[54] *"Qui tacet consentire videtur."*

[55] Ephesians 2:3

[56] II Corinthians 10:5

Chapter 11

Images of "Christ" and the Gospel

It was in 1981 while I was still a priest that I first struggled with the question of the images. It was my initial attempt to practice what the Bible says on the issue. After I saw that the Second Commandment prohibits the making of graven images, I was convicted that I should remove the four statues in the main church where I served. The Archbishop called me to his office for an explanation. After a heated debate he told me emphatically that Canon 188 of the Catholic Church states, **"The practice of displaying sacred images in the churches for the veneration of the faithful is to remain in force**." Although I was still not convinced that Catholic canon law overrode the law of God, I compromised because a devout Catholic threatened that my life would be in danger if I did not restore the statues of Mary and of the Sacred Heart of Jesus. It would be a few years before I was able to understand and actually live according to biblical truth.

The Idolatry of the Golden Calf
Everybody knows that the golden calf set up by Aaron was an idol, but most people do not realize that it was made intentionally to represent God (Elohîm) who had brought the people up out of Egypt. The Scripture states, "*and he [Aaron] received them [the people's golden earrings] at their hand, and fashioned it with a graving tool, after he had made it a molten calf: and **they said, These be thy gods, O Israel, which brought thee up out of the land of Egypt**. And when Aaron saw it, he built an altar before it; and Aaron made proclamation, and said, **Tomorrow is a feast to the LORD**.*"[1] The

---

[1] Exodus 32:4-5

Word of God also recounts that years later King Jeroboam, fearing that the people would return to Jerusalem, devised a plan *"whereupon the king took counsel, and made two calves of gold, and said unto them [the people], It is too much for you to go up to Jerusalem:* ***behold thy gods, O Israel, which brought thee up out of the land of Egypt.***"[2]   Both passages of Scripture make it clear that the people who made and used those images used them as images of the LORD God.[3]   But the Bible does not give God's name to any image. The context shows that the people intended to use these images to represent *Elohîm*, who delivered them from Egypt. Every attempt to make a similitude of God by representing Him in some materialistic form is basically a practice of the same sin as making the golden calf.

The Second Commandment clearly states, *"Thou shalt not make unto thee any graven image, or any likeness of any thing that is in heaven above, or that is in the earth beneath, or that is in the water under the earth. Thou shalt not bow down thyself to them, nor serve them: for I the Lord thy God am a jealous God, visiting the iniquity of the fathers upon the children unto the third and fourth generation of them that hate me, and showing mercy unto thousands of them that love me, and keep my commandments."*[4]

The making of idols is the primary issue in the Lord's explanation of the Second Commandment in Deuteronomy 4:12-13 and 15, *"and the LORD spake unto you out of the midst of the fire: ye heard the voice of the words, but saw no similitude; only ye heard a voice. And he declared unto you his covenant, which he commanded of you to perform, even ten commandments... Take ye therefore good heed unto yourselves; for ye saw no manner of similitude on the*

---

[2] I Kings 12:28

[3] Even though our English translations call the images "gods" with a small "g", the Hebrew word used, *Elohîm*, is the same word that is elsewhere translated as God. For example, *"In the beginning God (Elohîm) created the heaven and the earth."* (Gen. 1:1)

[4] Exodus 20:4-6

day that the LORD *spake unto you in Horeb out of the midst of the fire: lest ye corrupt yourselves, and make you a graven image, the similitude of any figure...."* The Lord warned His people to take heed of the sin of idolatry. That is the sin to which they would be most tempted through the traditions of the nations around them. They had seen no manner of similitude. All they saw was fire, darkness, and thick clouds, and nothing of which they could make an image of God. This was the Lord's infinite wisdom in so designing the manifestation of Himself to exclude all graphic equivalence.

Image as mediator
Because Holy God is totally other and separate from His creation, to picture a created man and to label that picture with the name of the Creator is to produce an image that confuses the Creator with the creation. Pictures and images convey a subjective reflection to the one who sees them. Thus, both the artist and the viewer blend God and His creation into a single entity in the image. Any image of Christ—pictures, statues, videos, cartoons—confuse and obscure the distinction between God and His created world, thus they are deceptions.

Any purported image of "God" has the potential to become a mediator between God and man because the viewer may think that he now has more information about God or, at least in some measure, knows better who He is through viewing the image. In this type of supposed knowledge of Christ, the viewer is allowed to go on silently thinking his own thoughts unhindered by the transforming power of God's written Word. Thus, the viewer's mind continues to be conformed to the world by the created image and by his own subjectivity. In this type of imaginary knowledge of Christ, pictures of "Jesus" silently appeal to the emotions of the viewer; but they do not appeal explicitly to the mind in any presentation of the objective truth concerning the Lord.[5] And

---

[5] Since such pictures lay a foundation for the pantheistic concept of "God" in the Church, it is no wonder the western Church is now being ravaged by the occult. Thus we are informed that, "Soaring Pagan numbers have churches worrying and calling for stricter controls on cult TV programs and films that celebrate sorcery like "Harry Potter," "Buffy the Vampire Slayer" and "Sabrina the Teenage Witch." 2003 Reuters Limited 6/20/03

even if in our modern media an image of "Jesus" is made to speak the Gospel, it gives a mixed signal because the words may be right but the image purporting to be Jesus is a lie. The thing is divided against itself and thus creates confusion because the mind and the senses do not agree. The written Word of God, however, addresses the mind, speaking truthfully to people by means of propositions, or clear statements, concerning who Christ Jesus really is.

Word totally adequate while visualizations delude

The Lord Christ Jesus said to His disciples, *"All things that I have heard of my Father I have made known unto you."*[6] Note that the emphasis is on hearing and from there to knowing. He reveals Himself in His Word that His own might know, *"what is the exceeding greatness of his power to us-ward who believe, according to the working of his mighty power, which he wrought in Christ, when he raised him from the dead, and set him at his own right hand in the heavenly places."*[7] God's mighty works are transcendent and show forth the inadequacies of the ways of man. Such is the copious revelation with which God has blessed His people. The Apostle Paul reminded the believers concerning Christ Jesus that in Him *"are hid all the treasures of wisdom and knowledge,"*[8] and *"In him dwelleth all the fullness of the Godhead bodily. And ye are complete in him."*[9]

To one who is in Christ, visualizations of Him are an abomination because they do not give a true and biblical understanding of who He is and how He works. They are fictions about Him—something one who is in Christ cannot long abide. Believers in Christ are *"His workmanship, created in Christ Jesus unto good works, which God hath before ordained that we should walk in them.*[10] To walk in those good works means that He will be shaping believers as they go, for they will be following the Lord Jesus Christ by walking daily with Him in the

---

[6] John 15:15
[7] Ephesians 1:19-20
[8] Colossians 2:3
[9] Colossians 2:9-10
[10] Ephesians 2:10

paths of righteousness that He has laid out for them. They know the voice of His Word and the voice of His Spirit and they will follow Him. This is the down-to-earth way that they know Him. Such experiential knowledge does not come by looking at some artist's imagination of Him.

The Apostle John proclaimed that Christ Jesus is the only true God; therefore, we cannot use images to stand for Him.[11] John also shows in the book of Revelation how God ultimately will destroy all idolatry and all idolaters from the world. The Apostle Paul preached to the idolatrous people of Athens that it is perverse to think that God is like art that people imagine and devise to epitomize Him. He declared, *"Forasmuch then as we are the offspring of God, we ought not to think that the Godhead is like unto gold, or silver, or stone, graven by art and man's device. And the times of this ignorance God winked at; but now commandeth all men every where to repent."*[12] The Lord God patiently overlooked the idolater's ignorance in times past, but now He commands everyone to repent of such idolatry. The same Apostle also explained how idolatry corrupts a man when he foolishly starts using images to stand for God, in fact, describing how idolaters, including the idol-makers, have corrupted the world, *"Professing themselves to be wise, they became fools, and **changed the glory of the incorruptible God into an image made like to corruptible man**, and to birds, and four footed beasts, and creeping things. Wherefore God also gave them up to uncleanness through the lusts of their own hearts, to dishonor their own bodies between themselves: Who **changed the truth of God into a lie, and worshipped and served the creature more than the Creator**, who is blessed for ever. Amen."*[13]

---

[11] I John 5: 20-21
[12] Acts 17:29-30
[13] Romans 1:22-25

How shall the God of the Bible be known?

The problem is this: since all routes to God through mysticism and images end in spiritual death, how shall the God of the Bible be known? *"To whom then will ye liken God? Or what likeness will ye compare unto Him?"*[14]. The scriptural answer is unequivocal: *"be not conformed to this world: but be ye transformed by the renewing of your **mind**, that ye may prove what is that good, and acceptable, and perfect will of God."*[15]

John 6:63 gives the Lord Jesus' answer, *"It is the Spirit that quickeneth; the flesh profiteth nothing: the words that I speak unto you, they are spirit, and they are life."* The Apostle Paul elucidates further, *"But if our gospel be hid, it is hid to them that are lost: In whom the god of this world hath blinded the **minds** of them which believe not, lest the light of the glorious gospel of Christ, who is the image of God, should shine unto them."* Again the emphasis is on delivering propositional information to the mind rather than addressing the emotions. The Apostle states of those in Christ that *"God, who commanded the light to shine out of darkness, hath shined in our hearts, to give the light of the knowledge of the glory of God in the face of Jesus Christ. But we have this treasure in earthen vessels, that the excellency of the power may be of God, and not of us."*[16] What image crafted in the cave of a man's darkened imagination can ever deliver *"the light of the knowledge of the glory of God in the face of Jesus Christ"*?

The Gospel is delivered in words that carry specific content that is either believed or disbelieved by the hearer. *"How then shall they call on him in whom they have not believed? And how shall they believe in him of whom they have not heard? And how shall they **hear** without a preacher? **And how shall they preach, except they be sent? As it is written,** How beautiful are the feet of them that **preach the gospel of peace, and bring glad tidings of***

---

[14] Isaiah 40:18
[15] Romans 12:2
[16] II Corinthians 4:3-7

good things!"[17] And again, "*Faith cometh by hearing and hearing by the word of God.*"[18]

Catholic defense of idolatry

What the Archbishop insisted with me in 1981 is now delineated in the *Catechism of the Catholic Church* (1994).

> "The Christian veneration of images **is not contrary to the first commandment which proscribes idols.**[19] Indeed, the honor rendered to an image passes to its prototype, and **whoever venerates an image venerates the person portrayed in it**. The honor paid to sacred images is a 'respectful veneration,' not the adoration due to God alone." (Para. 2132)

They have clearly stated that God now approves image worship because the honor rendered to the image passed to its prototype. Indeed, in the same passage the *Catechism* states,

> "Religious worship is not directed to images in themselves, considered as mere things, but under their distinctive aspect as **images leading us on to God incarnate. The movement toward the image does not terminate in it as image, but tends toward that whose image it is**."

Supposedly, using images leads people to God; but whose image is it if it is not genuinely Christ's? To what end does the religious worship then go? The image itself cannot answer.[20] How is such an image—whatever its form—any different than the statue that the Athenians set up on Mars Hill "*TO THE UNKNOWN GOD*" nearly two thousand years ago? And how is this modern rationale different from the Israelites' worship of the Golden Calf?

---

[17] Romans 10:14-15

[18] Romans 10:17

[19] The Catholic Church puts the first two Commandments of the Decalogue together but splits the commandment on covetousness into two.

[20] In instances of recorded phenomenon of statues weeping blood, etc., the answer is that the demonic is being demonstrated as the end of the religious worship directed through them because their message consistently leads the observer away from the commandments of Scripture and the Gospel into Mary worship and penance.

Because images work as mediators, as the *Catechism* has pointed out, this means that the Church of Rome has admitted that it has many mediators, does it not? Yet the Bible states, "*There is one mediator between God and men, the man Christ Jesus.*"[21] How shall the Catholic Church bring the message of one mediator, the man Christ Jesus, when they surround themselves with many purported mediators and point their faithful to them? Although the materials are now often film and electronics instead of wood and fine metals, are these modern image makers not like the idol-makers of old—ones of whom Isaiah says, "*a deceived heart hath turned him aside, that he cannot deliver his soul, nor say, Is there not a lie in my right hand?*" Since they have the Scripture in their hands, how is their anti-biblical rationale different from Jeroboam's?

The basis for the Roman Catholic Church's claim that idol worship does not countermand the Commandment on idolatry is that "…in the old Testament, God ordained or permitted the making of images that pointed symbolically toward salvation by the incarnate Word: so it was with the bronze serpent, the ark of the covenant, and the cherubim."[22] In citing the bronze serpent, the Ark of the Covenant, and the cherubim, the Catholic luminaries have made a serious error—for these items were neither images of God nor touted to be so. Regarding the bronze serpent, Matthew Henry points out that "It was God himself that devised and prescribed this antidote against the fiery serpents."[23] Since the Second Commandment was in force, clearly the Israelites were not to use the bronze serpent as an object of idolatrous worship, which later generations did, and for this reason God destroyed it.[24]

The *Catechism*, however, continues to expand on the idea that images of "Jesus" point "symbolically toward salvation by the incarnate

---

[21] I Timothy 2:5

[22] *Catechism of the Catholic Church* (1994), Para. 2130

[23] Matthew Henry's commentary on Numbers 21:4-9 on Biblesoft 3.1 (1993-2000).

[24] II Kings 18:3-4. They use the same logic regarding the Ark of the Covenant and the cherubim.

Word". But their argument fails to comprehend that God does not contradict Himself, so that making and bowing down—which means essentially rendering honor or "veneration"—to images of the Divine is still forbidden. Under the rubric of an historical authority for their position, they state,

"Basing itself on the mystery of the incarnate Word, the **seventh ecumenical council at Nicea (787) justified...the veneration of icons**—of Christ, but also of the Mother of God, the angels, and all the saints. **By becoming incarnate, the Son of God introduced a new 'economy' of images**."[25]

This paragraph of the *Catechism* stands in direct opposition to Acts 17:29-30 when it states that the incarnation of Christ brought in "a new economy of images" making it now permissible to have images of Christ. It countermands the Apostle Paul's preaching to the Athenians on Mars Hill on the very issue of idolatry—an incident that happened years after the incarnation of the Lord Jesus Christ. The Apostle stated, *"Forasmuch then as we are the offspring of God, we ought not to think that the Godhead is like unto gold, or silver, or stone, graven by art and man's device. And the times of this ignorance God winked at; but now commandeth all men every where to repent...."* These post-Incarnation idolaters were commanded to repent of their idolatry and believe the Gospel. Except that the Catholic authorities count their human rationalization of greater authority than God's written Word, how else can they deny this command? If they remain adamant, what then does I John 5:21, *"Little children, keep yourselves from idols"* mean—particularly when we are speaking of images made to represent Elohîm?

The Apostles went everywhere preaching that God sent His Son to save the world from sin, including idolatry and its consequences. The Apostle Paul states very clearly that the Lord Jesus Christ is now no more known after the flesh.[26] The Apostles, although having seen the Lord Jesus, never described what He looked like. They proclaimed what He said and what He did. They emphasized His death and

---

[25] *Catechism*, Para. 2131

[26] II Corinthians 5:15-16

resurrection, explaining what those events mean and how we must believe on His death and resurrection to be saved. They taught people that Christ Jesus Himself is the image of God in heaven. This is because God is only bodily portrayed in Christ Jesus the Lord, who is *"the express image of his person"*[27] The entire nature and character of God is shown forth perfectly in the Lord Christ Jesus. This is made clear by what the Apostles taught the Church.

The Catholic Church's argument also sets aside the Gospel and has refused to acknowledge that salvation is through God's grace alone and received by faith alone—and it was as true for the Old Testament saints as it is today.

"He [Abraham] staggered not at the promise of God through unbelief; but was strong in faith, giving glory to God; and being fully persuaded that what he had promised, he was able also to perform. And therefore it was imputed to him for righteousness."[28]
Abraham believed that God would deliver what He promised, and so was saved by faith because God accounted it to him as righteousness. This is the way believers have always been saved.

"Now it was not written for his sake alone, that it was imputed to him; but for us also, to whom it shall be imputed, if we believe on him that raised up Jesus our Lord from the dead; who was delivered for our offenses, and was raised again for our justification."[29]

The Gospel is *"the power of God unto salvation…for therein is the righteousness of God revealed from faith to faith."*[30] We receive this salvation through faith alone through the medium of the written Word of God, for *"faith cometh by hearing, and hearing by the word of God."*[31] The Gospel is the power of God unto salvation

---

[27] Hebrews 1:3 *"Who being the brightness of his glory, and the express image of his person, and upholding all things by the word of his power, when he had by himself purged our sins, sat down on the right hand of the Majesty on high."*

[28] Romans 4:20-22

[29] Romans 4:23-25

[30] Romans 1:16-17

when it is written, read, and spoken to one another. The power of the Word is that it is objective, rational, consistent truth rather than subjective speculations. *"The word of God is quick, and powerful, and sharper than any two-edged sword, piercing even to the dividing asunder of soul and spirit, and of the joints and marrow, and is a discerner of the thoughts and intents of the heart."*[32] Continually in the Old and New Testament are the commandment of God and the warning of God not to depict Him in a visual way. When Israel deviated from the written Word, a famine would come in the land. For example, *" Behold, the days come, saith the LORD GOD, that I will send a famine in the land, not a famine of bread, nor a thirst for water, but of hearing the words of the LORD."*[33] In our day, if people accept the Roman Catholic rationalization for pictures and videos of "Christ", they may think they have come to know Him or know Him better through the form of images and that their children might more easily be led to salvation through them. But in accepting such rationalization, they have entered into idolatry, which ever speaks only lies, while at the same time they have desecrated the very Gospel of God.

Idolatry within the church from early Christian history onwards
In the first two centuries of the church, Christians did not use images to represent Christ. During this infancy the early Christians would neither bow to the image of Caesar nor to any work of man's hands. They had no images, statues, or pictures; they well understood that the God they worshipped would never have accepted such an affront, for He alone is God. How then did idolatry come into the church? It was a process of time, indifference, ignorance and deceit. In the year 313 A.D., when the Roman Emperor Constantine declared Christianity to be the official religion of the Empire, pagans by governmental edict, and not regeneration, were declared Christians. Not knowing God or the Gospel, they flooded the church, idols in their arms, in their homes, in their minds, and in their hearts. Believers, however, opposed pictures and statues as representing Christ.

---

[31] Romans 10:17.
[32] Hebrews 4:12.
[33] Amos 8:11-12

The controversy raged back and forth for several centuries, and there was much turmoil over the matter. In the midst of this battle, Pope Gregory the Great I (604) presented a seemingly innocent and compellingly plausible argument in their favor. He wrote to Bishop Serenus of Marseilles, who had destroyed the images in his diocese, "What books are to those who can read, that is a picture to the ignorant who look at it; in a picture even the unlearned may see what example they should follow; in a picture they who know no letters may yet read. Hence, for barbarians especially a picture takes the place of a book."[34] Such carnal reasoning usurps authority from the Word of God. But in truth, if the illiterate cannot read, they can certainly "hear" and "*faith cometh by hearing and hearing by the Word of God*," because "*it pleased God by the foolishness of preaching to save them that believe.*" Then in the year 754 A.D., a large council of bishops declared that such pictures are not biblical and therefore are not acceptable in the Church. Twenty-three years later however another council of bishops reversed that teaching. The Second Council of Nicea, which met in 787 A.D, required the use of pictures and statues as signifying Christ. This inexcusable idolatry of the Roman Catholic Church led into the Dark Ages. When the Reformation came, and with it the true Gospel, there was also a condemnation of the evils of idolatry. To escape idolatry, many people left the Catholic Church, and Bible-based churches sprang up in many countries. John Calvin, one of the leaders of the Reformed churches at that time said, "Everything respecting God which is learned from images is futile and false."[35]   It is as true today as it was then, videos and movies notwithstanding.

---

[34] Ep. ix, 105, in P. L., LXXVII, 1027 http://landru.i-link-2.net/shnyves/Catholic_Tradition_art.html 3/15/04
[35] John Calvin, *Institutes of the Christian Religion,* in *The Library of Christian Classics,* John T. McNeill, ed. (Philadelphia: The Westminster Press, 1960) Vol. XX, Book I, Chapter XI, §5.

The Present Day

While many Christians today say that they do not worship images, they do in fact give them credibility by even frequenting events that feature images of Christ, or by having them to display as a symbol of their religiousness, or using them as reminders of the Lord Jesus Christ, or using them to teach others about Him. Such activity is neither worshiping God "*in spirit and in truth*"[36] nor proving "*what is that good, and acceptable, and perfect will of God*"[37] because it sets itself up directly against the Bible. Those who love God will obey Him by worshiping as He commands and by using His method of spreading the true Gospel.[38]

The commandment of God against idolatry is for the good of mankind because God's Law is Christological, pointing to Christ Jesus

---

[36] John 4:24

[37] Romans 12:2

[38] One of the Papacy's furious complaints against the Paulicians (later called Albigenses) from the ninth century on was that they used only the Scripture to convert people from paganism and Catholicism, both groups heavy users of idolatrous pictures and statues. Both Catholic and Protestant sources record that all across Europe from Bulgaria to Gascony in southern France and beyond, uncounted numbers of people responded to the Gospel given from the Scriptures. This first missionary work was done primarily by the Paulicians, who established sixteen major churches from Bulgaria to the Pyrenees. Through this effort the seeds of the Reformation of the sixteenth and seventeenth centuries were sown. See George Stanley Faber, *An Inquiry into the History of the Ancient Vallenses and Albigenses* (London, 1838; re-printed Dayton, OH: Church History Research & Archives, 1990) pp.51-66. See also Sir Samuel Morland's *The History of the Evangelical Churches of the Valleys of the Piemont* (London, 1658) Reprinted by The Baptist Standard Bearer, Inc., #1 Iron Oaks Drive, Paris, AR 72855 ISBN 1-57978-541-7. Morland was sent by Oliver Cromwell to Geneva to bring back a report regarding the persecution of the Vaudois in order that Cromwell might put pressure on other Protestant civil states to cause the Catholic Church to cease and desist in persecuting them because they would not ascribe to unbiblical Catholic rituals, including idolatry. Morland was able to obtain possession of several of the ancient original documents of the Vaudois that laid out the reasons why they had never and would not now accept the unbiblical practices of the Roman Church. Morland deposited these valuable documents in the Library of the University of Cambridge in April, 1658. They have since gone missing.

the Lord. In the Old Covenant, the Law was written on tables of stone. In the grace of the New Covenant, the Law is written on the hearts and in the minds of God's covenant people, *"this shall be the covenant that I will make with the house of Israel; after those days, saith the LORD, I will put my law in their inward parts, and write it in their hearts; and will be their God, and they shall be my people."*[39]

Image Breakers and Revival

The Apostle Paul was stirred to righteous anger against the use of images. Many of the major men of revival in the Bible, such as Moses, Elijah, Josiah, and Hezekiah were image breakers. Isaiah and Elijah mocked images and those who made and used them. Continually in the written Word, God commanded the Jews to destroy graven images. It is the Lord's final commandment given through the Apostle John, *"Little children, keep yourselves from idols."*[40] It is the glory of the Gospel which gives the best account of the true God and provides the best vantage point for our discerning the living and true God. The Catholic Church, however, keeps its members suspended above the abyss of everlasting darkness and death. For the Catholic there is no once-for-all finished atonement upon which one repents and believes, which brings direct access to the Father in Christ Jesus. Instead there are images, statues, relics and rituals. But biblical spiritual power can never rest with anything that has been attained in the natural order of things. Its spiritual vitality is solely in Christ Jesus by the Holy Spirit. The spirit of biblical faith is the person-to-person confrontation of the believer with Christ based upon direct conviction by the Holy Spirit.

What Then Should One Do?

What then should a sincere Christian do today? Idolatry is one of the sins for which Christ Jesus died. He offers forgiveness. Repent of idolatry and seek God's forgiveness. Believe God and do what His Word commands. The Bible tells us to *"flee from idolatry."*[41] Seek fellowship with people who do not use idols. *"Neither be ye idolaters,*

---

[39] Jeremiah 31:33
[40] I John 5:21
[41] I Corinthians 10:14; II Corinthians 6:17

as were some of them; as it is written, the people sat down to eat and drink, and rose up to play."[42] The treasure of the true knowledge of God comes from the written Word, the Bible, and it is loved out through the power of His Spirit. It is important to faithfully study the Bible, trusting the Holy Spirit to give biblical knowledge of the Father, Christ Jesus and the Holy Spirit Himself.

What will be our response to divine revelation of the person of Christ? Surely it is that we should *"abound in hope, through the power of the Holy Ghost."*[43] God makes known the Person and the excellencies of Christ Jesus impacting the hearts of His own with what He bestows on them in faith. The convincing work is the Holy Spirit's work. He can and does so, effectually, and none but He can open the heart. He silences the objections and prejudices of the world against the Gospel. He will do this by applying the truths of God to our minds so as to convince us with the evidence that we are sinners and cause us to feel the conviction that leads to faith. The result is to cause us to believe on Christ Jesus alone, as He is revealed in Scripture, and to come to God in that true worship that equips us for a closer and deeper fellowship with Him. *"And God is able to make all grace abound toward you; that ye, always having all sufficiency in all things, may abound to every good work."*[44] ◆

---

[42] I Corinthians 10: 7

[43] Romans 15:13

[44] II Corinthians 9:8

For the writing of this chapter and the section on the history of idolatry in particular, I am greatly indebted to Pastor J. Virgil Dunbar. He has written a book on this topic, *Christ Can't Be Pictured—God is not like Art.* Contact him by email at VDunbar@aol.com or write to Berean Beacon, P. O. Box 192, Del Valle, TX 78617.

With parents after ordination, 1963.

Performing a wedding ceremony, 1975.

9th July 1979.

His Grace the Archbishop,
The Most Rev. James Francis Carney D.D.,
Archbishop of Vancouver,
Archbishop's House,
150 Robson St.,
Vancouver 3, B.C.   V6B 2A7
Canada.

My dear brother-bishop,

I have great pleasure in introducing to
you, Father Richard Bennett O.P. He has been working
in this archdiocese for more than fifteen years.

He is now on a vacation in Vancouver with
some Canadian friends, and I would like you to know
that he is a very good personal friend and brother-
priest of mine.

He has been a most devoted and conscientious
priest and has been highly successful in promoting the
development of competent lay ladies in the parish of M^A
Pointe-a-Pierre which he has just left.

For some years now, he has been a great
admirer of the Catholic Charismatic Renewal and
gives it very effective support.

I recommend him very warmly to you and will
certainly consider as done to myself, whatever is
accorded to him by way of hospitality and encouragement.

I thank you most sincerely in advance for
your kind cooperation and remain in prayerful union

Yours fraternally in the Lord,

+ Anthony Pantin
  Archbishop of Port of Spain.

AP/JG

Recommendation from the Archbishop, 1979.

With first communion children, 1981.

Laying on hands at an ordination
ceremony, 1982.

About to celebrate Mass Trinidad,
1983.

At the end of Mass at the tabernacle, 1984.

Chapter 12

The Biblical Mary and Tradition

> "By asking Mary to pray for us, we acknowledge
> ourselves to be poor sinners and we address
> ourselves to the 'Mother of Mercy,' the All Holy
> One."[1]

Such is the superlative praise and veneration that Catholic teaching gives
to their Mary. The whole yearly cycle of feasts of the Catholic Church
is permeated with her festivals.[2] Pope John Paul II had dedicated

---

[1] *Catechism of the Catholic Church* (1994), Para. 2677
[2] 1 January Mary, Mother of God, 21 January, Our Lady of Altagracia, 23 January,
Espousal of the Virgin Mary, 24 January Madonna del Pianto (Our Lady of Tears), 2
February Purification of Mary, 11 February Our Lady of Lourdes, 25 March - Annuncia-
tion by Saint Gabriel, 25 April - Our Lady of Good Counsel (at Genazzano), 26 April
Our Lady of Good Counsel, 13 May Our Lady of Fatima, 13 May - Our Lady of the
Most Blessed Sacrament, 24 May, Mary, Help of Christians, 31 May, Mary, Mediatrix
of All Graces, 31 May - Visitation ,9 June - Mary, Virgin Mother of Grace, 27 June ,Our
Lady of Perpetual Help 2 July, Visitation by Mary to Saint Elizabeth, 16 July - Our Lady
of Mount Carmel, 17 July - Humility of the Blessed Virgin Mary, 2 August - Our Lady
of the Angels, 5 August - Our Lady of the Snow, 5 August - Our Lady of Copacabana ,13
August - Our Lady, Refuge of Sinners, 15 August - Assumption into Heaven, 21 August
Our Lady of Knock, 22 August - Immaculate Heart of Mary , 22 August Queenship of
Mary , 8 September - Nativity of Mary, 8 September - Our Lady of Charity, 12 Septem-
ber, Most Holy Name of Mary, 15 September, Feast of Our Lady of Sorrows 24 Septem-
ber, Our Lady of Mercy , 24 September, Our Lady of Walsingham, 1 October, Holy
Protection of the Mother of God, 7 October, Our Lady of the Most Holy Rosary, 11
October, Maternity of the Blessed Virgin Mary, 16 October, Purity of the Blessed Virgin
Mary, 21 November, Presentation of Mary at the Temple, 8 December, Mary's Immacu-
late Conception, 12 December Our Lady of Guadalupe, 18 December Expectation of the
Blessed Virgin Mary. [The] Moveable Feasts are: Our Lady, Queen of the Apostles,
Saturday after Ascension, Our Lady, Health of the Sick, Saturday before the last Sunday
in August, Our Lady of Consolation - Saturday after the Feast of Saint Augustine (28
August), Mary, Mother of Divine Providence, Saturday before 3rd Sunday of Novem-
ber." www.catholic-forum.com/saints/saintbvm.htm 3/20/03

himself and his pontificate to Mary. His personal motto was, "Totus Tuus", for "Totus Tuus sum Maria," meaning in English "I am all yours Mary." On October 8th, 2000, before the image of the Virgin of Fátima, he consecrated the world and the new millennium to "Mary Most Holy".[3] She is prominent in all his teachings and centerpiece to the lives of millions of Catholics.

With the constant charm and fascination of the apparitions, the world itself has become mystified and indeed seems to be becoming mesmerized by the same Mary. It is quite commonplace to find this Mary on the cover of *Life*, *Time*, and *Newsweek* magazines. She is becoming more and more a focal point of unity between the Church of Rome and the Muslims. The famous Archbishop Fulton Sheen stated, "It is our firm belief that the fears some entertain concerning the Moslems are not to be realized, but that Moslemism [*sic*], instead, will eventually be converted to Christianity—and in a way that even some of our missionaries never suspect. It is our belief that this will happen not through the direct teachings of Christianity, but through a summoning of the Moslems to a veneration of the Mother of God."[4] The ecumenism of the Papacy with Islam should be of grave concern to the true body of Christ, as recent events have shown. That the apparitions would play a role in this movement toward unity is not to be doubted.

Further, the apparitions are presently becoming more numerous, as Cardinal Ratzinger (now Pope Benedict XVI) noted some time ago, "In 1984 Joseph Cardinal Ratzinger, the head of the Roman Catholic Church's Congregation for the Doctrine of the Faith (CDF), declared that, 'one of the signs of our times is that the announcements of 'Marian Apparitions' are multiplying all over the world...' He made this observation as a comment on the many reports of the

---

[3] "The culminating moment of the Jubilee of Bishops was the Mass concelebrated by the Pope and Bishops in St Peter's Square on Sunday morning, 8 October. Tens of thousands of the faithful gathered for the sacred liturgy, which concluded with the Act of Entrustment to Mary Most Holy." *L'Osservatore Romano*, Weekly edition in English, 11 October 2000.htm

[4] www.oloswestriver.org/mary_koran.htm 3/20/03

appearance of the Blessed Virgin Mary to individuals located in a wide variety of countries, cultures and political systems."[5] Another typical Catholic webpage announces, "The last century-and-a-half has seen numerous accounts of appearances of the Blessed Virgin Mary. Jesus, Himself, is said to speak to a few of the seers. Some of the apparitions have received official approval by the Roman Catholic Church."[6] A sample of what is happening is the whole host appearances in Medjugorje in Bosnia, Herzegovina,

"Since the apparitions began in 1981, millions of people of all faiths, from all over the world, have visited Medjugorje and have left spiritually strengthened and renewed. Countless unbelievers and physically or mentally afflicted, have been converted and healed....Our Lady continues to give messages to six young people from the village of Medjugorje: Ivan, Jakov, Marija, Mirjana, Vicka, and Ivanka. These six young people (referred to as "visionaries") have had apparitions of the Blessed Virgin Mary since June 24, 1981. In addition to these messages, Our Lady is to give each of the six visionaries a total of ten 'secrets' or happenings that will occur on earth in the near future....Only one of the secrets so far has been revealed by the visionaries. Our Lady has promised to leave a supernatural, indestructible, and visible sign on the mountain where she first appeared....When each of the six visionaries has received all ten 'secrets', Our Lady will stop appearing to them on a daily basis. Currently, Marija, Vicka, and Ivan have received nine secrets, and Our Lady still appears to them every day, wherever they are, at 5:40 pm during daylight savings time, and 6:40 pm the rest of the year, Medjugorje time. Mirjana, Jakov, and Ivanka have received all ten secrets, and Our Lady appears to them once per year, and will do so for the rest of their lives."[7]

The adulation surrounding the Catholic Mary has reached such proportions that it is necessary to return to official Catholic teaching

---

[5] http://members.aol.com/bjw1106/marian1b.htm 3/20/03

[6] www.apparitions.org/ 3/20/03

[7] www.medjugorje.org/ 3/20/03

concerning her to see how such dramatic expressions of dedication to her could be part and parcel of the Catholic Church.

Catholic Parallel of Mary to Christ Jesus and to the Holy Spirit

In spite of the biblical truth, "*My glory will I not give to another*,"[8] the Church of Rome constructs a parallel of Mary to Jesus, and even of Mary to the Holy Spirit. The Catholic teaching consistently declares that attributes and offices of the Lord Christ Jesus are applicable to Mary. The table below shows the strategies underlying the presentation of the dogmas on Mary as if she were a parallel to the Lord Himself and to the Holy Spirit in some roles.

Biblical Truth
1. Jesus Christ's unique sinlessness
2. Grace and salvation are in Christ alone
3. Christ has ascended into heaven and is King of Kings
4. Jesus Christ is the one Mediator
5. The Holy Spirit is the believer's Helper and Advocate
6. Christ Himself with the Father and the Holy Spirit, is God, the all Holy One

Roman Catholic teaching
1. Mary's declared Immaculate Conception
2. Mary's place in grace and salvation
3. Mary's declared assumption into heaven and is declared Queen of Heaven.
4. Mary is declared Mediatrix
5. Mary is declared helper and advocate
6. Mary is also the All Holy One

---

[8] Isaiah 42:8

First Parallel

Catholicism attempts to claim a unique sinlessness, like that of the Lord, for the Catholic Mary. Thus the *Catechism*'s official dogma regarding Mary's so-called immaculate conception states that

"Through the centuries the [Catholic] Church has become ever more aware that Mary, 'full of grace' through God, was redeemed from the moment of her conception. That is what the dogma of the Immaculate Conception confesses, as Pope Pius IX proclaimed in 1854: The most Blessed Virgin Mary was, from the first moment of her conception, by a singular grace and privilege of almighty God and by virtue of the merits of Jesus Christ, Saviour of the human race, preserved immune from all stain of original sin." (Para. 491)

"...By the grace of God Mary remained free of every personal sin her whole life long." (Para. 493)

The idea of the "Immaculate Conception" assigned to Mary by the Catholic Church is totally unscriptural. The term as used by the Roman system has nothing to do with the Virgin birth of Jesus Christ but rather applies to Mary's own conception in the womb of her mother. The basis for Mary's claimed "Immaculate Conception" is found in the assertion that God and Jesus Christ totally preserved her from both original sin and personal sin.

The Scriptural truth, however, that "*all have sinned, and come short of the glory of God,*"[9] applies to Mary, as well as to all believers. Mary's position as a saved sinner is seen also in the following Scriptures, "*[Joseph and Mary came to Jerusalem] to offer a sacrifice according to that which is said in the law of the Lord, A pair of turtledoves, or two young pigeons.*"[10] That was accordance with the law of the Lord.[11] Mary's example teaches us both to give thanks to God for His mercies to us and to acknowledge ourselves as sinners saved by His grace alone. Further evidence that she understood that

---

[9] Romans 3:23

[10] Luke 2:24

[11] Leviticus 12:8

she was a sinner before God is Mary's famous song of praise in which she proclaimed, *"My soul doth magnify the Lord, and my spirit hath rejoiced in God my Savior...."*[12] God is called "Savior," as He saves His people from sin. Even the mother of the Lord had need of her Savior, as she clearly acknowledges.

Alleged perpetual virginity

The dogma that Mary was perpetually a virgin is part of the myth of sinlessness that the Roman Catholic Church ascribes to Mary. It is another step in the evolving doctrines that elevate Mary to the place of the Lord and Savior Jesus Christ. The doctrine states that Mary was not only a virgin before the birth of Christ but during the birth and afterward as well. Thus Rome teaches,

> "The deepening of faith in the virginal motherhood led the Church to confess Mary's real and perpetual virginity even in the act of giving birth to the Son of God made man. In fact, Christ's birth 'did not diminish his mother's virginal integrity but sanctified it.' And so the liturgy of the Church celebrates Mary as Aeiparthenos, the 'Ever-virgin'"[13]

The doctrine of the virginity of Mary before the birth of Jesus is a doctrine of the Scripture that is a very important part of biblical faith. But Scripture does not teach the perpetual virginity of Mary. In fact it teaches the opposite. Marriage is commended and called honorable on the pages of Scripture. The Scripture teaches, *"when as his mother Mary was espoused to Joseph, before they came together, she was found with child of the Holy Ghost."*[14] The term "came together" includes the idea of sexual intimacy. The implication clearly is that ultimately Mary and Joseph indeed "came together". Then the Scripture states, *"then Joseph...took unto him his wife: and did not know her till she had brought forth her firstborn Son: And he called His name JESUS."*[15] The language here makes it clear that she lived as

---

[12] Luke 1:46-47

[13] *Catechism*, Para. 499

[14] Matthew 1:18

[15] Matthew 1:24-25

the virgin wife of Joseph until Christ Jesus was born. Joseph did not know her sexually prior to that birth. Neither the word "till" nor "first-born" necessarily specifies what happened afterward. However, one would naturally infer that the normal relationship of marriage would follow, unless one is committed to defend the tradition of the perpetual virginity of Mary. The Holy Spirit through the writing of Matthew reveals no such inclination.

Alleged vow of virginity

Thomas Aquinas, Rome's leading authority, asks the question, "Whether the Mother of God took a vow of virginity?" He states, "Christ's Mother did not do this until she was espoused to Joseph. After her espousals, however, by their common consent she took a vow of virginity together with her spouse."[16] Likewise in our own day Catholic apologists, in a desperate attempt to justify Catholic teaching regarding Mary, maintain the same tradition. They hold the position that Mary kept her virginity vow and had no other children. This is absolutely absurd. The alleged perpetual celibate state of Joseph and Mary's relationship is contrary to the divine purpose. Marriage as designed by God is intended to bring a man and woman together as "one flesh".[17] Following the initial physical bonding as the marriage is consummated, the couple has the responsibility not defraud one another sexually. God appointed this means for the keeping of their bodies in sanctification and honor. If there is to be abstinence, it is to be by mutual consent, and that only temporarily.[18]

Had Joseph agreed to virginity in their marriage, it would have been a sin against the Lord's specific command to him, *"Thou son of David fear not to take unto thee Mary, thy wife."*[19] Joseph did

---

[16] *Summa Theologica* Third Part q 28 article 4 Reply to Objection www.newadvent.org/summa/402804.htm 3/20/03

[17] *"Have ye not read, that he which made them at the beginning made them male and female, And said, For this cause shall a man leave father and mother, and shall cleave to his wife: and they twain shall be one flesh?"* Matthew19: 4-5

[18] *"Defraud ye not the one the other, except it be with consent for a time, that ye may give yourselves to fasting and prayer; and come together again, that Satan tempt you not for your incontinency."* I Corinthians 7:5

[19] Matthew 1:20

exactly what he was directed to do by the Holy Spirit, as the Scripture records, "*and knew her not till she had brought forth her first born son. . .*" For Joseph, and all husbands, the Lord's command is clear and precise, "*Let thy fountain be blessed: and rejoice with the wife of thy youth. Let her be as the loving hind and pleasant roe; let her breasts satisfy thee at all times; and be thou ravished always with her love.*"[20] Had Mary and Joseph made vows of virginity within their marriage, they would sinned against God for to do so is against His command altogether.

Mary's real marriage and Christ's siblings

This "ever Virgin" role allotted to Mary by the Catholic Church is not scriptural. There are several passages that mention the brothers and sisters of Christ Jesus. An example is found in Mark's gospel, "*Is this not the carpenter, the Son of Mary, the brother of James, and Joses, and of Juda, and Simon? and are not His sisters here with us?*"[21] Another is found in Matthew's gospel account, "*Is this not the carpenter's son? Is not His mother called Mary? and His brethren, James, and Joses, and Simon, and Judas? And His sisters, are they not all with us?*"[22] From these and other texts, it is clear that Jesus had brothers and sisters. The Holy Spirit, as the author of all Scripture, used the precise language of Greek in which there is a clear distinction between brother, "adelphos" (literally, "a" meaning "from", and "delphus" meaning "womb"), and nephew, "anepsios", a cousin or sister's son. Likewise, the Apostle Paul, under the inspiration Holy Spirit calls James "the Lord's brother".[23] The word he used in the Greek is "adelphos" meaning brother rather than "anepsios" signifying cousin. The Holy Spirit again in the Gospel of Mark is utterly precise in using the distinct word for brother, "*Is not this the carpenter, the son of Mary, the brother [adelphos] of James.*"

---

[20] Proverbs 5:18-19

[21] Mark 6:3

[22] Matthew 13:55-56

[23] Galatians 1:19

While "adelphos" is employed on occasion in some writings in the New Testament to refer to the larger company of believers and disciples, the context of the passages in Mark and Matthew are such that anything other than the literal sense would involve an absurdity. "Brothers and sisters" signifying believers and disciples would be bizarre in the context. To claim the concept of "cousins" is equally ruled out; as such meaning is always given as "anepsioi" to signify that relationship. The Holy Spirit clearly states not only that Christ Jesus had siblings, but also in the gospel of John, He distinguishes between siblings and disciples, "... *He [the Lord], and His mother, and His brethren, and His disciples...*"[24]

In another and seemingly desperate attempt to preserve the tradition that Mary remained forever a virgin, the Church of Rome proposes that in the Scripture accounts, brothers and sisters of Jesus refer to another Mary. Thus it is stated,

"Against this doctrine the objection is sometimes raised that the Bible mentions brothers and sisters of Jesus. The Church has always understood these passages as not referring to other children of the Virgin Mary. In fact James and Joseph, 'brothers of Jesus', are the sons of another Mary, a disciple of Christ, whom St. Matthew significantly calls 'the other Mary'. They are close relations of Jesus, according to an Old Testament expression."[25]

Another Mary? Why the twisting of Scripture? This paragraph of the *Catechism* makes of no effect the Matthew verse defining His physical mother as Mary and naming His physical brothers. This is necessary to propagate an image of Mary as a quasi-divine creature who is above having a normal marital relationship with her husband, Joseph. This in turn is foundational to establishing her as a role model for nuns and priests to live celibate lives. The contrived tradition of Mary's " perpetual virginity" is held and promoted by the Roman Church to provide a foundation not only for viewing Mary as a special being in her own right, but also by extension to idolize the celibate state as a means

---

[24] John 2:12

[25] *Catechism,* Para. 500

to enter a higher plane of personal sanctity and access to God. Thus it is proclaimed, "The Blessed Mother's decision to commit herself completely to the Lord in virginity was the beginning and inspiration of consecrated virginity in the Church."[26]

True blessedness of Mary

The biblical Mary is truly a believer who all generations should call blessed among women—but she is not above them and she is not blessed on a par with Christ Jesus Himself. The blessedness of Mary was a demonstration of divine favor toward her, especially in calling her to be the mother of the Lord. This was an act of sovereign choice on God's part, and prophetically consequential to her lineage in the royal House of David. She, as a believer, and according to God's Word to her, conceived and brought forth Christ Jesus the Lord, as a virgin. Later in obedience to the Lord's Word (recorded infallibly for us in the Gospels), she was wife to Joseph and mother of their children. The unadorned truth is that like all other genuine believers, Mary of Bethlehem was a sinner saved by God's grace, through faith, not by any essential righteousness or preserving grace granted in her own birth, nor any elevation of virginity within marriage as a higher call than what the Lord has decreed in His Word. In this way she was and is truly blessed among women!

Second Parallel

According to Scripture, the Lord Jesus Christ completed the work of redemption. Grace and salvation are in Christ Jesus alone. In the tradition of Rome, however, the Catholic Mary is given a place in grace and salvation. Thus under the heading, "...she is our Mother in the order of grace", the Catholic *Catechism* teaches,

"Her role in relation to the Church and to all humanity goes still further. 'In a wholly singular way she cooperated by her obedience, faith, hope, and burning charity in the Savior's work of restoring supernatural life to souls. For this reason she is a mother to us in the order of grace.'"[27]

---

[26] www.miraclerosarymission.org/960821.htm 3/20/03

[27] *Catechism*, Para. 968

Fullness of grace and truth is distinctly Christ's own prerogative
God's grace and love in salvation does not come to us by means of a mother; rather God's grace and love in salvation is the high-priestly work of Christ and of Him alone. Grace is a distinct attribute of His Person. This unique feature in Scripture is ascribed to Christ Jesus the Lord alone. *"He dwelt among us, full of grace and truth,"*[28] all that went before Him was but a type and a representation of Him. All that came after Him points back to Him. *"Grace and truth came by Jesus Christ,"*[29] the Apostle John proclaimed, *"and of his fullness have all we received, and grace for grace."*[30] It is by His grace that true believers are made acceptable before the All Holy God. The Father's will was that all fullness of grace should dwell in Him. There is the abundance of grace only in the "Word made flesh". As the source of all grace to His people, He has fullness of merit and righteousness. It delighted the Father that in Him alone as Savior, all fullness should dwell, *"the fullness of him that filleth all in all."*[31] He alone abundantly gives to all that are His own people, *"grace for grace."* The assertion that Mary "is a mother to us in the order of grace" is an effrontery to both the Person and office of Christ Jesus. It implies that the working order of His grace needed a mother. Such "grace" is no grace at all. It is not grace properly possessed and freely given if it is not perfectly His own.

Alleged exaltation of Mary as having a saving office
The Catholic Church, however, continues to state that Mary has a place in the order of grace, and goes even further in her exaltation by declaring,
> "This motherhood of Mary in the order of grace continues uninterruptedly from the consent which she loyally gave at the Annunciation and which she sustained without wavering beneath the cross, until the eternal fulfillment of all the elect. Taken up to heaven she did not lay aside this saving office but by her manifold intercession continues to bring us the gifts of eternal salvation...Therefore the

---

[28] John 1:14

[29] John 1:17

[30] John 1:16

[31] Ephesians 1:23

Blessed Virgin is invoked in the [Roman Catholic] Church under the titles of Advocate, Helper, Benefactress, and Mediatrix."[32]

"...As St. Irenaeus says, 'Being obedient she became the cause of salvation for herself and for the whole human race.'"[33]

The claimed "motherhood of Mary in the order of grace" having a "saving office" "to bring us the gifts of eternal salvation" is straight blasphemy against the Person of Christ Jesus, who alone is full of grace and truth. It is also an insult to the true character of the Mary of Scripture. Likewise the citation from Irenaeus is blasphemy because it absurdly claims "she became the cause of salvation for herself and for the whole human race." This infers a power of influence of her will with God and actually credits her as being an effective cause in salvation of souls, including her own. It is also shows an arrogant disrespect for the love of God as the original cause of the salvation of souls. The Bible teaches that the salvation of men is a divine initiative because, *"God so loved the world, that he gave his only begotten Son, that whosoever believeth in him should not perish, but have everlasting life."*[34] Scripture teaches that God is, *"merciful and gracious, longsuffering, and abundant in goodness and truth"*[35] and *"longsuffering, and of great mercy, forgiving iniquity and transgression."*[36] To direct anyone toward Mary in the hope of finding mercy through her influence with God is an outright betrayal of a soul's only hope, which is in Christ Jesus alone. It is also attempted thievery of the glory and honor due to God alone for His provision of the hope of salvation.[37]

Third Parallel

In this parallel, the biblical fact that Christ Jesus has ascended into heaven as King of Kings is matched in the Catholic Church with the claim that

---

[32] *Catechism*, Para. 969

[33] *Catechism*, Para. 494

[34] John.3:16

[35] Exodus 34:6

[36] Numbers 14:18; Psalms 86:15, 103:8, 111:4, 130:7 and elsewhere

[37] Psalms 42:5, 61:2, Isaiah 45:22, Micah 7:7

Mary has been assumed into heaven and is now the Queen over all things. Thus Rome officially teaches,

> "Finally the Immaculate Virgin, preserved free from all stain of original sin, when the course of her earthly life was finished, was taken up body and soul into heavenly glory, and exalted by the Lord as Queen over all things, so that she might be the more fully conformed to her Son, the Lord of lords and conqueror of sin and death. The Assumption of the Blessed Virgin is a singular participation in her Son's Resurrection and an anticipation of the resurrection of other Christians:
> "In giving birth you kept your virginity; in your Dormition you did not leave the world, O Mother of God, but were joined to the source of Life. You conceived the living God and, by your prayers, will deliver our souls from death."[38]

A biblical response to the Third Parallel

The Roman Catholic doctrine of the Assumption of Mary teaches that she was assumed body and soul into heaven either without dying or shortly after death. It was made a dogma of faith in 1950. To deny this doctrine is a mortal sin according to Rome's teaching. This is truly an absurd dogma since there is no scriptural mention of it and there was not even any early tradition on the subject. This is admitted by Roman Catholic scholars such as Ludwig Ott when he states, "The idea of the bodily assumption of Mary is first expressed in certain transitus–narratives of the fifth and sixth centuries. Even though these are apocryphal they bear witness to the faith of the generation in which they were written despite their legendary clothing. The first Church author to speak of the bodily ascension of Mary, in association with an apocryphal transitus B.M.V., is St. Gregory of Tours (594)."[39] In the teaching of the Assumption of Mary, the Roman Church has embraced and is responsible for promoting teachings that originated with heretical writings, which were officially condemned by the early Church.

---

[38] *Catechism*, Para. 966
[39] Ludwig Ott, *Fundamentals of Catholic Dogma* (Rockford: Tan, 1974), pp. 209–210

Besides the official teaching of the Assumption, the same assumed Mary is proclaimed "Queen over all things." For the Catholics, the popular prayer following the Rosary is the "Hail Holy Queen." It starts, "Hail Holy Queen, mother of mercy, hail our life, our sweetness and our hope." This is the offering of one's life and hope to the Queen of Heaven. The official litany of the Roman Mary calls her, "Queen of Angels, Queen of Patriarchs, Queen of Prophets, Queen of Apostles, Queen of Martyrs, Queen of Confessors, Queen of Virgins, Queen of all Saints, Queen conceived without original sin, Queen assumed into heaven, Queen of the most holy Rosary, Queen of Peace".[40]

This is quite similar to what the perverse Israelites did in Old Testament times as recorded by the Prophet Jeremiah, *"The children gather wood, and the fathers kindle the fire, and the women knead their dough, to make cakes to the queen of heaven, and to pour out drink offerings unto other gods, that they may provoke me to anger."*[41] It is also reminiscent of the ancient Phoenicians who called the moon Ahstoreth or Astarte, the wife of Baal and the Queen of Heaven. In the same way, the Babylonians worshipped the Queen of Heaven as Mylitta.

In Chapters Four and Five of the Book of Revelation, a quite detailed picture of Heaven is given. God is seated on the throne, surrounded by twenty-four elders and four living creatures. The Lamb, the Lord Christ Jesus, is on the throne. Many thousands of angels circle the throne, singing God's praises. There is no Queen of Heaven, for such would be an abomination to the Lord. The Lord God alone is glorified. *"Look to Me, and be ye saved, all the ends of the earth: for I am God, and there is none else."*[42] Those who promote such worship to the Queen of Heaven *"shall drink of the wine of the wrath of God, which is poured out without mixture into the cup of his indignation."*[43]

---

[40] www.webdesk.com/catholic/prayers/litany-of-the-blessed-virgin-mary.html 2/1/2002

[41] Jeremiah 7:18

Fourth Parallel

Over and above all that has been documented here, the Church of Rome constructs Mary as Mediatrix in equivalence to Christ Jesus as the one Mediator. Thus the Vatican teaches, "...Therefore the Blessed Virgin is invoked in the [Roman Catholic] Church under the titles of Advocate, Helper, Benefactress, and Mediatrix."[44] More details of the fabrication are given in the Vatican Council II documents,

> "In the words of the apostle there is but one mediator: 'for there is but one God and one mediator of God and men, the man Christ Jesus, who gave himself a redemption for all' (I Tim. 2:5-6). But Mary's function as mother of men in no way obscures or diminishes this unique mediation of Christ, but rather shows its power. But the Blessed Virgin's salutary influence on men originates not in any inner necessity but in the disposition of God...."[45]

> "...Therefore the Blessed Virgin is invoked in the [Roman Catholic] Church under the titles of Advocate, Helper, Benefactress, and Mediatrix. This, however, is so understood that it neither takes away anything from nor adds anything to the dignity and efficacy of Christ the one Mediator"[46]

A biblical Response to the Fourth Parallel

The Church of Rome looks upon Mary as having also the role of mediator in the feminine form, mediatrix. The issue of mediation between God and man is very serious because it is only in the one who is truly the God-man, Christ Jesus, that an individual can be brought into relationship with the All Holy God. The Lord Himself said, "*I am the way, the truth, and the life: no man cometh unto the Father,*

---

[42] Isaiah 45:22

[43] Revelation 14:10

[44] *Catechism*, Para. 969

[45] *Vatican Council II: The Conciliar and Post Conciliar Documents*, No. 28, *Lumen Gentium*, 21 Nov. 1964, Austin Flannery, Gen. Ed., Vol. I, Para. 60, p.418

[46] *Ibid.*, Para. 62, p. 419

but by me."[47]   The Father is God. Jesus, the Son, is the only way to the Father. The Apostle Paul also wrote, *"there is one God and one mediator between God and man, the man Christ Jesus."*[48]   The Heavenly Father sent His only Son so that sinners can come to Him directly through *"the man Christ Jesus"*.

The Vatican Council II explanation of how it is possible to have Mary in the role of a mediatrix is a classic example of Roman Catholic prevarication. While presenting two mediators, the claim is made that Mary does not "obscure or diminish from this unique mediation of Christ." The teaching of Rome directly contradicts the truth of the Scripture. And the actual practice of ordinary Catholics based on such dogma in catechisms and prayer books shows Rome's estimation to be a long-standing lie. The ordinary Catholic who looks to Mary as feminine mediator is thereby impeded and hindered from putting his trust in Christ Jesus alone. Jesus Christ is the only way to the Father. The Man Christ Jesus is the **one** Mediator in heaven, *"believe on the Lord Jesus Christ, and thou shalt be saved."*[49]   This is solid fact. Yet historically, and at present, the Vatican officially denies this truth by proclaiming Mary as a feminine Mediator and as the Queen of heaven.

The Apparitions of Mary

The apparitions of "Mary" throughout the world endorse the official teachings of the Vatican and show how such teachings of a feminine Mediator, who is also the Queen of heaven, are lived out. Sometimes these apparitions present Mary as a co-mediator with Christ Himself, and also as a high priestess with Him on behalf of believers. She often appears as the Queen from heaven.

The apparitions preach a message that is always the same. Consider the most popular site of the apparitions, Fátima, in Portugal. In 1917, the apparition of Mary at Fátima stated that the children there needed to increase the level of their sacrifices, because, "…many souls

---

[47] John 14:6

[48] I Timothy 2:5

[49] Acts 16:31

go to hell because they have no one to sacrifice and pray for them."[50] This message stands in direct contradiction to the teaching of Scripture, which plainly states that Christ's sacrifice on the Cross was the first, last, and only meritorious sacrifice for the remission of sins. Thus the visions of Mary at Fátima serve to contradict directly the message of the Cross and, indeed, to deny altogether its efficacy. The same is true of visions of Mary at Medjugorje; at Denver, Colorado; Phoenix, Arizona; Conyers, Georgia, and across the world. Through His all-sufficient offering on the cross, Christ *"by Himself purged our sins"* and *"sat down on the right hand of the Majesty on high."*[51] The Holy Spirit's clear instruction is that the Gospel message is of one sacrifice of the one Mediator, *"But this man, after he had offered one sacrifice for sins for ever, sat down on the right hand of God... For by one offering he hath perfected for ever them that are sanctified."*[52] Clearly, the visions of Mary at Fátima and elsewhere contradict the message of the Cross and, indeed, deny its efficacy. The visions of Mary have shown contempt for the sanctity and purpose of the cross of Christ. They lied about its identity (i.e., Mary) and lied about its origins (i.e., heaven). The authority of the Apostle Paul weighs in on the matter, *"...and no marvel; for Satan himself is transformed into an angel of light."*[53]

Detailed analyses of the messages of the apparitions of Mary, their demonic origins, and their interactions with popes are contained the books *Quite Contrary* and *Graven Bread*.[54] Upon further investigation, one finds the Roman Catholic Church allied with a demon and its messages of establishing one's own righteousness by self-suffering, reparation, and prayer and obedience to one claiming to be co-Mediator, co-High Priestess, and even elevated to the throne of God.

---

[50] www.vatican.va/holy_father/john_p.../hf_jp-ii_hom_20000513_beatification-fatima_en.htm 6/1/00.

[51] Hebrews 1:3

[52] Hebrews 10: 12,14

[53] II Corinthians 11:14

[54] Both books by Timothy Kauffman are available from White Horse Publications, CWRC, PO Box 325, Herndon, VA 20172-0325

Fifth Parallel

The Holy Spirit is the believer's Helper and Advocate. The Vatican, however, endeavors to teach that Mary is also the believer's Advocate and Helper. Thus it is officially stated, "...Therefore the Blessed Virgin is invoked in the [Roman Catholic] Church under the titles of **Advocate, Helper, Benefactress**...."[55] What is so serious regarding these titles is the fact that in the Bible the Comforter, the Helper sent to take the Lord's place on earth for believers and to indwell them, is the Holy Spirit. He abides with believers forever (John 14:16). He brings to mind Christ's words (John 14:26). He testifies not to Himself but to Christ (John 15:26). He guides believers into all truth (John 16:13). Truly the Holy Spirit is another Advocate, a divine Helper, the Comforter, and the Spirit of Truth. The seriousness of teaching that these divine roles—those of the Holy Spirit as well as Christ Jesus' role as sole mediator—belong also to "Mary" is that such teaching blasphemes the divine Persons of the Lord Christ Jesus and of the Holy Spirit. This teaching is heresy.

The knowledge of the way of salvation comes by the declaration of the Word of God, and by an individual's true appreciation of the urgent need to be reconciled to God. This is conveyed to the soul, who hears that Word declared through the convicting ministry of the Holy Spirit, and not by some female substitute. The Word of Truth alone is the means of the Holy Spirit, and the Holy Spirit alone is the only effective minister in applying it. On May 13th, 2000, at Fatima, Portugal, Pope John Paul II proclaimed the Roman Catholic concept of "Mary" subsuming the role of the Holy Spirit in leading people to God. He said,

> "According to the divine plan, 'a woman clothed with the sun' (Rev. 12:1) came down from heaven to this earth to visit the privileged children....She asks them to offer themselves as victims of reparation, **saying that she was ready to lead them safely to God**. And behold, they see a light shining from her maternal hands which

---

[55] *Catechism* Para #969

penetrates them inwardly, so that they feel immersed in God..."[56] The Pope's assertive language at Fatima was mystically flavored Marian fanaticism. He, in his position as supreme teacher of the Catholic Church, misused the Word of God itself to arrogate to an ordinary woman the Holy Spirit's role of leading people to God. No one would be more appalled at this than the true Mary of Bethlehem. The official teaching of Rome, and the appealing words of the Pope, are summarized in the famous Catholic prayer called the "The Memorare,"

"Remember, O most gracious Virgin Mary, that never was it known that anyone who fled to your protection, implored your help, or sought your intercession, was left unaided. Inspired then with confidence, I fly unto you, O Virgin of virgins, my Mother! To you do I come, before you I stand, sinful and sorrowful. O Mother of the Word Incarnate, despise not my petitions, but in your mercy, hear and answer me. Amen"

This prayer implies that though God may fail to answer, the "most gracious Virgin Mary" never will. This is the very height of idolatry. Polytheism has always been a besetting sin. The Lord God's commandment still stands. *"Thou shalt have no other gods before me."*[57]

Sixth Parallel
Attribute that separates God from all beings

Christ Jesus Himself with the Father and the Holy Spirit, is God—the all Holy One. In Roman Catholicism, an attempt is made to proclaim that Mary also is the All Holy One. The parallels in which the Roman Catholic "Mary" is declared to be the cause of salvation, Advocate, Helper, and Mediatrix are blasphemous, that is, they are attempts to place divine roles on a human person. The official teaching of Rome, however, adds insult to blasphemy in attempting to call "Mary" the All Holy One, and the source of holiness. This irreverent teaching is an attempted theft on the very essence of the divine glory. The Vatican

---

[56] www.vatican.va/holy_father/john_p.../hf_jp-ii_hom_20000513_beatification-fatima_en.htm 6/1/00. See our critique of the same in "Fatima: JP II, RCC Contradict Gospel: Where Do Evangelical ECT Signatories Now Stand?", www.bereanbeacon.org

[57] Exodus 20:3

teaching declares,

> "By asking Mary to pray for us, we acknowledge ourselves to be poor sinners and we address ourselves to the 'Mother of Mercy,' the All Holy One."[58]

> "From the [Roman Catholic] Church he [the Catholic] learns the *example of holiness* and recognizes its model and source in the all-holy Virgin Mary..."[59]

The Bible clearly teaches that God alone is infinite, eternal, and unchangeable in His being, wisdom, power, holiness, justice, goodness and truth. He is **the** all Holy One. His holiness is the attribute that covers all attributes so that His righteousness is holy, His truth is holy, and His justice is holy. He **is** each of His attributes. **The overall attribute of holiness is that which separates Him from all beings.** He is totally other. The reason why we need to be saved before the All Holy God is because in the words of Scripture, *"there is none holy as the Lord: for there is besides Thee: neither is there any rock like our God."*[60] And, again the Word of the Lord proclaims, *"Who shall not fear thee, O Lord, and glorify Thy name? for thou only art holy: for all nations shall come and worship before thee."*[61] This is of utter seriousness in the words of the Prophet Isaiah, *"Holy, Holy, Holy, is the Lord of hosts: the whole earth is full of his glory."*[62] To attempt to address a creature as the "All Holy One" is consummate blasphemy and idolatry of the first order.

Conclusion

The Bible not only establishes who God is, but it excludes all others from that glory. Similarly, the Bible not only teaches who the Lord Jesus Christ is, but it also excludes all others from His roles. And finally, Scripture declares the Person and role of the Holy Spirit and bars all others from His role. These Bible truths exclude all Roman

---

[58] *Catechism*, Para. 2677

[59] *Catechism*, Para. 2030 Emphasis in the original

[60] I Samuel 2:2

[61] Revelation 15:4

[62] Isaiah. 6:3

Catholic teaching that parades their "Mary" as "the All Holy One," as one of "Immaculate Conception," "Mother in the order of grace", "Queen of Heaven", "Mediatrix", "Advocate", and "Heavenly Helper". *"I am the Lord; that is My name: and My glory will I not give to another, neither My praise to graven images."*[63]

The false Mary of Roman Catholicism is not parallel to Christ Jesus, nor the Holy Spirit but an abomination before God and His Word. There is, however, a revealing parallel between the Roman Catholic "Mary" and pagan goddesses. Similar to the Roman Mary, some pagan goddesses, it is claimed, do not need salvation as they are the ones who cause it. Often goddesses do not have human children and they are often called the "Queen of Heaven" and are invoked to make supernatural things happen through special objects and special verbal formulas. Goddesses do not die and they are prayed to in worship. The Catholic Cult of the ever-virgin Mary, the Queen of Heaven, leads one into the occult and, not surprisingly, is found in the occult. The Roman Virgin Mary is included among the goddesses that are listed on, for example, the following WebPages: The Spiral Goddess Grove, The White Moon, and Goddess 2000. They consider Mary to be the "Divine Feminine" and say that for centuries, many people have blended their ancient goddesses with Mary.[64] While the Scriptures states that *"Satan himself is transformed into an angel of light"*[65], it still comes as a shock to see the Prince of Darkness misuse the wonderful believer, Mary, until she appears as a goddess. The Lord's judgment will come upon all who teach and practice this malicious doctrine. The Lord Christ Jesus Himself declared, *"For the Father judgeth no man, but hath committed all judgment unto the Son...And hath given him authority to execute judgment also, because he is the Son of man."*[66] All right and power of administrative judgment and correction has been given to Christ Jesus as ruling King of Kings and Lord of Lords. The

---

[63] Isaiah 42:8

[64] www.goddess2000.org/Mary.html   www.thewhitemoon.com/mary/main.html
www.spiralgoddess.com/Mary.html

[65] II Corinthians 11:14

Lord Himself declared, *"All things are delivered unto me of my Father;"*[67] and *"All power is given unto me in heaven and in earth."*[68] He will be true to His Word, *"Vengeance belongeth unto me, I will recompense, saith the Lord."*[69]

Turn to Him in faith alone for the salvation that He alone gives by the conviction of the Holy Spirit, and based on his death and resurrection. Believe on Him alone, *"to the praise of the glory of his grace."*[70] The Pope makes no secret of where he stands. Whether done in ignorance or not, Catholics (even sincere ones) who remain loyal to the Pope in exalting Mary, spurn the exclusivity and splendor of Christ and His Gospel. The Word of the Lord speaks clearly to the choice that is before all Catholics. *"See that ye refuse not him that speaketh. For if they escaped not who refused him that spake on earth, much more shall not we escape, if we turn away from him that speaketh from heaven."*[71] When God speaks to men in the Scripture, the guilt of those who refuse Him is the greater—and their punishment will be more intolerable. He justly expects from them the strictest attention in the Gospel that demands faith on Christ Jesus the Lord, who alone is full of grace and truth. This is no time to presume on the grace of God, but rather to pray urgently for it! The Lord's glory, Gospel, and promise are at stake! *"Wherefore we receiving a kingdom which cannot be moved, let us have grace, whereby we may serve God acceptably with reverence and godly fear: For our God is a consuming fire."*[72] ◆

---

[66] John 5:22, 27.

[67] Matthew 11:27.

[68] Matthew 28:18.

[69] Hebrews 10:30.

[70] Ephesians 1:6

[71] Hebrews 12:25

[72] Hebrews 12:28-29.

Chapter 13

God's Institution of Marriage
and Rome's Infringement on It

The old adage that states, 'the hand that rocks the cradle rules the world', ought more correctly to be declared as 'the hand that controls marriage rules the world'. Before critiquing the Catholic Church's control of marriage by her laws, marriage must be seen coming directly from the creator Himself. As creator and sovereign Lord over His creation, God in His wisdom instituted and commanded that male and female should at a proper time leave mother and father and be married, *"therefore shall a man leave his father and his mother, and shall cleave unto his wife: and they shall be one flesh."*[1]

Scripture shows that from the beginning both, believers[2] and non-believers[3], married because the ordinance of marriage is for all mankind. Mankind cannot overthrow or put an end to this creation command. God has used families, clans, tribes, kingdoms and states as instruments to facilitate, enforce and watch over the bonds of marriage. But because of fallen man's sinful nature and darkness, these institutions in varying degrees have not followed the command of permanent monogamy as the divine law of marriage. Even some of God's people have followed the corrupted norms of the societies rather than the law of God. When some kingdoms and states allow marriage to fall into disrepute, God's judgment is on these institutions and their societies.[4]

---

[1] Genesis 2:24

[2] For example see Genesis 5

[3] For example see Genesis 4:16-17

[4] *"For the wrath of God is revealed from heaven against all ungodliness and unrighteousness of men who hold the truth in unrighteousness."* (Romans 1:18) The word "ungodliness" includes all crimes against God and all crimes against fellow men in marriage or otherwise.

The Lord Jesus Christ reinforced the creation command and explained how it was God's will for His people, *"What therefore God hath joined together, let not man put asunder."*[5] True believers in the Lord Jesus Christ should reflect their union with their Lord in their marriages, as a light to a fallen world.[6] The true people of God should be the preeminent instrument that God uses to uphold marriage because they have the revelation of Scripture and the power of the Holy Spirit. No church or so-called church has authority to make laws concerning the validity of marriage or its unmaking. Marriage is a creation ordinance, belonging to all mankind.

The Word of God does not prescribe anything in respect to the mode of performing the marriage ceremony. Ceremonies differ in various nations but should never be regarded as anything more than a public recognition of a relationship entered into by a man and woman before God their creator. Yet as marriage is a matter of important consequence involving public as well as private obligations, it is appropriate and necessary that some ceremony should be performed, and that is should be public so as to leave no doubt as to its reality.

Alleged absolute power over marriage

While the Catholic Church gives lip service to marriage as fashioned by God in its basic meaning and structure, in its law and practice it is totally different. The Catholic Church claims to have absolute authority over marriage and therefore exercises total legislation over marriage, even its validity and unmaking. For example, Pope Leo XIII tried to vindicate the Catholic Church's usurped authority over the institution of marriage when he declared,

> "When Christ, therefore, renewed matrimony and raised it to such a great [i.e., sacramental] excellence, He gave and confided to the Church the entire legislation in the matter."[7]

---

[5] Matthew 19:6

[6] *"Therefore as the church is subject unto Christ, so let the wives be to their own husbands in every thing... This is a great mystery: but I speak concerning Christ and the church."* Ephesians 5:24, 32

[7] *The Christian Faith in the Doctrinal Documents of the Catholic Church*, Neuner, J., and Dupuis, J., eds. (Cork: The Mercier Press, 1967) Para. 1821

In Papal Rome's *Code of Canon Law* she states, "Marriage cases of the baptized belong to the ecclesiastical judge by the proper right."[8] She is quite definite in giving the basis for her wholesale claim that marriage belongs to her. Thus she officially proclaims,

"But the grace which was to perfect that natural love, and confirm the indissoluble union, and sanctify those united in marriage, Christ Himself, institutor and perfector of the venerable Sacraments, merited for us by His passion. The Apostle Paul intimates this, when he says: 'Men, love your wives as Christ loved the Church, and delivered Himself up for it', directly adding: '**This is a great Sacrament**; but I speak in Christ and in the Church.'"[9]

This statement is a fabricated lie. The proof of this is in Scripture text itself, "*This is a great mystery: **but I speak concerning Christ and the church.***"[10] The Apostle gives express warning that no man should understand him as speaking of marriage. The subject that the Apostle was exalting is "*Christ is the head of the church.*"[11] He explains that this truth is more fully expressed as **"a great mystery"**, that is to say, that Christ breathes into the church His own life and power. To twist this to mean that marriage is "a great sacrament" and thus give a foothold for the Catholic claim to power over marriage is one the grossest examples of the perversion of Scripture. The Roman Church substitutes the word "Sacrament" for the word "mystery".[12] This was because of the Vulgate translation of the Bible by Jerome. Thus, on the mistranslation of a Bible word, the Catholic Church has constructed a whole theology whereby she claims absolute power over the most intimate and private

---

[8] *Code of Canon Law,* Latin-English Ed., New English Tr. (Canon Law Society of America, 1983) Canon1671. All canons are taken from this source unless otherwise stated.

[9] Henry Denzinger, *The Sources of Catholic Dogma*, Tr. by Roy J Deferrari from *Enchiridion Symbolorum*, 30th ed. (St. Louis, MO: B. Herder Book Co., 1957) # 969

[10] Ephesians 5:32

[11] Ephesians 5:23

[12] In Para 1616 of the *Catechism of the Catholic Church* (1994) she does use the correct word "mystery"; but like some other dogmas in Papal Rome, once the tradition is established, the original basis for it can be ignored.

relationship of millions of people. This error is no small thing when one sees the havoc it wreaks upon the lives of those who belong to the Catholic Church and how much pain and difficulty it brings to those who are trying to live out their marriage under her jurisdiction. Nevertheless, the Catholic Church is so adamant in maintaining her claim that she puts a curse on anyone who denies that marriage is truly a sacrament,

> "If anyone says that matrimony is not truly and properly one of the seven sacraments of the evangelical Law, instituted by Christ the Lord, but that it has been invented by men in the Church, and does not confer grace: let him be anathema."[13]

Megalomaniac power even in civil law

The Roman Catholic laws on marriages are a shock to anyone who knows the nature of marriage as coming from the creator Himself. In Scripture it is declared to be respectable in all its components, *"Marriage is honorable in all, and the bed undefiled."*[14] It is the institution of God designed in such a way that men and women in every part of the habitable world should be free to be united in this bond. It is God's ordinance and not that of any church. It ought to be so esteemed by all and not denied to any of those for whom God has made it. It is honorable because God instituted it for man from the beginning. He married and blessed the first couple, the first parents of mankind, to direct all to look to God in this great institution. This is so abundantly clear that one would think that all humankind would be in agreement. But the Church of Rome does not agree.[15] All of the secular features of marriage expressed above are strongly opposed by the Roman Catholic Church. This first happened in the twelfth century when Papal Rome gained control over marriage and began legislating on the validity or invalidity of all marriages, whether kings or peasants.[16]

---

[13] Denzinger, # 971

[14] Hebrews 13:4

[15] Marriage in Muslim societies is unfeasible in Biblical terms, and there are other exceptions such as Communist China where the State dictates even the number of children that a couple is allowed to have.

[16] For most of its history from the sixth century to the time of the Reformation, the

This takeover of marriage by Rome in her drive for power is one of the most influential tools that she has in her control of Catholics worldwide. In her 1983 *Code of Canon Law*, the Vatican has moved to consolidate her power over marriage. For example, the Vatican sets the age that a person may enter marriage when it legislates that "a man before he has completed his sixteenth year of age and a woman before she has completed her fourteenth year of age cannot enter into a valid marriage."[17] Further, according to Catholic law, the marriage of a Catholic with an unbaptized person is legally invalid,

> "A marriage between two persons, one of whom has been baptized in the Catholic Church or received into it and has not defected from it by a formal act and the other of whom is not baptized, is invalid."[18]

The same Vatican also legislates that sexual impotence on the part of a man and wife make a marriage legally invalid.

> "Antecedent and perpetual impotence to have intercourse, whether on the part of the man or the woman, whether absolute or relative, nullifies marriage by its very nature."[19]

Catholic Church controlled religion, morals, politics, art and education in what was known as the Holy Roman Empire. In all those centuries of the Dark Ages, it was the priest and bishop who governed peoples' lives in regards to morality and therefore, marriage. It was not until the Reformation that the institution of marriage achieved any freedom from Roman ecclesiastical control. In 18th and 19th centuries, some governments established an independent civil institution of marriage for all people on an equal basis. There were, of course, Christian groups independent of the Catholic Church throughout all of the Christian era, as, for example, the Vaudois, the Waldenses, and others. From its beginning, the United States as a nation built its governmental structures in both church and state upon the Reformation understanding of separation of religious and civil jurisdictions. Because of this biblical understanding, the United States was free from Catholic dominion from the very beginning. The United States is compromised however by the fact that it now has civil relations with the Vatican. The general state of affairs in Europe for most of its history was that the Catholic law was the moral law.

[17] Canon 1083, §1

[18] Canon 1086 §1

[19] Canon 1084 §1

The Pope further reserves the right to dissolve a non-consummated marriage, even if a person is unwilling. Thus the Vatican in Canon 1142 legislates,

> "For a just cause, the Roman Pontiff can dissolve a non-consummated marriage between baptized persons or between a baptized party and a non-baptized party at the request of both parties or of one of them, even if the other party is unwilling."

While public recognition of a relationship is essential to marriage, the Vatican in Canon 1130 legislates even for secret marriages, "For a grave and urgent cause, the local ordinary [the bishop] can permit a marriage to be celebrated secretly." This "secret marriage" is so covert and surreptitious that the Vatican solemnly declares, "A marriage celebrated secretly is to be noted only in a special register to be kept in the secret archive of the curia."[20] This is only a small portion of the more than 110 laws that the Cardinals and Bishops Church of Rome legislate for Catholic people around the world.[21]

On the issue of marriage, the Vatican acts as if she has the power of God, as for example, in what we quoted of the Pope's alleged power to dissolve a non-consummated marriage even if one party is unwilling. If this alleged power were just theoretical and strictly within the confines of the Papal Church, it would still be unacceptable although predictable. The difficulty is that the Vatican power is that of both a Church and a civil state.[22] As a sovereign state, the Vatican is recognized by one hundred seventy-four other nations with whom she

---

[20] Canon 1133

[21] So comprehensive are these laws that they are organized into chapters. Canons 1055 – 1165: Ch. I. Pastoral Care and Those Things Which Must Precede the Celebration of Marriage. Ch. II. Diriment Impediments in General. Ch. III. Specific Diriment Impediments. Chapter IV. Matrimonial Consent. Ch. V. The Form of the Celebration of Marriage. Ch. VI. Mixed marriages. Ch. VII. Marriage Celebrated Secretly. Ch. VIII. The Effects of Marriage. Ch. IX. The Separation of Spouses, Art. 1. Dissolution of the Bond. Art. 2. Separation with the Bond Remaining. Ch. X. The Convalidation of Marriage, Art. 1. Simple Convalidation. Art. 2. Radical Sanation.

[22] The term "Holy See" always refers to the Roman Catholic Church as a political entity and is used in her relationships with other nations.

exchanges ambassadors. With some of these nations she also legally enters into what is called a "concordat". A "concordat" is an international contract legally binding the nation involved and the Vatican. It guarantees to the Roman Catholic Church and Catholics such 'rights' as worship, instruction of their people in their religion, and the acceptance of Roman Catholic law regarding marriage and annulment. This last factor, the control of marriages within nations, is recognized even by secular academic writings. We quote from *The International Journal of Not-for-Profit Law*,

> "The Catholic Church [in most Latin American countries] was basically the only church with a legal presence, and it did not operate under the aegis of governmental laws or regulations. The law applicable to the Catholic Church was its own canon law. The Catholic Church's dealings with governments were not regulated by legislation or executive decree, but by treaties or agreements with the Vatican. Other churches, to the extent they existed or operated at all, could not enter into such treaties because they were not independent sovereigns."[23]

The age-old ambitions of the Vatican have not changed nor has the desire to control her people minutely even in the most intimate of all relationships, marriage. This means that her hold on Catholic marriages will not be relinquished without the Gospel. Under the Gospel, men and women are brought into a state of liberty in which they are freed from the yoke of Roman Catholic marriage law and the rigorous control it engenders. It is therefore the glorious duty of men and women to stand fast in this liberty and to adhere to the Gospel of grace and the freedom it brings. This is the basic and essential way for Catholics to be rid of the yoke of bondage.

Mixed marriages

The Vatican's control over marriages and the marriage bed becomes especially manipulative in what they call "mixed marriages". Mixed

---

[23] The International Journal of Not-for-Profit Law, Volume Six, Issue One, Sept 2003, p. 3
http://www.icnl.org/JOURNAL/vol6iss1/rel_isaacsonprint.htm 5/28/05

marriages have been and continue to be one of the more successful ways of increasing the numbers of those who submit to Catholic ways. I remember in all my twenty-one years as a priest in Trinidad how stringently I insisted on the Catholic laws. I performed marriage after marriage in which the papers were filled with the resolution that all children born of the union would be brought up in the Catholic Church. This is the Catholic law, "Without express permission of the competent authority, a marriage is prohibited between two baptized persons of whom one is baptized in the Catholic Church or received into it after baptism and has not defected from it by a formal act and the other of whom is enrolled in a Church or ecclesial community not in full communion with the Catholic Church."[24] The real clinching law is Canon 1125,

> "The local ordinary [i.e., a bishop] can a grant permission of this kind if there is a just and reasonable cause. He is not to grant it unless the following conditions have been fulfilled. 1. the Catholic party is to declare that he or she is prepared to remove dangers of defecting from the faith and to make a sincere promise to do all in his or her power so that all offspring are baptized and brought up in the Catholic Church; 2. the other party is to be informed at an appropriate time about the promises which the Catholic party is to make, in such a way that it is certain that he or she is truly aware of the promise and obligation of the Catholic party; 3. both parties are to be instructed about the purposes and essential properties of marriage, which neither of the contracting parties is to exclude."

When Rome first set about winning Protestants to Catholicism in the United States of America, one strategy of its documented plan was to entice them by mixed marriages. In 1810, Roman Catholic Bishop Brute wrote a report to be sent back to Rome in which he mentions under the topic of "Conversion of Protestants" that "It is necessary to consider the conversions: By direct teachings. By education among Catholics. By mixed marriages…"[25] Regrettably, these

---

[24] Canon 1124
[25] *Documentary Reports on Early American Catholicism* selected and introduced by Philip Gleason (New York: Arno Press, 1978) p. 229

humanistic plans have been quite successful in augmenting the power of Rome, mixed marriages being one of the most successful means. Such unbiblical practices, however, are in total opposition to the means of establishing the kingdom of God as taught in the Scriptures. Christ Jesus declared, *"My kingdom is not of this world."*[26] His is not a political institution regulated by worldly laws to gain more subjects. Rather, His kingdom is a spiritual regime, regulated by the Truth. The means He uses for its enlargement is His gracious Gospel.

Divorce
Biblically, when it comes to divorce, there are four main statements by the Lord Jesus Christ. Two of these reflect total opposition to divorce whereas two others indicate acceptance of divorce on the grounds of sexual unfaithfulness, and the right to remarriage for the innocent party. Before God, marriage is a lifetime relationship that should never be brought to an end by human action. The fundamental divine law of marriage is that a man shall leave father and mother, and shall cleave to his wife. The nature of the marriage contract is that the two persons joined in such a union become one flesh, *"Wherefore they are no more twain, but one flesh. What therefore God hath joined together, let not man put asunder."*[27] Husband and wife, being joined together by the ordinance of God, are not to be put asunder by any decree of man. God says that He hates divorce.[28] God's perfect will is the safeguarding of society and future generations by the preservation of marriages. God will give anyone great help in sustaining a marriage of estranged marriage partners. There are only two grounds for divorce and remarriage. When sexual unfaithfulness has taken place, a divorce can be obtained because adultery has already severed the marriage relationship and divorce is a formal acknowledgment of what has already taken place. *"Whosoever shall put away his wife, except it be for fornication, and shall marry another, committeth adultery: and whoso marrieth her which is put away doth commit adultery."*[29]

---

[26] John 18:36
[27] Matthew 19:6
[28] Malachi 2:16
[29] Matthew 19:9

The law of Christ reinstated man in his initial integrity; the law of married love was from the beginning. When we consider what evil is perpetrated on families and nations through Papal laws on annulment of marriage, and the arbitrary civil divorces are that are prevalent in society, we shall see how much this law of Christ stands in the interest of all mankind.

Divorce—annulment style

The Catholic Church declares that all marriages between baptized people are in fact a sacrament. This is reiterated in canon law, "…a valid matrimonial contract cannot exist between the baptized without it being by that fact a sacrament."[30] In declaring marriage to be a sacrament, the Catholic Church means that it is an institution by which God gives grace and over which she has control. Rome sets up a hierarchy of marriages whereby the Catholic marriage takes precedence over other marriages. Marriages that are civilly valid can be considered null and void from the point of view of Catholic law. A marriage of a Catholic to a non-Catholic that did not take place before a Catholic priest is considered null and void and it is only a matter of time before the parties can be released from their marriage covenant.

The whole idea of marriage as a sacrament is to set up a system whereby Catholic marriage surpasses other marriages and takes precedence over them. Catholics are conditioned from childhood to accept the idea that marriage must be done before a priest and they look down on marriages that have not been so performed. The way that this teaching is lived out under Catholic law is very serious because it is quite easy to get a decree of annulment when a marriage was not performed before a priest. It is much more difficult to get an annulment for those marriages that have been carried out before a priest and are called Sacramental.

The Catholic Church continually enunciates that there is no divorce for a marriage that is lawfully performed between a consenting,

---

[30] Canon 1055, §2

baptized man and woman. However, study of the Roman laws regarding an annulment shows that great technical skill and ingenuity is used in dispensing Ecclesiastical annulments. An annulment in actual fact amounts to exactly the same thing as a divorce in practice. In law it goes beyond the concept of a divorce. The Catholic Church, in granting an annulment, declares legally that a marriage never was. This means that one can end up in the absurd situation of having been married and having had children from that marriage—a tangible fact of the marriage—and yet the marriage is declared to never have been!

Further, without an annulment, civil divorce is not recognized by the Catholic Church as valid. This in turn keeps Catholics from taking the Eucharist, which, after baptism, is the central means of obtaining ongoing grace that purportedly flows through the sacrament. This in turn has extreme consequences when Catholics think of dying without the necessary sacramental grace in which they have been taught to believe.

One of the chief implements used in gaining an annulment is what is called a "diriment impediment". A diriment impediment is an impediment that is serious enough to nullify a marriage automatically. This could be a lack of consent of either party or a deficiency in "the form of marriage". The required form of marriage according to Rome is that it is performed before a priest and two witnesses. Many marriages are declared null because of the laws the Catholic Church has regarding "diriment impediments". Then, too, the Catholic Church has evolved a terminology that outclasses even the Pharisees. An example of this is a "radical sanation". A "radical sanation" is a decree that is retroactive and can stabilize and make a marriage valid that had started out invalidly. Present day canon law states,

> "The radical sanation of an invalid marriage is its convalidation without the renewal of consent, which is granted by the competent authority and entails the dispensation from an impediment, if there is one, and from canonical form, if it was not observed, and the retroactivity of canonical effects."[31]

---

[31] Canon 1161

Even the Pharisees would have marveled at this intricate legislation that is purportedly able to retroactively make a marriage valid that had not been valid. The same canon continues,

> "Convalidation occurs at the moment of the granting of the favor. Retroactivity, however, is understood to extend to the moment of the celebration of the marriage unless other provision is expressly made."[32]

Such making and unmaking of marriages contravenes Divine law. It is done by the same Papal Rome that outlaws marriage for her priests.

Papal making and unmaking of marriage

The making and the unmaking of marriage is claimed to be all within the apostolic power of the Catholic Church. The Catholic Church exercises such power even if both parties know nothing of what is being done. Thus Rome proclaims in her law, "A sanation can be granted validly even if either or both of the parties do not know of it; nevertheless it is not to be granted except for a grave cause."[33] This mysterious power she declares is held in the heart of Rome herself, "The Apostolic See can grant a radical sanation."[34] Marriage is not made valid at the command of Rome; in Scripture marriage is regulated according to the will and counsel of God. The Lord Christ Jesus said *"a man shall leave father and mother, and shall cleave to his wife."*[35] This alone is how a marriage becomes valid before God. To decree that celibate prelates in Rome, even though the parties themselves do not know of it, can make a marriage is pharisaic totalitarianism gone wild! This bizarre power is claimed because Rome claims that marriage is a sacrament. It is therefore within her power to make or break marriages according to her own will and purposes.

The unmaking of marriages is sometimes done by what is called "interior consent", that is, the consent that either the man or woman had or did not have from the beginning. On different ecclesiastical

---

[32] Canon 1161, §2

[33] Canon 1164

[34] Canon 1165

[35] Matthew 19:5

investigations, this can come out in an ecclesiastical court, either to make or to break a marriage. Catholic annulments are a big business inside the Catholic Church, and in the United States it is known in which of the states it is easier to get an annulment.

"The statistics are interesting. In 1968 there were in the US a total of 338 annulments. In 1992 there were no less than 59,030, that is one hundred and seventy-five times as many. Another interesting figure is that the total number of annulments in the Catholic Church world wide in 1992 was 76,286, which means that no less than 75% of all annulments were from the US, that is from a little over 5% of the world's Catholic population. Moreover, not only do one in two Catholic marriages here in the States end up with a divorce, but one in five is officially annulled, 90% of the demands for annulment being successful."[36]

"During 1984 and 1986- 1994, U.S. Second Instance tribunals ratified 342,218 ordinary process decrees of nullity, retried and ruled for nullity in 13,303, and decided against nullity in 1,412. Second Instance tribunals in the rest of the world, despite adjudicating 250,000 fewer cases, ruled against nullity in 5,890 cases. Putting this another way, an American ordinary process annulment had four chances in a thousand of being overturned at Second Instance, as opposed to 56 chances in a thousand for ordinary process annulments granted elsewhere."[37]

Procedure for obtaining an annulment
The procedure to obtain an annulment is laid out by some archdioceses. For example, the Archdiocese of New York's *modus operandi* is explained by Holy Name of Mary Parish,

"PROCEDURE (1) The Petitioner's Packet is given to the petitioner with a general explanation concerning the filling out of the fact sheet (names, addresses, phone numbers, etc.) (2) The Petitioner should understand that the case, in all probability, will be tried on the grounds of lack of due discretion (Canon 1095) on the

---

[36] http://www.sspx.org/Canonical_Commission/august_1995_ltr.htm 5/30/05

[37] www.familylifecenter.net/txt/annulments-in-america.html 5/30/05

part of the PETITIONER. This means that the petitioner bears the burden of proof that he/she failed to exercise reasonable judgment about himself/herself or the other party before marrying. The proof includes the following: (a) The BIOGRAPHY of the PETITIONER. (b) Statements from at least TWO WITNESSES. (c) Evaluation of the PETITIONER by a PSYCHOLOGICAL or PSYCHIATRIC EXPERT. (d) All pertinent DOCUMENTS and CERTIFICATES. (3) The Petitioner should understand that the RESPONDENT or FORMER SPOUSE must be contacted under Canon Law by the ADVOCATE and the TRIBUNAL. The petitioner should be reassured that he/she will not have to come into contact with the former spouse. (4) The PETITIONER should understand that at some point he/she MUST make a PERSONAL APPEARANCE before the Tribunal for a FORMAL HEARING UNDER OATH. WITNESSES should also understand that they will be called upon to provide testimony under oath either IN PERSON or BY PHONE. (5) When you have received the PRELIMINARY STATEMENT and the WITNESS STATEMENTS (in sealed enveloped), you are to refer the Petitioner to one of our psychological experts for an evaluation. After the petitioner makes the appointment, you may mail copies of the petitioner's biography and witness statements to the expert. If the petitioner has been currently seeing a therapist or has seen a therapist in the last two years, you may have the petitioner sign a release form (sample included). This MAY avoid the necessity of the petitioner consulting with one of our experts. It should be noted, however, that quite often these reports from therapists offer very little insight about the individual on the day of marriage. (6) After you have received the expert's evaluation, fill out the PETITION and MANDATE (samples are included). (7) Forward everything to the Mt. Kisco office of the Tribunal with a DEPOSIT of $350.00 made payable to ARCH-DIOCESE OF NEW YORK. Please inform the petitioner that at the time of the FORMAL HEARING, the remaining balance is

---

[38] http://www.catholic-church.org/holyname/procedur.htm 12/10/2000 Capital letters are in the original.

due: $650.00. Enclosed in this packet and the petitioner's packet is a STATEMENT OF UNDERSTANDING ABOUT THE EXPENSES OF THE CASE. Please ensure that the petitioner understands the agreement. If the petitioner is in financial difficulty, of course, part of the fee or all of the fee may be waived. In such a case, I would ask that you, as the ADVOCATE, write a letter to that effect and place it in the file forwarded to the Tribunal. (8) The petitioner should understand that NO DATE should be set for a future wedding until a definitive decision is reached by the REVIEW COURT. Since we will be instituting a new REVIEW COURT, probably located at Dunwoodie (with a completely different staff), in accordance with Rome's request, the time element for completing cases will be more UNCERTAIN. Also, the petitioner should not be led to think that an AFFIRMATIVE DECISION is a foregone conclusion. With RESPONDENTS becoming more contentious and adversarial, at times, appeals to Rome are not uncommon. (9) Once the FORMAL HEARING has taken place in Mt. Kisco, the petitioner should be informed that further inquiries about the progress of the case should be directed to this office."[38]

The casual and arrogant manner of dealing with marriage and the dissolution of marriage is not surprising, given the bishops and priests who make papal judgments on marriages. A pastor in Scripture is to be *"one that ruleth well his own house, having his children in subjection with all gravity; for if a man know not how to rule his own house, how shall he take care of the church of God?"*[39] These qualifications exclude the celibate judges who grant annulments. Like Indulgences, the whole annulment industry of the Roman Catholic Church—from the propounding of the laws to the sale of the contraband article—is in total violation of Scripture.

Marriage and the Catholic travesty against it
The Lord Jesus Christ, the Incarnate Son of God, clearly spoke of the dignity and sanctity of marriage. When questioned about marriage, He

---

[39] I Timothy 3:4-5

went back to the narrative in Genesis, *"Have you not read that he which made them from the beginning made them male and female, and said, 'For this cause shall a man leave father and mother, and shall cleave to his wife: and they twain shall be one flesh'?"*[40] Christ Jesus' endorsement of the sanctity of marriage was simply a re-endorsement of the original revelation given by God. Marriage is a creation ordinance. It is not like baptism and the Lord's Supper, which are ordinances of the New Testament directly from Christ Himself and for believers only.

Marriage is from the beginning and it comes under the jurisdiction of the civil state as instituted by God. For Christians, the laws regarding marriage are clearly laid out in the Bible, both in the Old and New Testaments. A Christian pastor can counsel a couple regarding their marriage according to these biblical norms. He is never to take jurisdiction over their marriage to make or break it. The Lord Jesus Christ is abundantly clear when He states that what God has joined together, no man should put asunder. The only biblical case that can be found for divorce is what the Lord Himself allows for in the case of sexual unfaithfulness and the case that of the desertion of a believer by an unbelieving spouse as described I Corinthians 7:12-15.[41]

Nevertheless, the Catholic Church has manufactured a whole set of rules and regulations that requires a Roman Catholic canon lawyer to fully understand. They are such that even the Pharisees would blush. Since cases of the validity of marriage abound with many different technical terms, Rome says she upholds the sanctity of marriage, but she allows marriages to be declared null and void based upon a

---

[40] Matthew 19:4-5

[41] *"If any brother hath a wife that believeth not, and she be pleased to dwell with him, let him not put her away. And the woman which hath an husband that believeth not, and if he be pleased to dwell with her, let her not leave him. For the unbelieving husband is sanctified by the wife, and the unbelieving wife is sanctified by the husband: else were your children unclean; but now are they holy. But if the unbelieving depart, let him depart. A brother or a sister is not under bondage in such cases: but God hath called us to peace."*

terminology of her own making. For example, "validity" when granted by Rome's ecclesial courts is not just a simple statement. It allows for different interpretations. For example Canon 1684 states,

"After the sentence which first declared the nullity of the marriage has been confirmed at the appellate grade either by a decree or by a second sentence, the persons whose marriage has been declared null can contract a new marriage as soon as the decree or second sentence has been communicated to them unless a prohibition attached to the sentence or decree or established by the local ordinary [the bishop] has forbidden this."

Thus the very decree that a marriage is null and void is muddied by theological terminology whereby, if someone is to act on Catholic teaching, he needs trained lawyers to lead him through the labyrinth of canon law. In total contrast the Bible gives a clear message that God, who is the All Holy One, has decreed what makes a marriage. This is wonderful for both the people of God and for all mankind. It is a common blessing of God's grace. The Catholic Church has abducted this divine institution and used it for its own purposes. Papal Rome has granted hundreds of thousands of annulments and allowed remarriage. Many of these unions, called marriages, are in fact, before the Lord and His Word, nothing more than officially blessed whoredoms. Such sinful unions take away the hearts and souls of men and women. These are living situations, blessed by the priest and the Church of Rome; they are like a deep ditch and a narrow pit, out of which it is almost impossible to escape.

An example from early American history

John Adams, the second President of the United States, addressed ecclesiastical tyranny as he asked the question, "Can a free government possibly exist with the Roman Catholic religion?"[42] . He so clearly saw the dangers that he called "Catholic Christianity" "Cabalistic Christianity".[43] In his "Dissertation on the Canon and the Feudal Law", Adams pinpointed the problem when he wrote of the early Christian Puritans in

---

[42] John Adams, Letter to Thomas Jefferson, May 19, 1821 www.historicist.com/articles2/historicwarnings.htm

[43] *Ibid.*, John Adams, letter to Thomas Jefferson, July 16, 1814. "Cabalistic Christianity, which is Catholic Christianity, and which has prevailed for 1,500 years, has received a mortal wound...."

America, that their "greatest concern seems to have been to establish a government of the church more consistent with the Scriptures, and a government of the state more agreeable to the dignity of human nature, than any they had seen in Europe, and to transmit such a government down to their posterity, with the means of securing and preserving it forever....They saw clearly, that of all the nonsense and delusion which had ever passed through the mind of man, none had ever been more extravagant than the notions of absolutions, indelible characters, uninterrupted successions, and the rest of those fantastical ideas, derived from the canon law, which had thrown such a glare of mystery, sanctity, reverence, and right reverend eminence and holiness, around the idea of a priest, as no mortal could deserve, and as always must, from the constitution of human nature, be dangerous in society."[44]

In this day of false ecumenism with the same Roman Catholic Church, John Adams' question should again be asked, can a free government possibly exist with the Roman Catholic marriage laws?

Conclusion

The extravagant demands of Roman Catholic law impinge on the freedom of any nation. If Christian people are truly informed, they must become aware that marriage, the very basis of society, is being controlled and manipulated for millions of Catholics.[45] It applies to not only the millions of Catholics in United States, in different Western nations, and

---

[44] John Adams, "A Dissertation on the Canon and the Feudal Law", printed in the *Boston Gazette*, August 1765. Text is on: www.ashbrook.org/library/18/adams/canonlaw.html 5/30/05

[45] On September 12, 2005 FoxNews.com brought to light one of the insidious tactics used by the Roman system to gain greater control of Catholic marriage through civil law in its article, "Ontario Rejects Use of Islamic Law". "Ontario, the most populous province in Canada, has allowed Catholic and Jewish faith-based tribunals to settle family law matters on a voluntary basis since 1991. The practice got little attention until Muslim leaders demanded the same rights. Officials had to decide whether to exclude one religion, or whether to scrap the religious family courts altogether. McGuinty [Premier of Ontario] said such courts 'threaten our common ground,' and promised his Liberal government would introduce legislation as soon as possible to outlaw them in Ontario. 'Ontarians will always have the right to seek advice from anyone in matters of family law, including religious advice,' he said, 'But no longer will religious arbitration be deciding matters of family law.'" The Catholic Church's foothold into Canadian civil law has suffered a set-back for the moment by this decision of Premier McGuinty.

across the world, but it also applies to the millions of the Christians and others who are also deeply ensnared by Papal canon law as they enter into a marriage with a Catholic. If Catholicism is to be addressed seriously, the infringement on marriage must be dealt with scripturally, as it stands at the very heart and structure of civil society as given by God.

The true believer can understand that the contrast between the Church of Rome and the true Church is the difference that there is between a wanton woman adorned with gold and jewels, scarlet and purple, and a pure virgin chastely and modestly adorned, about to be united in bonds of love to a upright husband. Thus the Scripture declares, *"Blessed are they which are called unto the marriage supper of the Lamb."*[46] The true believer has washed his robes and made them white in the blood of the Lamb; the wedding blessings he did not purchase by any price of his own, but received them as the gift and inheritance of his blessed Lord. Great and awe-inspiring events are before the true believer. Now is not the time for flabby Christianity that will not face the legal consequences of faith. It is time to fully investigate the social price tag of Papal law on marriages.

There is no way to maintain a biblical and evangelical testimony for the Gospel of salvation by faith alone in Christ alone while granting legitimacy to Roman Catholic laws on marriage. It is impossible to hold that one is a Bible-believing Evangelical Christian who accepts both the inspiration and authority of the Word of God and still give legality to Roman Catholicism, which forthrightly rejects that principle, as their laws on marriage show. Such behavior is an affront to Christ in His work of redemption and likewise to the Holy Spirit in His ministry of convicting the world of sin, righteousness and judgment. The Apostle Paul wrote under the direction of the Holy Spirit, *"the wrath of God is revealed from heaven against all ungodliness and unrighteousness of men, who hold the truth in unrighteousness."*[47] Who can bear with the devouring fire of God's everlasting wrath? The good news is

---

[46] Revelation 19:9

[47] Romans 1:18.

that personal faith and salvation is also from His hand, *"Him hath God exalted with his right hand to be a Prince and a Savior, for to give repentance to Israel, and forgiveness of sins."*[48]   The Scripture proclaims, *"Believe on the Lord Jesus Christ, and thou shalt be saved."*[49]   The Lord Himself declared, *"He that believeth, and is baptized, shall be saved; he that believeth not shall be damned."*[50] The Lord will always be merciful to those who turn to Him in faith for the remission of sins. *"Come unto me, all ye that labor and are heavy laden, and I will give you rest. Take my yoke upon you, and learn of me; for I am meek and lowly in heart: and ye shall find rest unto your souls. For my yoke is easy and my burden is light."*[51] Before the all-holy God, according to the Bible, an individual is saved by grace alone, through faith alone, in Christ alone. Following on this, all glory and praise is to God alone! ◆

---

[48] Acts 5:31.

[49] Acts 16:31

[50] Mark 16:16

[51] Matthew 11:28-30

Chapter 14

Convent Life

Convent life involves over 800,000 women and is a very big part of Catholicism. The principles behind convent life are basically the same as those behind monastic life, but this chapter will deal with the convent in particular. It is particularly significant that many women have been fascinated by this form of life as an alternative to marriage, and many of them have only faced with the abnormalities in convent life after it was much too late, they thought, to leave.

The idea of young maidens dedicated to the service of God, leaving their homes and introduced into convents under the care of elderly matrons, did not begin with Roman Catholicism. This was, for example, the lifestyle of the vestal virgins in pagan Rome, whose duty it was to watch the sacred fire and who were bound to perpetual virginity. It was also the lifestyle of the holy virgins of Peru during the reign of the Incas. There is also the strong tradition of Buddhist Nuns. This idea goes back many centuries before Christ. Thus the pagan tradition of women becoming nuns is a long one.

"The form of life which the Son of God made his own"
The teaching of the Catholic Church regarding convent and monastic life has invaded the lives of millions of men and women in history, and there are over a million men and women in religious orders of nuns, priests, and brothers at the present time. The philosophy is given clearly in Catholic teaching, which declares,

"...Furthermore the religious state constitutes a closer imitation and an abiding reenactment in the Church of the form of life which the

Son of God made his own when he came into the world to do the will of the Father and which he propounded to the disciples who followed him."[1]

To assert that Christ made the Religious state (i.e., the monastic and convent system) "his own and he propounded it to his disciples" is a falsehood which flatly denies the historical facts. Nowhere in Scripture does He "make it his own" nor "propound it to his disciples". Monasticism was known in the Lord's time, for the Essenes at Qumran lived in monastic fashion. It is clear from the Scriptures that the Lord had nothing to do with the Essenes or any monastery. The Gospel accounts give neither hint of Christ setting up such a way of life nor of Him instructing His disciples in that way of life. According to the Lord's teaching, believers are sanctified by the work of the Holy Spirit in applying the biblical Word of Truth to their lives—not by trying to escape from the world. Christ Jesus prayed, *"I pray not that thou shouldest take them out of the world, but that thou shouldest keep them from the evil...Sanctify them through thy truth: thy word is truth."*[2]

The claim that the monastic and convent system is a stable form of living
The Vatican declares that monastic and convent is a stable form of living. "The life consecrated through the profession of the evangelical counsels is a **stable form of living** by which the faithful, following Christ more closely under the action of the Holy Spirit, are totally dedicated to God..."[3] In reading news reports regarding the life of nuns it is evident that such a way of living is anything but stable. Recently there have been many news items regarding the precariousness of the lives of nuns. The Catholic news on January 6, 2003 carried the announcement that,

"The St Louis Post-Dispatch carried a disturbing report on Sunday, picked up by other major media outlets around the world, of

---

[1] *Vatican Council II: The Conciliar and Post Conciliar Documents*, No. 28, *Lumen Gentium*, 21 November 1964, Austin Flannery, O. P., Gen. Ed., 1981 ed., 2 vols., (Northport, NY : Costello Publ. Co., 1975) Vol. I, Para. 44, p. 404

[2] John 17:15,17

[3] *Code of Canon Law*, Latin-English Ed., New English Translation (Canon Law Society of America, 1983, 1999) Canon 573, §1. All canons are taken from this volume unless otherwise stated.

research at the St Louis University paid for by several orders of religious nuns that shows 'about 40 percent of all nuns in the United States, have suffered some form of sexual trauma'. The study was undertaken in 1996 and reported in some respected but small circulation religious journals in 1998 but not picked up by the mainstream media....One in eight nuns said she had been sexually exploited. Of those, nearly three of every four maintained she was victimized by a priest, nun or other religious person. The exploitation included everything from pressure for 'dates' to requests for sexual favors to sexual intercourse."[4]

The cover story of the *National Catholic Reporter* November 1, 2002, was a report on abuse by nuns, which has been reported in the USA. It stated, "Experts on abuse by church figures say the scenario has played out at convents, Catholic schools, churches and orphanages across the country. Over the last decade, at least a dozen lawsuits alleging sexual abuse by nuns have been filed, and cases in Minnesota, Vermont, New York and Michigan have been settled. None of them are known to have been prosecuted."[5] From these Catholic news sources it is obvious that the lives of nuns are anything but stable, and for many it is quite abnormal at best.

Catholic distinction between the commandments of God and the counsels of God

The Catholic Church in its traditions makes a distinction between the commandments of God and the counsels of God. Thus she proclaims,

"The consecrated life through the profession of the evangelical counsels is stable form of living....The Christian faithful freely assume this form of living in institutes of consecrated life....Through vows or other sacred bonds according to the proper laws of the institutions, they profess the **evangelical counsels** of chastity, poverty, and obedience..." (Can. 573, §2)

"Besides its precepts, the New Law also includes the *evangelical counsels*. The traditional distinction between God's commandments

---

[4] http://www.cathnews.com/news/301/20.php
[5] www.natcath.org/crisis/110102h.htm 8/6/03

and the **evangelical counsels** is drawn in relation to charity, the perfection of Christian life."[6]

This distinction is not biblical. There is no such thing in Scripture. Whatever falls under counsel in moral matters in Scripture falls also under commandment. What God counsels is what He commands. For example, in the book of Revelation the Lord says "*I counsel thee to buy of me gold tried in the fire, that thou mayest be rich; and white raiment, that thou mayest be clothed, and that the shame of thy nakedness do not appear; and anoint thine eyes with eye salve, that thou mayest see.*"[7] The commandment of Christ Jesus is to part with sin and self-sufficiency, and come to Him with a sense of your spiritual poverty and emptiness, that you may be secure in His salvation. Thus it was also when the Apostle Paul had made known all the commandments of God he said, "*For I have not shunned to declare unto you all the counsel of God.*"[8] Paul made known all the moral law to God's people. God rejected the Pharisees and the lawyers in the Lord's time because they refused His commandments, "*Pharisees and lawyers rejected the counsel of God against themselves.*"[9] The counsel of God toward them was the solemn warning by John to repent and be baptized, and be prepared to receive the Messiah.

There is nothing in the moral law of God that is not included in the commandment to love God with all our mind, soul, heart and spirit and to love our neighbor as Christ has loved us. The Lord commands us in what He counsels us, for example the Lord says, "*So likewise, whosoever he be of you that forsaketh not all that he hath, he cannot be my disciple.*"[10] And, "*if any man will come after me, let him deny himself, and take up his cross, and follow me.*"[11] Nevertheless, the account of the rich man and the Lord Jesus Christ is

---

[6] *Catechism of the Catholic Church* (1994), Para. 1973

[7] Revelation 3:18

[8] Acts 20:27

[9] Luke 7:30

[10] Luke 14:33

[11] Matthew 16:24

used by the Catholic Church to denote a distinction between commandment and counsel that is utterly false. Christ Jesus did not give a counsel but rather a commandment that is common to all because no one can have any hope for salvation unless he follows Christ alone. The particulars of that story were to expose the hypocrisy of the rich young ruler. By using this scriptural event as the basis by which to fabricate a distinction between the commands of God and His counsels, the Roman Catholic Church has taken authority, based on this "new" distinction, to build for herself the institution she calls "the religious form of life". The conclusion from her falsehood is proclaimed officially in her own words,

> "Besides giving legal sanction to the religious form of life and thus raising it to the dignity of a canonical state, the Church sets it forth liturgically also as a state of consecration to God. She herself, in virtue of her God-given authority, receives the vows of those who profess this form of life...."[12]

Testimony of Patricia Nolan Savas

Patricia Nolan Savas was in religious life for ten years.[13] I interviewed her on a radio program, asking her if she found that religious life was a more stable form of living. This is what she had to say,

> *Patricia:* "No, I'd have to say so on the surface, as we were told to maintain, always to smile and never to let people know anything was happening, and that was part of the rule we had to obey. On the surface it looked very stable, but you see underneath was a terrible [thing]....all kinds of psychological and physical problems we were dealing with because we were just human beings, trying to obtain superhuman perfection. It cannot be done. It cannot be done!"

> *Richard:* "And you talk [in your book] about mortification of the flesh, we were always, even in the monastery also told to offer things up and to try to become holy by doing works of penance. Was this the same for you?"

---

[12] Flannery, Vatican Council II Document No. 28, *Lumen Gentium*, Para. 45, p. 406
[13] Patricia Nolan Savas, *Gus: A Nun's Story* (GNFC, 1444 Nimitz Way, Mesquite, TX 75181 Ph: (800) 228-7412)

Patricia: "Constantly, constantly, and underlying that, we didn't really know God….Our concept of God was of a far off, angry, punishing God and we were doing all these works and killing our flesh in order to try to somehow work our way 'up on our knees' as it were, to His throne."

Richard: "So, Patricia, it was not a stable and more solidly based type of life then the ordinary married life?"

Patricia: "Oh by far no! I'd like to say also what I actually put into the book was what I really experienced and saw. Nothing that I heard, no hearsay, and it was not stable because it is not God-ordained and it's not natural actually to be in this environment. Actually it's a homosexual environment. 'Homo' means same and 'Hetero', of course, means other, but we were even told to deny that other part of ourselves."

Richard: " We have [in the convent] an unnatural type of existence?"

Patricia: "Yes, very, very. And trying during all this…. leading this unnatural type of existence, trying to punish your flesh, mortify it, bring it into subjection, trying to reach that, what we thought at that time was a far off, angry, punishing God. This compounded this enormous psychological and physical illnesses."

Richard: "You speak about some sisters getting really annoyed. One sister was very offended; finally when she was being shunned she just threw a whole plate of spaghetti over the table and walked out?

Patricia: "Yes"

Richard: "Did you have many such incidences?"

Patricia: "Well, they weren't spoken of because people were just sort of whisked away and that sister actually now is a nurse and in the New Orleans area. So she came out relatively sane. She was a young nurse; very capable, promoted over older nurses. Of course I go into this and what happened to me also and because of this great jealousy and tension they do little things that become big things and just make life miserable for you. This was normally a very quiet, mild mannered person, but she just broke one day. She had asked them to pass I think it was the butter or sugar three times and they ignored her. They were giving her the freeze and she just threw the whole platter of spaghetti down the table and literally walked out in her full habit and everything. She's one of the survivors."

Richard: "Something much more difficult was Sister R that you mention who had a particular friendship with another nun and had been reprimanded and then when she leaves the convent she's found with a pistol in her hand?"

Patricia: "Yes, yes and that is one of the persons who didn't survive and there were many that lost their minds completely or their lives, and I do think without becoming salacious, I do mention the incidents of homosexuality. You have to realize what homosexual environment this is and these are augmented again which they wouldn't be in a normal heterosexual environment, but this woman did have those tendencies and unfortunately she was found one day with a revolver. She had blown her brains out. I still grieve for these sisters. I grieve for the ones that are still in mental institutions and they call them retreats and other things, but we know what they are."

Rocio Zwirner, in her testimony concerning convent life in Spain, speaks of

"another nun, because of her distress of mind threw herself into the convent's well. Her cries, not for help but of inconsolable mental torment, were heard throughout the entire convent, 'I'm condemned, I'm condemned'. She didn't know how to swim; yet she was floating and we were able to take her out alive. Her panic because of eternal condemnation gave me food for thought. During 'Operation Rescue', Mother Superior kept repeating, 'My daughter, stop condemning yourself' but the nun kept on wailing, 'I'm condemned'. Even now I remember this terrible experience with pain, for many still follow the same path, believing in what is dead and empty."[14]

There are many written accounts from those who lived in the convent life depicting that way of living as very unstable and disturbed.

---

[14] Rocio P. Zwirner, "The Woman at the Well" in *The Truth Set Us Free: Twenty Former Nuns Tell Their Stories* (Mukilteo, WA: Winepress Publishing, 1997) p. 87. Available through www.bereanbeacon.org.

Enticing the young

The Catholic system's primary tactic is to whet the appetite of her youths' zeal and idealism for such lives with dramatic words as,

> "The profound meaning of obedience is revealed in the fullness of this mystery of death and resurrection in which the supernatural destiny of man is brought to realization in a perfect manner. It is in fact through sacrifice, suffering and death that man attains true life. Exercising authority in the midst of your brethren means therefore being their servants, in accordance with the example of him who gave 'his life as a ransom for many.'"[15]

The sentiment and feeling of sentences such as this one, "...It is in fact through sacrifice, suffering and death that man attains true life...", leads many women to enter the convent, and men to join a religious order. That souls can be saved through the penitential work of other human beings has been Satan's message consistently in the cults and pagan religions. It appeals to a person's spiritual pride, even in the convent. "...*Ye shall be as gods...*"[16] was the message of Satan's original lie, and the game plan continues.

One of the very subtle ways the Catholic system entices young women into the "religious state" is declaring that by making public vows, a young woman is able through the Catholic institution to consecrate herself to God "ad mortem", "until death". "Religious profession" is defined by Rome,

> "By religious profession, members assume the observance of the three evangelical counsels by public vow, are consecrated to God through the ministry of the Church, and are incorporated into the institute **with rights and duties** defined by law."[17]

A close reading shows that this is a very subtle way of offering to a young woman a substitute for marriage, a substitute that purportedly would make her a very special individual and, like marriage, incorporate

---

[15] Flannery, Post Vatican Council II Document No. 53, S.C.R.S.I., *Evangelica Testificatio*, 29 June 1971, Vol. I, Para. 24, p. 691

[16] Genesis 3:5

[17] Canon 654

her into a publicly acceptable state "with rights and duties". It is declared that the members are thus "consecrated to God". As the Catholic laws regarding Religious life unfolds, however, it becomes clear that the young woman's consecration was not to God but rather to the Catholic Church, and that in this state she is, in fact, special to no one. If this were not so, how else could Rome's Canon 701 be explained, "By legitimate dismissal, vows as well as the rights and obligations deriving from profession cease *ipso facto*..." If one's vows truly consecrated one to God, no human "legitimate dismissal" could cause them to automatically cease.

Well-heeled poverty

In return for swearing fidelity to the vow of poverty, a nun is promised complete economic security by the Catholic Church. In such a state of poverty, she may own nothing but, usually as a corporate member of the community, she is well endowed with material goods. This circumvention interferes with the biblical pattern of responsibility of personal ownership, as well as the spiritual maturation acquired when a person trusts God for daily bread.

Question of obedience
Christ Jesus lived in the world, but was not of the world. He was absolutely obedient to His Father, even as the believer is told to be obedient to Him and to His Word, *"my sheep know my voice,"* *"whoever loves me will keep My word."* A nun's vow of obedience, however, brings in a concept alien to biblical thought. Rome teaches,

"The evangelical counsel of obedience, undertaken in a spirit of faith and love in the following of Christ obedient unto death, requires a submission of the will to **legitimate superiors, who stand in the place of God** when they command according to the proper constitutions." (Can. 601)

Obedience to the Lord commanded in the Bible is turned by in the Catholic world into obedience to one's local superior "who stands in the place of God." The Lord utterly condemned the Pharisees who were heading in that idolatrous direction when they sought to be called "Father" or "Master" by the people. Though the Pharisees imposed burdens on the people, they never came anywhere near to declaring a submission to "superiors, who stand in the place of God". The Catholic Church, however, declares, "Likewise, Religious are obliged to observe all those prescriptions which episcopal councils or conferences legitimately decree as binding on all."[18] And Rome is ready and willing to enforce the same standard, "The local ordinary can coerce religious with penalties in all those matters in which they are subject to him."[19] Such dictates as these, however, run contrary to the Lord's command to His servants, *"Stand fast therefore in the liberty wherewith Christ hath made us free, and be not entangled again with the yoke of bondage."*[20] John Wycliffe's words thundered in England in 1382 still resound today, "Since Jesus Christ shed His blood to free His Church, I demand its freedom. I demand that every one may leave these gloomy walls [the convents] within which a tyrannical law prevails, and embrace a simple and peaceful life under the open vault of heaven."[21]

Illegal pattern imposed

The Roman Catholic system must have new blood in each generation. Nuns are the backbone of the Catholic parochial schools and of the Catholic hospitals, both institutions having been proven to be places in which many Evangelicals are converted to Catholicism. To acquire this workforce, Rome seeks to circumvent the vows of marriage by requiring fidelity to her own definition of "chaste self-dedication", thereby instituting celibacy as the required state for the Religious,

> "The life consecrated through the profession of the evangelical counsels is a stable form of living by which the faithful, following Christ **more closely** under the action of the Holy Spirit, **are totally dedicated to God**…" (Can. 573, §1)

The words "more closely" therefore, contrast to the vows of marriage, meaning that consecrated life is a closer following of Christ than is

---

[18] Flannery, *More Post Conciliar Documents*, No. 92, S.C.R.S.I., *Mutuae Relationes*, 23 April 1978, Vol. II, Para. 44, p. 235.

[19] Canon 1320

[20] Galatians 5:1

[21] J. A. Wylie, *The History of Protestantism*, Vol. II, Book Second, Ch. XII, p. 124

marriage. But God has never declared this to be so. The Bible declares to all true believers, *"But ye are a chosen generation, a royal priesthood, a holy nation, a peculiar people; that ye should show forth the praises of him who hath called you out of darkness into his marvelous light."*[22]

The gift of celibacy is given only to a few. The time and circumstances of that celibate life are solely between the Lord and the individual, *"He that is able to receive it, let him receive it."*[23] It is in this exact context that the Lord speaks of the eunuchs for the kingdom of heaven's sake. It is to be noted in this case that there is no new institution authorized. It is within the stability of the family life established by the Lord that an individual with God's gift of celibacy may attempt to live out his calling. What the Lord did NOT say was this: "for this cause shall a man also leave father and mother and join himself to a group of other celibates, and their way of life shall be established." No such form of life was ever established by the Lord! Putting the Lord absolutely first in relationships is what He taught again and again, *"He that loveth father or mother more than me is not worthy of me: and he that loveth son or daughter more than me is not worthy of me."*[24] Thus the leaving of house, parents, brethren, wife, or children for His sake is what every believer must do. Nothing and no one is to become more precious to any of the believers than He is. But that such living does not constitute a religious house is made absolutely clear by the Lord's promise to believers who do follow His commands, for they are rewarded within the context of family life, *"but he shall receive an hundredfold now in this time, houses, and brethren, and sisters, and mothers, and children, and lands, with persecutions..."*[25]

These very relationships are deepened and more properly realized as one leaves all to put the Lord first in his or her life. God's

---

[22] I Peter 2:9

[23] Matthew 19:12

[24] Matthew 10:37

[25] Mark 10:30

Word is clear and precise. Had the Lord envisaged convents with Mother Superiors and Father Generals, He would have said so in this context. The hundredfold that is given to the believer is of the same fabric of what God Himself has ordained. There is no hint of a separate "stable form of living" in a "life consecrated" or of, "following Christ more closely." To decree that there is such is to denigrate marriage.

"Mystical espousal"

Sometimes the basic understanding is not only that Religious life is a "closer following of Christ," but the idea is also given that it is a mystical marriage with Christ. An example of this double assertion of superiority is the text of "The Consecrated Life and Its Role in the Church and in the World",

> "...Similar to these forms of consecrated life is the order of virgins, who, hearkening to the sacred call **to follow Christ more closely**, are consecrated to God by the diocesan bishop according to the approved liturgical rite; **are mystically espoused to Christ**, Son of God; and are dedicated to the service of the Church..."[26]

Here again the words "more closely" contrast to the vows of marriage ordained in His written Word; but the second claim, that such "an order of virgins" is "mystically espoused to Christ" is simply not true. In the Bible, the Lord rejoices over who are all born of the Spirit as a bridegroom rejoices over the bride. To go beyond what God Himself has instituted is sin. The biblical admonition is straightforward, "...*not to think above that which is written.*"[27]

The real call

By nature, every person is born a sinner destined for Hell. Salvation comes through Jesus Christ alone. The real call of Scripture is to believe on the Lord Jesus Christ alone, for it is by grace alone through

---

[26] "The Consecrated Life: Excerpts from the Lineamenta for the 9th Ordinary General Assembly of the Snyod of Bishops", *Catholic International*, (Brighton, MA 02135: North American Province of the Augustinians of the Assumption) Vol. 4, No. 2, February, 1993, p. 58. English text as published by the Libreria Editrice Vaticana, Vatican City.

[27] I Corinthians 4:6

faith alone that a person is born again to new life in Christ. *"The Father loveth the Son, and hath given all things into His hand. He that believeth on the Son hath everlasting life: and he that believeth not the Son shall not see life; but the wrath of God abideth on him."*[28]

To those in convent life

If you are in the convent and understand that salvation is by grace alone and that you must depend only on the righteousness of Christ Jesus alone, perhaps you now can see why thousands left monasteries and convents at the time of the Reformation. You may know very well the Catholic law, "Those who depart from a religious institute legitimately or have been dismissed from it legitimately can request nothing from the institution for any work done in it."[29] From inside the system, it looks impossible to face any future, for not only can one leave with "nothing from it for any work done" but also often one leaves with the disapproval of family and friends. This is the point at which the testimonies of former nuns to the faithfulness of the Lord become doubly precious. The Father's love is personal; He calls individual by individual. He calls you by name and provides for you. He, the mighty God, the Father, says to you, *"Wherefore come out from among them, and be ye separate, saith the Lord, and touch not the unclean thing; and I will receive you, and will be a Father unto you, and ye shall be my sons and daughters, saith the Lord Almighty."*[30] The experience of Catherine von Bora at the time of the Reformation was the same, who in studying the Scriptures came to see that her vows were not binding. Convent vows are made on the false ideology that there is a state of life more pleasing to God than marriage, and that the Church of Rome is delegated in the name of God to receive such vows. Once you see that the basis is untrue, you see that your vows are false and ought to be renounced before God.

---

[28] John 3:36

[29] Canon 702, §1

[30] II Corinthians 6:17-18

The Word of God opens the door of the convent cell

You probably are aware of the huge obstacles that stand before you, like those which were faced by Peggy O'Neill, Mary Ann Pakiz, and Eileen Donnelly and others as accounted in *The Truth Set Us Free: Twenty Former Nuns Tell Their Stories.* The Word of the Lord is clear and the evidence of His gracious presence in the lives of those who truly have been born again is indisputable, *"for He hath said, I will never leave thee nor forsake thee. So that we may boldly say, The Lord is my helper, and I will not fear what man shall do unto me."*[31] God's presence, providence and protection are an assurance to the true believer. Resting on the divine pledge, one can curb desires and alleviate fears. *"I will never leave thee nor forsake thee"* is a guarantee of the Lord's continual provision and protection, and a rebuke against all inordinate desires and anxious fears.

Conclusion, with a personal word from Carmen Da Mota

While compiling a book of testimonies of former nuns to be published in Brazil, I received the delightful testimony of Carmen Da Mota. After years of devoted religion as a nun in Brazil, Carmen found rest in the Lord. At the very end of her testimony she has a word on how difficult it is for a nun to leave the convent and yet how faithful the Lord is to give His grace to supply all needs. She speaks of another nun whom she met after she herself had left the convent,

> "When I was working at The Christian Reader bookstore, a nun came in one day. She said she had read my life story in the small book, 'Searching'. It had touched her heart and she pled with me to help her leave the convent. After talking it over with the missionary, Earl Mets, he opened his home so she would have a place to stay for a while. I made the necessary plans and went to fetch that nun. The whole situation wasn't easy. But, thanks to God's grace, I managed to bring her home. You simply can't imagine the extent of her insecurity. Ruth had entered the convent when she was twenty, and left when she was fifty-seven years old. During thirty-seven years inside the convent, she taught seven subjects but her nerves

---

[31] Hebrews 13:5-6

268

were gone. Her self-image was fragile and psychologically, she was in bad shape. Only God could help her. After many battles, Ruth accepted Jesus as her Savior, for which we praise God. We went together to speak about the Lord Jesus Christ at a few churches. Afterward I traveled some, she also traveled to different places, and we lost track of each other. I can only thank the Lord that one more soul was delivered from the power of darkness and transferred to the wonderful light of Christ. Here you have read a summary of critical parts of my life, and of what the Lord did for me! If you are truly seeking Him, He will do the same for you! Take refuge in these words of Christ, '*Come to Me, all ye that labor and are heavy laden, and I will give you rest.*'"[32] ◆

---

[32] Matthew 11:28

Chapter 15

Biblical Unity in the Lord and Papal Conformity

The unity for which Christ Jesus prayed in John Chapter 17 is a unity that already exists. His intercession is not an appeal to produce unity among His own. It is a prayer to the Father in Heaven to preserve the unity that already exists. Therefore, He prayed, *"Holy Father, keep through thine own name those whom thou hast given me, that they may be one, as we are."*[1] The Lord is not speaking primarily of a visible, external, organizational unity; rather He is speaking of the exact opposite. It concerns the very essence of Christian unity. The Lord compares Christian unity to the ultimate unity, the Trinity. It has always existed between the Father, Son, and the Holy Spirit, three Persons yet One God. There is not a more profound and exact definition of the essence of biblical unity than that which He proclaimed in prayer, *"That they all may be one; as thou, Father, art in me, and I in thee, that they also may be one in us."*[2]

The fact that the Lord Jesus Christ prayed to the Father for the maintenance of Christian unity means that such unity **is** preserved. There is, therefore, among true Christians a spiritual union like that which is in God Himself. It is an answered prayer, as the Lord Himself declared, *"Father, I thank thee that thou hast heard me and I knew that thou hearest me always."*[3] The Church, called in Scripture the Body of Christ, is a spiritual organism. God before the world existed chose the believers to be in Christ His Son. Over the centuries, He has justified them through Christ's righteousness. In saving them He places them in

---

[1] John 17:11
[2] John 17:21
[3] John 11:42

Christ and will preserve them in that unity to the end of all things. This promise is sure.

The only unity of which the New Testament speaks
The foundation of Christian unity is the position of believers "*in God the Father and in the Lord Jesus Christ.*"[4] It is more fully defined in the words of the Apostle, "*According as he hath chosen us in him before the foundation of the world...Having predestinated us unto the adoption of children by Jesus Christ to himself, according to the good pleasure of his will...wherein he hath made us accepted in the beloved.*"[5] This is the foundation and the source of all Christian unity. There is no unity apart from the Person of the Lord Jesus Christ. There is no Christian oneness apart from His work of redemption. To speak about Christian unity without this essential foundation of the redemption that is in Christ Jesus is futile. It is similar to speaking about a family as if the family were the house, and not a husband, wife, and their children.

Unity as fellowship with God
Seeing unity as it is in Scripture—being in fellowship with God, alienation from God is not possible for true believers. The Lord had previously stated, "*My sheep hear my voice, and I know them, and they follow me: and I give unto them eternal life; and they shall never perish, neither shall any man pluck them out of my hand. My Father, which gave them me, is greater than all; and no man is able to pluck them out of my Father's hand.*"[6] Thus, true believers are placed into a unity, which is in the Father and in Christ Jesus. This unity is an accord which they themselves did not establish, but which they are commanded to keep. In the words of the Apostle Paul, they are "*to keep the unity of the Spirit in the bond of peace. There is one body, and one Spirit, even as ye are called in one hope of your calling; one Lord, one faith, one baptism, one God and Father of*

---

[4] I Thessalonians 1:1
[5] Ephesians 1:4-6
[6] John 10:27-29

all, who is above all, and through all, and in you all."[7] The nature of that unity is the unity of the Spirit. The basis of the unity is the one Lord; Christ Jesus as the Head of the Church, and the one faith that is the Gospel, and the one baptism. All of this culminates in the one God who "*is above all, and through all, and in you all.*" This concluding factor reinforces the fact that the essence of unity is spiritual oneness with God through the Lord Jesus Christ alone.

Perfect unity as the Lord returns

The unity for which the Lord prayed is undeniable as believers are spiritually one in the Father and in the Son; but it is not now fully realized in a faultless, impeccable unity. This is clearly seen as the Lord continued His prayer, "*and the glory which thou gavest me I have given them; that they may be one, even as we are one: I in them, and thou in me, that they may **be made perfect in one**.*"[8]   The prayer is in accord with what the Word of truth declares, "*whom he justified, them he also glorified.*"[9] The future glorification of true believers is so absolutely certain that it is spoken of as a thing already accomplished. Believers are to "*be made perfect in one*", which is a consequence of the glory to be given to them. This spiritual union is already begun, but will come to full fruition only in the life to come. Thus being "*made perfect in one*" is to have its full realization when Christ returns. It is then that Christ will "*present it to himself a glorious church, not having spot, or wrinkle, or any such thing; but that it should be holy and without blemish.*"[10] Then and only then will there be perfect oneness in faith, knowledge, love, holiness, justice and truth. When the glory that Christ received from the Father has been given to believers on the Lord's return, then there will be perfect unity.

God Himself chooses, seeks out, finds, redeems and loves His people in Christ. The number one question is, are you one of His people? The only way to be sure is to believe in what He has promised and

---

[7] Ephesians 4:3-6
[8] John 17:22-23
[9] Romans 8:30
[10] Ephesians 5:27

fulfilled in Christ Jesus. God promises are your surety, *"for all the promises of God in him are yea, and in him amen, unto the glory of God."*[11] The veracity of God, the mediation of Christ, and the operation of the Spirit are all connected to the promises that God has made. The promises of God guarantee pardon of sin for those who believe on Christ Jesus alone. He will be their sanctification and their support in temptation and trial. All of these promises are made through the Redeemer and are one hundred percent certain. The promise made and on which you today must stand is, *"for whosoever shall call upon the name of the Lord shall be saved."*[12] This promise is without exception. As you hear the Gospel of salvation, and obey the command for repentance, you will not approach the throne of grace in vain. As you call upon the name of the Lord Jesus Christ, the Savior of sinners, you shall be saved. Your guilt will be pardoned, your heart purified, and you shall be saved with all the power of an eternal life. When you believe on Christ Jesus, you will have a growing sense of your dependence upon His grace so that you will learn to look to God and trust in His power and goodness alone. Then in spirit you will hear and personally accept the wonder of these words, *"I have loved thee with an everlasting love."*[13] You will begin to understand that God loves Christ unchangeably, and so in Christ He loves true believers consistently. *"God is not a man, that he should lie; neither the son of man, that he should repent: hath he said, and shall he not do it? or hath he spoken, and shall he not make it good?"*[14] Then you will begin to understand the intimacies of unity in Him. As the Lord Himself said, *"if a man love me, he will keep my words: and my Father will love him, and we will come unto him, and make our abode with him."*[15] And in the words of the Apostle John, *"we know that the Son of God is come, and hath given us an understanding, that we may*

---

[11] II Corinthians 1:20

[12] Romans 10:13

[13] Jeremiah 31:3

[14] Numbers 23:19

[15] John 14:23

know him that is true, and we are in him that is true, even in his Son Jesus Christ. This is the true God, and eternal life."[16]

True believers have union with the true God in His Son, and He sustains this intimate relation, which is eternal life. This is strong language denoting the spiritual unity, which exists among believers. They await the New Jerusalem, the Church of God in a perfect state, prepared as a bride adorned for her husband, decorated with all perfection of wisdom and holiness, prepared for the full revelation of the Lord Jesus Christ in glory. This will be that external unity promised in the Word, *"behold, the tabernacle of God is with men, and he will dwell with them, and they shall be his people, and God himself shall be with them, and be their God."*[17] Then their souls will more fully understand Him, as they will be filled with all the love and delight of Him as their Lord. God Himself will be their God; His immediate presence will be with them; His glory will be upon them in perfect joy and unity. Thus, Christ Jesus' prayer for unity while fulfilled now spiritually, will be perfectly realized in all the excellence of the Kingdom to come.

True ecumenism

There is genuine unity of all true believers throughout the world. There is but one faith. All believers are converted by the same Holy Spirit, and by the same work of grace have been placed in Christ Jesus. Though all do not have the same measure of wisdom and spiritual knowledge, yet they all are believers who trust in God alone and His Written Word alone. They are saved by the all-Holy God, by grace alone, through faith alone, in Christ alone, and all praise is to God alone. These five biblical principles show forth the foundation of true unity in the Lord. These principles have helped the persecuted Church through the centuries to hold fast to the simplicity of the Gospel. True ecumenism is fellowship or working together in adherence to the five basic biblical principles that maintain the foundation of true unity in the Lord. To the

---

[16] I John 5:20
[17] Revelation 21:3

degree to which these key basic biblical standards are embraced, true unity will be evident.

False ecumenism

False ecumenism, on the other hand, is typically institutionalized and joins together professing Christian groups in a purported "common cause". In such endeavors, few are concerned that one or more of the parties involved are unconverted. While purporting to confess the Lord Jesus Christ according to the Scriptures, these groups often in fact compromise the five biblical principles that display the basis of true unity in the Lord. The extent to which these principles are not upheld usually shows the inclination of a church or group to submit to Rome. The World Council of Churches is such an institution. Within it, there is no agreement on any of the five biblical principles. The Church of Rome, likewise in apostasy, repudiates all of the five biblical standards. Counterfeiting the body of the Lord Jesus Christ, Rome is intent on finding successful ways to bind all "believers" to a visible and formal unity achieved through the dominion of ecclesiastical machinery. This institutionalized "unity" generates only infidelity to the Lord and the Gospel.

Vatican drama aspiring towards institutionalized "unity"

The gathering of mainstream churches at St. Paul's Basilica in Rome early in the year 2000 was thought to have been the largest assembly of Christian leaders with a Pope since Vatican Council II in the early 1960s. On January 18th, the Tuesday of the week which had been designated "The Week of Christian Unity" in the "Holy Year, 2000", leaders representing four-fifths of Eastern Orthodoxy gathered alongside Anglicans, Lutherans, Methodists, and Pentecostals. They were participating in the celebration of the opening of the "Holy Door at St. Paul Outside the Walls". Archbishop George Carey, at that time Primate of the Church of England, and Metropolitan Athanasius, representing Bartholomew, Patriarch of Constantinople and head of the Orthodox Church, knelt on either side of Pope John Paul II before the newly opened door. Only one cushion had been provided as it was thought that only the Pope would kneel, but when both Carey and

Athanasius also fell to their knees, the Pope called out, "Unity! Thank you!" It was a highly pretentious moment.

The Pontiff had every reason to express his gratitude to the churches represented and the two men flanking him. After all, in May 1999, the joint Anglican Roman Catholic International Commission (ARCIC) had issued a statement "recognizing the Pope as the overall authority in the Christian World" and describing him as "a gift to be received by all Churches". Five months later in October 1999 on Reformation Day, the Roman Catholic and Lutheran Churches signed a joint declaration announcing that their opposing views on justification had been reconciled.[18] With this declaration of reconciliation and unity, the way is clear for the Lutherans to join the Anglicans in accepting Papal primacy. The frosty relationship from earlier years with the Russian Orthodox Church has warmed up, which led to a papal visit to Moscow and a meeting with Patriarch Alexy II. In the 1994 signing of "Evangelicals and Catholics Together: The Christian Mission in the Third Millennium" (ECT), Evangelical leaders have led large numbers of Evangelicals to kneel before the open "holy" door that the Roman Catholic Church offers them. Pentecostals and Charismatics have also accelerated their journey toward Rome.

The Pope's words that January day were couched in language that associated equality with freedom. Carefully concealed in his response, however, was the non-negotiable agenda of the Roman Catholic Church. Rather than looking for unity based on truth, the Papacy, as ever, is seeking to secure conformity through the compromise of others. The "ecumenical dialogue" referred to by the Pope during the January 18th ceremony is clearly governed by a special set of rules. Vatican Council II's Post Conciliar Document on ecumenism states that "…

---

[18] Of the three Lutheran Synods in the USA, Missouri (2.6 million), Wisconsin (0.4 million) and Evangelical Lutheran Church of America (ELCA, 5.4 million), only the ELCA signed this accord with Rome. See our analysis, "The Roman Catholic-Lutheran 'Joint Declaration on the Doctrine of Justification': A Denial of the Gospel and the Righteousness of Christ" on our WebPage: www.bereanbeacon.com

dialogue is not an end in itself...it is not just an academic discussion."[19] Rather, "ecumenical dialogue...serves to transform modes of thought and behavior and the daily life of those [non-Catholic] communities. In this way, it **aims at preparing the way for their unity of faith in the bosom of a Church one and visible**."[20] The Papacy expects this process of dialogue to take time to accomplish its stated aim, for it continues, "....little by little, as the obstacles to perfect ecclesial communion are overcome, **all Christians will be gathered, in a common celebration of the Eucharist [the Mass] into that unity of the one and only Church....** This unity, we believe, dwells in the Catholic Church as something she can never lose."[21] The "little by little" approach of the Vatican II document is now marching forward! How many present at the January 18th, 2000, gathering understood what was really happening? The final goal of any dialogue with the Roman Catholic Church is, first and foremost, "unity" in a visible and specific ritual under the authority of the Roman Catholic Church. She could hardly have stated her position more clearly.

---

[19] *Vatican Council II: The Conciliar and Post Conciliar Documents*, Post Vatican Council II Document No. 42, "Reflections and Suggestions Concerning Ecumenical Dialogue", S.P.U.C., Austin Flannery, O. P., Gen. Ed., 1981 ed., (Northport, NY : Costello Publ. Co., 1975) Vol. I, Sect. VI, p.549

[20] *Ibid.*, Sect. II, pp. 540-1.

[21] *Ibid.*, p. 541. The issue of visible unity is not a new issue. In the mid-seventeenth century, the Bishop of Meaux published a treatise entitled *The History of the Variations of Protestants*. In 1690, Dr. Peter Allix first published his book against the Bishop, for he maintained that the Bishop's object "is to deceive those, who by ways of violence have been made to enter into the bosom of the Romish Church, and whom the same violence keeps there, against the sense of their conscience." Allix's work was originally published as *Churches of the Piedmont* (1690) and *Churches of the Albigenses* (1692). Re-printed from the 1821 edition entitled *The Ecclesiastical History of the Ancient Churches of Piedmont and of the Albigenses* (Dayton, OH: Church History Research & Archives, 1989) Preface. For another very substantial rebuttal to the Bishop of Meaux, see George Stanley Faber, *The History of the Ancient Vallenses and Albigenses* (London: R. B. Seeley & W. Burnside, 1838) Reprinted by Church History Research & Archives, 1990.

The Pope defines conformity

In Pope John Paul's official letter, "That They May Be One", he defined the subjection that is demanded in order to be in communion with Rome,

> "The Catholic Church, both in her praxis and in her solemn documents, holds that the communion of the particular Churches with the Church of Rome, and of their Bishops with the Bishops of Rome is, in God's plan, an essential requisite of full and visible communion."[22]

To arrive at that point of full subjection, a set of five principles must be adopted—principles that actually deny all five parameters of that define a true believer. According to the Pope,

"It is already possible to identify the areas in need of fuller study before a true consensus of faith can be achieved:

> (1) the relationship between Sacred Scripture, as the highest authority in matters of faith, and Sacred Tradition, as indispensable to the interpretation of the Word of God;
>
> (2) the Eucharist, as the Sacrament of the Body and Blood of Christ, an offering of praise to the Father, the sacrificial memorial and Real Presence of Christ and the sanctifying outpouring of the Holy Spirit;
>
> (3) Ordination, as a Sacrament, to the threefold Ministry of the episcopate, presbyterate and diaconate;
>
> (4) the Magisterium of the Church, entrusted to the Pope and the Bishops in communion with him, understood as a responsibility and an authority exercised in the name of Christ for teaching and safe guarding the faith;
>
> (5) the Virgin Mary, as Mother of God and Icon of the Church, the spiritual Mother who intercedes for Christ's disciples and for all humanity."[23]

The Pope's objective in declaring his five principles is to lay out the basis of a ubiquitous visible conformity to the Church of Rome. This

---

[22] *Ut Unum Sint*, "That They May Be One: On Commitment to Ecumenism", John Paul II (Washington, DC: United States Catholic Conference) Publ. No. 5-050, 5/25/95, Para. 97.

[23] *Ibid.*, Para. 79.

visible conformity will be forged in accordance with the norms of her institution alone. Thus the Pope decrees,

"…it is now necessary to advance towards **the visible unity** which is required and sufficient and which is manifested in a real and concrete way, so that the Churches may truly become a sign of that full communion in the one, holy, catholic and apostolic Church **which will be expressed in the common celebration of the Eucharist**."[24]

Without a doubt the Roman Catholic Church is attempting to forge **a man-made unity**, visible by means of an institution to which all must conform.[25] Such a conception stands in direct contradiction to the reality of believers who are placed invisibly in Christ by God, and are to maintain the bond of unity given to them by the Holy Spirit.

External unity attained by power and penalty

What is this conformity now so passionately advocated by the Pope? How would it be applied in practice? From all previous experience,

---

[24] *Ibid.*, Para. 78.

[25] The Oxford Movement of the 19th century, which has issued in ARCIC [Anglican-Roman Catholic International Commission] of today, was according to John Henry Newman begun in July of 1833. It was a thrust of the Papacy to take over the Church of England from the inside by encouraging Anglicans who were basically Roman Catholic in sympathy, to stay within the English Church to transform it to Roman Catholic standards rather than to defect to Rome. What terms the Papacy would require of the Church of England was spelled out in 1833 to Newman. "A few months before that date, Newman, in company with his friend, Richard Hurrell Froude, while travelling on the Continent, had visited Monsignor (subsequently Cardinal) Wiseman at Rome. 'We got introduced to him, 'wrote Froude, 'to find out whether they would take us in [i.e., to the Church of Rome] on any terms to which we could twist our consciences, and we found to our dismay that not one step could be gained without swallowing the Council of Trent as a whole.' (*Froude's Remains,* Vol. I., p. 306) While on this journey Newman fell seriously ill with a fever…While in a weak condition…he tells us: 'I sat down on my bed, and began to sob violently. My servant, who had acted as my nurse, asked what ailed me. I could only answer him:—'*I have a work to do in England.* ' (Newman's *Apologia Pro Vita Sua,* p. 35, 1889 ed.) What that work was we now know full well. It was that of Romanizing the Church of England." Walter Walsh, *The Secret History of the Oxford Movement,* Fourth Ed. (London: Swan Sonneshine & Co., Ltd., 1898) p. 263.

and the official teaching of the same Pope in his canon law, those fully participating will be obliged to submit both their mind and their will to "the Holy Father" (i.e., the Pope), to his decrees, and to the dogma of his Church. Thus present day Roman law decrees,

> "Although not an assent of faith, a religious submission of the intellect and will must be given to a doctrine which the Supreme Pontiff or the college of bishops declares concerning faith or morals when they exercise the authentic magisterium, even if they do not intend to proclaim it by a definitive act."[26]

In this official law Rome states, in clearer terms than any cult, the necessity for her followers to suppress their God-given faculties of mind and will. This is demanded under duress, for the new canon law, the "Papal Code" codified by the Pope John Paul II, includes a section entitled "Punishment of Offenses against Ecclesiastical Authorities and the Freedom of the Church". Under the heading, "The Punishment of Offenses in General", the Inquisition appears again, for Canon 1311 states, "The Church has the innate and proper right **to coerce** offending members of the Christian faithful with penal sanctions."[27] A brief acquaintance with history readily reveals that coercion is indeed a term that the Roman Church understands very well. Naturally, when ushering all comers into her big tent, she makes light of its implications. But if ever the Papacy is again directing the levers of political power, Canon 1311 could acquire that same notoriety as other measures that have so darkened the pages of history with the blood of the martyrs.

Historical records of oppression to impose conformity

In the mid-nineteenth century, Lord Acton, one of the greatest of Roman Catholic historians, said famously, "Power corrupts, and absolute power corrupts absolutely." He was pinpointing clearly Papal Rome's compulsion to conformity by her legal imposition of more than six hundred years of the Inquisition. Calculated and premeditated legal

---

[26] *Code of Canon Law*, Latin-English Ed., New English Tr. (Canon Law Society of America, 1983, 1999) Canon 752

[27] *Ibid.*

agreements between Papal Rome and the civil powers established these horrors of history. In these dreadful centuries, the Roman Catholic Church needed the appearance of legality to silence the true Gospel and bring nations into her fold. Her apostasy from the Gospel has not changed since the Inquisition, but her strategy has indeed changed.

Chapter 12 recounted some of the persecution that the Vaudois believers suffered because they would not attend the Roman Mass. In the middle of the 16th century, there was a short period of comparative peace for the Vaudois churches of the Valleys. This was only a relative peace, however, for at this same time troops were dispatched by Papal orders to either massacre multitudes of believers or convert them to Rome's creed. Also at that time, individual inquisitors still hounded and afflicted some individual Vaudois believers. The historian, J. A. Wylie, cites some gruesome details. We give them to illustrate the length to which Bishops and priests of the Roman system were willing to go to bring about submission to the Church of Rome. If you are very sensitive to the particulars of horrific torture, please omit this quotation,

"Some of these martyrs perished by cruel, barbarous, and most horrible methods. To recite all these cases would be beyond our purpose, and to depict the revolting and infamous details would be to narrate what no reader could peruse. We shall only quote part of the brief summary of Muston. 'There is no town in Piedmont,' says he, 'under a Vaudois pastor, where some of our brethren have not been put to death. Hugo Chiamps of Finestrelle had his entrails torn from his living body, at Turin. Peter Geymarali of Bobbio, in like manner, had his entrails taken out at Luzerna, and a fierce cat thrust in their place to torture him further; Maria Romano was buried alive at Rocco-patia; Magdalen Foulano underwent the same fate at San Giovanni; Susan Michelini was bound hand and foot, and left to perish of cold and hunger at Saracena. Bartholomew Fache, gashed with sabres, had the wounds filled up with quicklime, and perished thus in agony at Fenile; Daniel Michelini had his tongue torn out at Bobbio for having praised God. James Baridari perished covered with sulphurous matches, which had been forced into his flesh under the nails, between the fingers, in the nostrils, in the lips, and over all his body, and then lighted. Daniel Revelli had his mouth filled with gunpowder, which, being lighted, blew his head to pieces. Maria Monnen, taken at Liousa, had the flesh cut from her cheek and chin bones, so that her jaw was left bare, and she was thus left to perish. Paul Garnier was slowly sliced to pieces at Rora. Thomas Margueti was mutilated in an indescribable manner at Miraboco, and Susan Jaquin cut in bits at La Torre. Sara Rostagnol was slit open from the legs to the bosom, and so left to perish on the road between Eyral and Luzerna. Anne Charbonnier was impaled and carried thus on a pike, as a standard, from San Giovanni to La Torre. Daniel Rambaud, at Paesano, had his nails torn off, then his fingers chopped off, then his feet and his hands, then his arms and his legs, with each successive refusal on his part to abjure the Gospel. Thus the roll of martyrs runs on, and with each new sufferer comes a new, a more excruciating and more horrible mode of torture and death."[28]

These appalling details have been included only to demonstrate the length to which Papal Rome was willing to go to enforce conformity to her control. The current tactic is that of a false ecumenism to win "converts" to a false "unity" in the midst of what is called Christianity; however, Rome's laws on control and coercion have not changed.

Summary and application

The Lord's prayer for unity is answered in the life of every believer who is justified by God's saving grace alone, which is through faith alone, and is in Christ alone. Christ Jesus prayed, *"that they all may be one;*

---

[28] J. A. Wylie, *The History of Protestantism,* Book 13, Ch 6. See also Jean Paul Perrin [a Waldensian pastor], *History of the Ancient Christmas Inhabiting the Valleys of the Alps,* "III. The Vaudois" (1847) republished by Christian History Research & Archives, 1991; Henry Charles Lea, *A History of The Inquisition of the Middle Ages,* three vols. (New York: Russell & Russell, 1955); William Shaw Kerr, *A Handbook on the Papacy,* (London: Marshall, Morgan & Scott, Ltd., 1950) pp. 232-245; John Knox, *The History of the Reformation of Religion Within the Realm of Scotland,* (Edinburgh: The Banner of Truth Trust, first ed. 1898; first Banner ed., 1982); John Foxe, *Book of Martyrs*; etc.

[29] John 17:21

as thou, Father, art in me, and I in thee, that they also may be one in us: that the world may believe that thou hast sent me."[29] The Lord knew very well those for whom He prayed. The objects of His prayer were clear to Him. These believers embrace eternal life as they are regenerated by the Holy Spirit. The foundation of Biblical unity is of God, not man. Those for whom the Lord prayed are *"born, not of blood, nor of the will of the flesh, nor of the will of man, but of God."*[30] The inheritance which you receive by believing the Gospel is wonderfully described in the Word of God, *"wherefore we receiving a kingdom which cannot be moved, let us have grace, whereby we may serve God acceptably with reverence and godly fear: For our God is a consuming fire."*[31] As a true believer, you come into the kingdom of God in Christ, a spiritual kingdom in this world, and heavenly kingdom to come. Both aspects of the kingdom are enhanced with boundless blessings. The Holy Spirit emphasizes the specific characteristic of the kingdom; it *"cannot be moved"*. As you embrace true faith, you come into *"the everlasting kingdom of our Lord and Savior Jesus Christ."*[32] The immutable Word of truth in Scripture gives you the right and title to eternal life. Then there is the correlation between your inheritance and your duty. The greater the privilege, the greater the obligation to express our gratitude in a suitable and becoming manner. Thus the Word of God instructs us, *"whereby we may serve God acceptably with reverence and godly fear."* The true believer has two powerful motives, *"receiving a kingdom"* and *"our God is a consuming fire."*

The same truth has a grave warning for one who is still bound to his church, the one who believes in Christ Jesus on the authority of his church rather than directly on the Lord by the authority of His written Word. God is the same just and righteous God under the Gospel as He was under the law in the Old Testament. He deals with us in love and grace yet He in Himself remains *"a consuming fire"*. He is the God of strict justice, who will avenge Himself on all who have not received the

---

[30] John 1:13

[31] Hebrews 12:28-29

[32] II Peter 1:11

love of the truth, but rather look to a church or some person other than the Lord Jesus Christ alone for life. The Lord Jesus Christ has lived the perfect life and has made the faultless propitiatory sacrifice for sin; to refuse to believe in Him alone is a critical offence. When the Lord dealt with the sincere and devout Pharisees, He gave them a very strong word. *"I said therefore unto you, that you shall die in your sins: for if ye believe not that I am he, ye shall die in your sins."*[33] You may say that you are a good Catholic and that you want to please God in this present life and hope to live with Him forever. That is a noble goal, and you may be as sincere and devout as the Pharisees, but like them, if you neglect personally to believe on Him alone, you likewise will die in your sins. Distinct faith and trust on the Lord Jesus Christ is essential and frequently highlighted in Scripture. *"God so loved the world that he gave his only begotten Son, that whosoever believeth in him should not perish, but have everlasting life."*[34] *"He that believeth on him is not condemned..."*[35] *"He that believeth on the son hath everlasting life."*[36] *"He that believeth on the Son of God hath the witness in himself: he that believeth not God hath made him a liar; because he believeth not the record that God gave of his Son."*[37] The whole underpinning question is placed before you: *"but whom say ye that I am?"*[38] Because man is a fallen being, the Gospel presents a personal direct faith in Christ Jesus the Lord alone. To substitute faith in a church as the way to believe on Him is a dangerously subtle deceit. It has all the appearance of piety and devotion, but in the final analysis, the choice is an institution in the place of the Lord Jesus Christ. True faith must be personal. A faith through the mediation of a church has all the trappings of religion and produces church people in large numbers, as were the Pharisees, but devoid of the life of God. If you do not have true faith, you also shall die in your sins; *"for our God is a consuming fire."* ◆

---

[33] John 8:24

[34] John 3:16

[35] John 3:18

[36] John 3:36

[37] I John 5:10

[38] Luke 9:20

Chapter 16

The Alignment of New Evangelicals with Catholicism

As a Catholic priest, I had great difficulties with the New Evangelicals. The essential problem was with the false gospel message that is given by them. It was frustrating for me to find that many of the teachings of Catholicism seemed quite similar to what the New Evangelicals were preaching. If the problem was frustrating for me as a Catholic priest back in the seventies and eighties, it is even more difficult now for anyone inside Catholicism who is seeking for the truth. Besides a false gospel that is given by many New Evangelicals, there is also an increase in false ecumenism. In recent times there has been a great impetus in the movement of New Evangelicals seeking to embrace Catholics as "brothers and sisters in Christ". It is necessary therefore to address this false ecumenism.

Evangelicals throughout the centuries have maintained that through justification by faith—and by faith alone—sinful human beings are made right in Christ before the all Holy God.[1] Justification itself is a judicial, declarative act on the part of God alone. By it, He declares that only in Christ is a man perfectly just. His judicial, declarative act is not made on the basis of anything within a man, but rather it is made solely and wholly upon the righteous life and sacrificial death of the Lord Jesus Christ. Our Saviour lived a perfect life and on the cross

---

[1] *The Westminster Confession of Faith*, 1646; *The Baptist Confession of Faith*, 1689; *The Philadelphia Confession of Faith*, Adopted by The Baptist Association, 1742; and others.

paid the just penalty for all the sins of His people. Historically, Evangelicals have been in agreement with the Apostle Paul, *"to him that worketh not, but believeth on him that justifieth the ungodly, his faith is counted for righteousness."*[2]

A person calling himself Evangelical is professing to be committed to the Gospel of Christ as proclaimed in Scripture. The true Gospel demands separation from all who teach another Gospel. As the Apostle declared, *"But though we, or an angel from heaven, preach any other gospel unto you than that which we have preached unto you, let him be accursed. As we said before, so say I now again, if any man preach any other gospel unto you than that ye have received, let him be accursed."*[3] *"Have no fellowship with the unfruitful works of darkness, but rather reprove them."*[4] Without such separation the name Evangelical **signifies nothing**. "New Evangelicalism", which willingly compromises with and accommodates *another Gospel*, has gained ground everywhere, beginning in the early 1960s. Since then, the Evangelical world has changed beyond recognition.[5]

The first and second National Evangelical Anglican Conferences that met at Keele and Nottingham in the UK in 1967 and 1977, respectively, were primed to launch and further the new policy of Anglican Evangelicals towards ecumenism. There was a now a desire on the part of New Evangelicals to be united with ritualistic Anglicans, who were essentially Roman Catholic in belief and practice[6], and liberals

---

[2] Romans 4:5.

[3] Galatians 1:8-9.

[4] Ephesians 5:11

[5] This is fully documented in Iain Murray's *Evangelicalism Divided* (Banner of Truth, 2000).

[6] The background for this development is thoroughly laid out by Walter Walsh in *The Secret History of the Oxford Movement* (London: Swan Sonnenschein & Co., Inc., 1898) in which he states, "The great object of the Ritualistic Movement from its very birth, in 1833, was that of *Corporate* Reunion with the Church of Rome...As far back as 1867 a leading quarterly of the advanced Ritualists declared that, instead of seceding to Rome, 'it would be much better for us to

who believed in a fallible Bible. Leading Evangelicals, such as John Stott and J.I. Packer, endorsed the statements from these. John Stott, who chaired the first conference at Keele, made it clear that the conference was accepting not only Anglo-Catholics and liberals, but Roman Catholics also: "All who confess the Lord Jesus Christ as God and Saviour according to the Scriptures and therefore seek to fulfill together their common calling to the glory of one God, Father, Son and Holy Spirit have a right to be treated as Christians, and it is on this basis that we wish to talk with them."[7] The conference at Nottingham went further than Keele, giving the compromise already proclaimed a complete seal of approval. Nottingham also endorsed and praised the Charismatic movement and is remembered for David Watson's reference to the Reformation as "one of the greatest tragedies that ever happened to the church."[8]

The most extensive exodus from biblical faith

The most drastic departure from true Evangelicalism, however, took place in the United States in 1994, some seventeen years after the Nottingham Conference. At the end of March 1994, a group of twenty leading Evangelicals and twenty leading Roman Catholics produced a document entitled "Evangelicals and Catholics Together: The Christian Mission in the Third Millennium" (ECT).

---

remain working where we are—for what would become of England if we [Ritualists] were to leave her Church? She would be simply lost to Catholicism…Depend upon it, it is only through the English Church itself that England can be Catholicised' (*Union Review,* Volume for 1867, p. 410). …But in order to realize such a reunion it is first of all necessary to make the Church of England look as much like the Church of Rome as possible. 'A Colonial Priest' of the Ritualistic party, writing to the *Church Review,* of September 21st, 1888, remarked: 'It seems to me utterly premature to consider reunion, especially with the great Patriarchal See of the West [Rome] as within even distant probability, until the Anglican Communion as a whole is Catholicised. *There lies our work…'"* pp. 260-261. Eighty years later, post-Vatican Council II documents declare that Rome desires dialogue with Bible believers, whom she now calls "separated brethren". At the same time, the New Evangelicals are being wooed openly by the Ritualistic Anglicans.

[7] Quoted in Michael de Semlyen's *The Foundations Under Attack: The Roots of Apostasy*, (Herts., WD3 5SJ: Dorchester House Publications, 1998) p.6

[8] *Ibid.*, pp.7-8; also John Capon, *Evangelicals Tomorrow* (Glasgow: Scotland).

The two main instigators of this ecumenical thrust were Charles Colson and Richard John Neuhaus, a Lutheran pastor turned Roman Catholic priest. The specific task was begun in September, 1992. Larry Lewis of the Home Mission Board of the Southern Baptist Convention, Jesse Miranda of Assemblies of God, John White of the Geneva College and National Association of Evangelicals; and others, including two Jesuits, Avery Dulles and Juan Diaz-Vilar, joined Colson and Neuhaus in the writing process. Cardinal Idris Cassidy, the Head of the Pontifical Council for Promoting Christian Unity, was said by Richard Neuhaus to have given "very active support throughout the process." The Evangelical signatories included J. I. Packer, Bill Bright of Campus Crusade for Christ, Mark Noll of Wheaton College, and Pat Robertson of The 700 Club. Roman Catholic signers included such well know figures as Cardinal John O'Connor, now deceased, Archbishop Sevilla, Archbishop Stafford, and Bishop Francis George, now Archbishop of Chicago.

The Gospel according to ECT
The signers of ECT readily admit to "differences that cannot be resolved here". Nevertheless, motivated by the desire to face important moral issues together, the authors of ECT flatly state that Evangelicals and Catholics are one in Christ, and that all are truly Christians.[9] The primary fallacy of the lengthy document is its declaration on the Gospel. The signers state what they believe comes closest to the Gospel of Christ when they declare, "We affirm together that we are justified by grace through faith because of Christ. Living faith is active in love that is nothing less than the love of Christ...."[10] To be biblical, this statement should read, "We affirm together that we are justified by grace **alone,** through faith **alone, in Christ alone**." The word "alone" signifies that the perfect righteousness of Christ Jesus—and that alone—is sufficient before the all Holy God to justify unholy sinners.[11] To so define justification, however, would exclude the Catholic sacraments and the

---

[9] ECT, § I "We Affirm Together"
[10] *Ibid.*
[11] Romans 4:5-8, II Corinthians 5:19-21, Romans 3:22-28, Titus 3:5-7, Ephesians 1:7, Jeremiah 23:6, I Corinthians 1:30-31, Romans 5:17-19. and elsewhere.

priests who control them, both of which are necessary for the Catholic people.[12]   Thus a <u>subtraction</u> had to be made from the Gospel of Christ by excluding what is signified by the word "alone". In a similar manner an <u>addition</u> had to made to the Gospel.   The ECT addition that redefines faith is, "<u>living faith active in love</u>." "Living faith" implies works and to Catholics, baptism in particular.   This is documented in present day official teaching of the Church of Rome where Rome teaches, "the very root of the Church's living faith [is] principally by means of Baptism."[13]   It is the same addition to faith that was proclaimed by the Roman Catholic Church at her Council of Trent in 1547, "For faith, unless hope and charity be added to it, neither unites one perfectly with Christ, nor makes him a living member of his body…."[14]   The theology of the Church of Rome always comes back to the concept of "living faith" so as to include "works righteousness" and particularly in her sacraments, that she defines as necessary for salvation.[15]

The New Evangelical signers of ECT have concurred with the Roman Catholic definition of "living faith active in love", and thus they have formally agreed to an addition to the Gospel that nullifies its message.

"If anyone shall say that by faith **alone** the sinner is justified, so as to understand that nothing else is required to cooperate in the attainment of the grace of justification, and that it is in no way necessary that he be prepared and disposed by the action of his own will: let him be anathema [cursed]."[16]

To endorse Roman Catholic teaching, therefore, is to deny the clear teaching of Scripture, "*But after that the kindness and love of God*

---

[12] *Catechism of the Catholic Church* (1994), Para. 987.

[13] *Catechism*, Para. 249.

[14] Henry Denzinger, *The Sources of Catholic Dogma,* Tr. by Roy Deferrari from Thirtieth ed. of *Enchiridion Symbolorum* (St. Louis, MO: B Herder Book Co., 1957) #800.

[15] *Catechism*, Para 1129.

[16] Denzinger, Para. 819.

our Savior toward man appeared, not by works of righteousness which we have done, but according to His mercy He saved us."[17]

Disturbing effects of ECT

The devastating effect of the New Evangelical compromise with the Gospel is to put a stop to the evangelizing of Roman Catholics across the world. If this compromise of the true Gospel of Jesus Christ is accepted, then Bible-believing Churches will refrain from evangelizing Catholics. The impact on the true Church in third world Catholic countries of Central and South America, in Africa, as well as in Spain, Portugal, and the Philippines, is already apparent. If this anti-evangelical trend continues unchecked it will become ruinous to the spiritual welfare of millions of souls. But this is exactly the policy the ECT signatories promote when they state, "...it is neither theologically legitimate nor a prudent use of resources for one Christian community [church] to proselytize [evangelize] among active adherents of another Christian community."[18] Since when has it been theologically illegitimate to expose error and heresy?

Compounded endorsement of Rome

On November 12, 1997, a second document, entitled "The Gift of Salvation", was signed and published by Evangelical and Roman Catholic leaders. Its expressed intention was to demonstrate the "common faith" of Evangelicals and Roman Catholics, and to further "acknowledge one another as brothers and sisters in Christ." It was published in the December 8, 1997, issue of *Christianity Today.* Explicitly, the Roman Catholic signatories such as Richard John Neuhaus and Avery Dulles, S.J., state in the document that they are "Catholics who are conscientiously faithful to the teaching of the Catholic Church." The Roman Catholic doctrine of conferred justification is taught as the Gospel. The New Evangelicals are now joined together in not only giving a clouded Gospel-Justification message, but also in a distinctively erudite manner, endorsing Rome's doctrine of conferred inner righteousness.

---

[17] Titus 3:4-5.
[18] ECT, §V, "We Witness Together"

A studied denial of the Gospel

This second ecumenical document states, "Justification is central to the scriptural account of salvation, and its meaning has been much debated between Protestants and Catholics." Then it claims that the signers have reached agreement. Their statement of accord is,

> "We agree that justification is not earned by any good works or merits of our own; it is entirely God's gift, conferred through the Father's sheer graciousness, out of the love that he bears us in his Son, who suffered on our behalf and rose from the dead for our justification. Jesus was 'put to death for our trespasses and raised for our justification' (Romans 4:25). In justification, God, on the basis of Christ's righteousness alone, declares us to be no longer his rebellious enemies but his forgiven friends, and by virtue of his declaration it is so."[19]

The subject under review is stated clearly in the first sentence. "We agree that justification...is conferred through the Father's sheer graciousness." But it is only by careful reading that one comes to see what the two pivotal sentences state grammatically, "...it [justification] is entirely God's gift, conferred [rather than imputed]...and by virtue of his [God's] declaration it [justification conferred] is so." This is traditional Roman Catholic doctrine. To employ the Roman Catholic word "conferred" instead of the biblical word "imputed" is tantamount to putting aside the authority of Scripture on the issue of justification. Since medieval times, the Roman Catholic Church has clearly distinguished between the concept of imputation and the Thomist concept of God's grace conferred as a quality of the soul.[20] Since the Council of Trent she has condemned the biblical doctrine of justification by faith alone. Present day dogma of the Roman Catholic Church not only upholds the teaching of the Council of Trent but also declares that such Councils are infallible.[21] The Council of Trent proclaims the following curse:

---

[19] *Christianity Today,* Dec. 8, 1997
[20] Thomas Aquinas, *Summa Theologica*, 2 vols., *Great Books of the Western World,* Tr. by Fathers of the English Dominican Province (Chicago: Encyclopedia Britannica, Inc., 1952) Part I of the Second Part, Question 110, Article 1, Obj. 3 and Article 2, Reply Obj. 1.
[21] *Catechism*, Para. 891.

"If anyone shall say that by the said sacraments of the New Law, grace is not **conferred** from the work which has been worked [*ex opere operato*] **but that faith alone in the divine promise suffices to obtain grace: let him be anathema.**"[22]

Rome's reason for such a curse on those who hold to "justification by faith alone" and to "justification imputed" is logical because of what she refuses to concede. For her, justification is not an immediate one-time act of God received by faith alone. Rather, she teaches that grace is conferred continually through her sacraments. Thus she is able to make a place for herself as a necessary means through which inner righteousness is given. She teaches this in her *Catechism*, "**Justification is conferred in** Baptism, the sacrament of faith. It conforms us to the righteousness of God, who makes us inwardly just by the power of his mercy."[23] Because inner righteousness, which is claimed to have been conferred, is located in the person, and not located in Christ, it can be lost and may need to be conferred again and again. Thus Rome officially states, "…the sacrament of Penance offers a new possibility to convert and to recover the grace of justification. The Fathers of the Church present this sacrament as 'the second plank [of salvation] after the shipwreck which is the loss of grace.'"[24]

"Conferred justification" is necessary for Rome because of her claim that the work of her sacraments is the work of the Holy Spirit. Thus she states, "**'Sacramental grace' is the grace of the Holy Spirit**, given by Christ and proper to each sacrament."[25] Identification of "sacramental grace" with the "grace of the Holy Spirit" is a pretentious blasphemy against the All Holy God. No church ritual can be identified with the grace of the Holy Spirit. The Spirit of God is absolutely sovereign in all His operations—He may or may not act when either Baptism or the Lord's Table are biblically administered—but His power is not synonymous with any Church rite. The Roman Catholic Church's

---

[22] Denzinger, Para. 851, Can. 8.

[23] *Catechism*, Para. 1992.

[24] *Catechism*, Para. 1446.

[25] *Catechism*, Para 1129.

persistence in using the word **"conferred"** is an attempt to substitute her sacraments for the sovereign grace of the Holy Spirit. The concept that the sacraments automatically[26] convey the grace of the Holy Spirit to people is pivotal to Papal Rome. However what is proclaimed in Scripture is that the Holy Spirit is infinite, supreme, omnipotent, and all sufficient in convicting of sin, and in bringing a person directly to new life in Christ Jesus.[27] Nevertheless Rome will not repudiate the concept of "conferred" because for her the sacraments are "necessary for salvation".[28] Without her seven sacraments, she has no function as a Church in the lives of people.

Defense of "Evangelicals and Catholics Together"

The most serious apologetic for the document entitled "Evangelicals and Catholics Together: The Christian Mission in the Third Millennium"(ECT) is in the book of the same title *Evangelicals & Catholics Together: Toward a Common Mission*.[29] The architects of ECT were well aware of the crucial distinctions with regards to the Gospel separating Catholics and Evangelicals, but they chose to by-pass them. J.I. Packer writes in *Common Mission*, "Neither evangelicals nor Roman Catholics can stipulate that things they believe, which the other side does not believe, be made foundational to partnership at this point; so ECT lets go Protestant precision on the doctrine of justification and the correlation between conversion and new birth...."[30]

---

[26] The technical Latin phrase that Rome uses is, 'ex *opere operato*', that is the sacraments function irrespective of the spiritual condition of the Priest giving them or the layperson receiving them. In a word, they work automatically.

[27] "He [The Holy Spirit] will reprove the world of sin, and of righteousness, and of judgment." John 16:8, "That which is born of the flesh is flesh; and that which is born of the Spirit is spirit." See also John 3:6, John 3:8, Romans 8:2, Ephesians 2:1, I John 5:11.

[28] *Catechism* Para 1129, "The Church affirms that for believers the sacraments of the New Covenant are ***necessary for salvation.***" Italic in the original. Bolding added here for emphasis.

[29] *Evangelicals & Catholics Together: Toward a Common Mission,* Charles Colson and Richard John Neuhaus, editors (Dallas, TX: Word Publishing, 1995). Hereafter referred to as *Common Mission*.

[30] *Common Mission*, p 167.

That such compromise is unbiblical is seen from his statements earlier in the same article when he said, "...Roman teaching obscures the Gospel and indeed distorts it in a tragically anti-spiritual and unpastoral manner..."[31] and "Rome's official doctrinal disorders, particularly on justification, merit, and the Mass-sacrifice, so obscure the Gospel that were I, as a gesture of unity, invited to mass—which of course as a Protestant I am not, nor shall be—I would not feel free to accept the invitation."[32]

Packer towards the end of the article speaks of the evils of "humanism", "materialism, hedonism and nihilism". To rebuild a Christian consensus, he proposes that "...**domestic differences about salvation** and the Church should not hinder us from joint action in seeking to re-Christianize the North American milieu..."[33] These are amazing words from the author of *Knowing God*. The orthodox Evangelical J. I. Packer of old spoke of the doctrine of justification by faith alone, *sola fide,* as "like Atlas, it bears a world on its shoulders, the entire evangelical knowledge of saving grace"! Now the same saving faith is downgraded to the "domestic differences about salvation." In a 1994 article, "Why I Signed It", he refers to *sola fide* (faith alone) as "small print."

Most serious and bizarre defense

Packer, who leads the New "Reformed" Evangelicals, has struggled to explain his position. In a 1996 article he asks,

"Can conservative Protestants, Eastern Orthodox and mainstream Roman Catholics join together in bearing witness to all that I have spoken of? I urge that we can, despite our known and continuing differences about the specifics of the salvation process and the place of the church in that process...To be sure fundamentalists within our three traditions are unlikely to join us in this, for it is the way of fundamentalists to follow the path of contentious orthodoxy, as if the mercy of God in Christ automatically rests on persons who are notionally correct and is just as automatically withheld from those

---

[31] *Ibid.,* p. 153.

[32] *Ibid.,* pp 162,163.

[33] *Common Mission*, p. 172.

who fall short of notional correctness on any point of substance. But this concept of, in effect, justification, not of works, but of words—words, that is, of notional soundness and precision—is near to being a cultic heresy in its own right and need not detain us further now, however much we may regret the fact that some in all our traditions are bogged down in it."[34]

No orthodox Evangelical has ever maintained that "notional soundness and precision", that is, doctrinal theory, ever saved anyone. Rather, orthodox Evangelicals have always held to Romans 10:10, *"For with the heart man believeth unto righteousness; and with the mouth confession is made unto salvation."* It appears that Packer is here conducting a little casuistry of his own. He is attempting to preempt his critics by raising an anti-biblical dichotomy between head and heart. This is an old liberal tactic to create an unbiblical dichotomy and then imply and insinuate that any party who refuses to acknowledge it, must in the nature of the case, be unspiritual, opposed to Christian love. None of the historic Evangelical confessions of faith hold out that mere doctrinal "soundness" saves anyone. This is an absurd caricature. Rather orthodox Evangelicals today, even as they did in the days of the Apostle Paul and at the Reformation, declare that it is the righteousness of Christ Jesus alone that saves a person!

What Packer does in setting aside the crux of the issue— justification is by grace alone through faith alone in Christ Jesus alone— is thoroughly in tune with the practice of the Church of Rome. For *Sola Fide*, faith alone, is **the** issue for which the Apostle Paul contended against the Judaisers and for which the Reformers contended against the Roman Catholics of their day. It was the burning issue, foundational to why so many thousands of Evangelicals gave their lives at the stake— John Huss, William Tyndale, John Rogers, Hugh Latimer, Nicholas Ridley, Anne Askew, John Bradford, and John Philpot, to name but a few. The ardent desire of true Evangelicals to *"be found in him, not having mine own righteousness, which is of the law, but that which*

---

[34] J. I. Packer, "On from Orr", *The J. I. Packer Collection*, Selected and Introduced by Alister McGrath (Downers Grove, IL: InterVarsity Press, 1999) p. 264.

[35] Philippians 3:9

is through the faith of Christ, the righteousness which is of God by faith,"[35] was and is the heart of the Gospel, not "contentious orthodoxy" nor "cultic heresy". Christ Jesus' righteousness is the crown jewel of orthodoxy, the pivotal doctrine of truth revealed again by God in its rediscovery, which began the Reformation.

Dr. Packer has chosen to deny the very doctrine that once stood for him like Atlas and bore a world on its shoulders. What Packer has done is to deny the importance of the Scriptures on the precise point of *Sola Fide*. He also denies the Reformation history of those Evangelicals who under the Roman Catholic Inquisition gave their lives, not for any correctness in words, but rather for their faith in Christ Jesus alone.

"Separation for the sake of the gospel is not necessary"
In the same book, Richard Neuhaus stated emphatically, "If, at the end of the twentieth century, separation for the sake of the gospel is not necessary, it is not justified."[36] What Neuhaus was effectively saying is that the Gospel is no longer relevant to Christian unity. This seems to be the precise intent of the 1994 ECT document and equally the 1997 "The Gift of Salvation" document. If true Evangelicals do not combat this heinous attack on the Gospel, then Neuhaus' anti-Scriptural words "separation for the sake of the gospel is not necessary or justified" might well fall on them and their children after them. If the lie is swallowed that separation for the sake of the Gospel is not justified, then the logical conclusion is that churches should cave in and submit to the Church of Rome. This has always been the avowed goal of the Roman Catholic Church, as her documents verify.

Neuhaus argues that "to declare it [justification by faith alone] to be the article by which the Church stands or falls in a manner that excludes other ways of saying the gospel is to turn it into a sectarian doctrine."[37] The true Gospel of grace has in this statement not simply

---

[36] Richard John Neuhaus, "The Catholic Difference", *Common Mission*, p. 199. Emphasis is in the original document.

[37] *Common Mission*, p. 207.

been declared unnecessary, but it has also been labeled a "sectarian doctrine". This statement by Neuhaus shows the intent of Catholics who have planned and fostered the whole deceitful compromise with Evangelicals. Their purpose is to make the true Gospel of grace through faith in Christ alone to be irrelevant, all the while promoting as truly Christian the Catholic "salvation by works-gospel"—which is no gospel at all but which is so acceptable to the natural man.

C. H. Spurgeon's timely words apply now even more than his own day, "Since he was cursed who rebuilt Jericho, much more the man who labors to restore Popery among us. In our fathers' days the gigantic walls of Popery fell by the power of their faith, the perseverance of their efforts, and the blast of their gospel trumpets...."[38] The Gospel trumpet is the very issue at stake, for the Roman Catholic and Evangelical signers of ECT I & II first give the false message of Rome, go on to uphold baptismal regeneration and then in defense of what they have written, declare that the Gospel of Christ is a "domestic matter" or even "a sectarian doctrine".

Practical evaluation
As I said at the beginning of this chapter, if the alignment of new Evangelicals was frustrating for me, as a priest, it is even more difficult for anyone who is seeking for the truth at the present time. The questions that one must ask are these. Do I know the truth about myself according to what the Scripture says is true? Do I believe what the Scripture tells me? Do I believe that I am a sinner? Is my only hope in Christ Jesus? The Lord Christ Jesus saves His people from their sins. He sends His Holy Spirit into their hearts, so that they are radically changed from what they were previously. The Holy Spirit sends forth the love of God in the hearts of those whom He regenerates. That love is manifested by a deep desire and honest resolve to please the Lord and to serve Him. When Christ Jesus saves a soul, He also delivers that soul from the power of sin. It is true that the Lord has not yet completed His work in believers, and there are still sins that need to be eradicated, but any person that He has truly saved is delivered from the

---

[38] Morning and Evening, on Joshua 6:26

dominion of sin. We thank God for those who are saved that do not live in sin. Can you say that this is true for you? In the difficult age of compromise in which we live, do you act under the guidance of the Holy Spirit? Do you make the Word of God your measure of truth and the grace of God your assurance of life? If you can honestly say yes to these questions you will understand that you are not under the condemnation the law, but your faith is in Christ Jesus and His righteousness alone! Then with the Apostle Paul you will have great joy in proclaiming, *"There is therefore now no condemnation to them which are in Christ Jesus, who walk not after the flesh, but after the Spirit...for as many as are led by the Spirit of God, they are the sons of God."*[39] ◆

---

[39] Romans 8:1, 14

Chapter 17

Conclusion

In this book I have consistently tried to show that salvation is of God and not of any church. Why is the Gospel so important? The Gospel of Jesus Christ is the fullest proof of God's infinite love and the only way to salvation. It is vital because it affects all of one's life. First, it is a question of eternal life and of eternal security in the Lord, then it affects families, social life, political life, in fact every fiber and aspect of life.

The oldest error

The Catholic Church's teaching—that it is the Church itself that gives salvation[1]—is accomplished through the oldest method known to man. In Catholicism physical things are presented as instrumental in approaching God and in finding salvation. Looking to physical things to give spiritual life was the first lie of Satan, "...*in the day ye eat thereof, then your eyes shall be opened, and ye shall be as gods, knowing good and evil.*"[2] Satan offered the fruit as the efficacious means of bestowing good upon Eve. She believed in the inherent efficacy of the physical object to open her eyes to the knowledge of good and evil.

In the same way, as we have documented throughout the book, the Catholic Church presents her seven physical sacraments as the inherent means of obtaining the grace of the Holy Spirit. The Vatican's pretense is to present her physical symbolic sacraments as the efficacious cause of sanctity and salvation. To summarize, she claims that baptism

---

[1] *Catechism of the Catholic Church* (1994) Second Edition, Para. 824 "**It is in the Church** that 'the fullness of the means of salvation' has been deposited. It is in her that 'by the grace of God we acquire holiness.'"

[2] Genesis 3:5

regenerates the soul of man,[3] and by anointing with the oil of chrism young people and adults are filled with the Holy Spirit by the sacrament of confirmation.[4] By the words "I absolve you from your sins in the name of the Father, and of the Son, and of the Holy Spirit" uttered in the confession box, she purports to forgive sins.[5] Four words uttered at the altar during Mass, she believes, changes the bread into the body of Christ.[6] These enticing ways to be touched by God are but the age-old temptation of looking to physical substances to obtain life. Such teachings as these come under the eternal curse of perverting the Gospel of Christ.[7] Her priests implement the alluring ways presented by the Vatican. These priests, she holds, "have received from God a power that he has given neither to angels nor to archangels...God above confirms what priests do here below."[8] The New Testament established pastors and elders to lead the Lord's flock; the Vatican, however, conveniently bridges over twenty centuries to join its sacrificial priests to Christ Himself.[9] Thus the Catholic Church belief system expresses some of the greatest temptations that can be imposed on the souls of men and women.

A way that satisfies many

The Gospel is never more dangerously attacked than when the counterfeit is concealed under the pretence of having divine power. However, people seem well pleased with papal Rome. Generally speaking, the world and those inside Catholicism love the ways of Rome. People

---

[3] *Code of Canon Law*, Latin-English Ed., New English Tr. (Canon Law Society of America, 1983, 1999) Canon 849 All canons are taken from this volume unless otherwise noted.

[4] *Catechism*, Para. 1316

[5] *Catechism*, Para. 1493

[6] *Catechism* Para 1413

[7] *"If any man preach any other gospel unto you than that ye have received, let him be accursed."* Galatians 1:9

[8] *Catechism*, Para. 983

[9] *Vatican Council II: The Conciliar and Post Conciliar Documents*, No. 63, *Presbyterorum Ordinis*, 7 Dec. 1965, Austin Flannery, Gen. Ed. (Northport, NY: Costello Publ. Co., 1975) Vol. I, Sect. 7, p. 875.

love a religion that has everything, as it were, "on tap". In Catholicism there is something that corresponds to every class and liking, emphasizing adaptability to most tastes and receiving the support of men of diverse intellectual and moral temperament. To the person who likes rituals and pomp, here is everything to satisfy his heart's content, sacramental rituals being acted out amidst candles, palms, charcoals, ashes, and the perfume of incense, by men in multicolored vestments. It has some of the finest architecture in the world and some of the most captivating music. To the politician or military man, it has all the grandeur of rank and hierarchy. For one seeking direct communication with God, it has a long tradition of mysticism. To the ascetic, there are penances and sacrifices in monastic and convent life. For the Catholic charismatic, there is drama, signs and wonders. For those captivated by visions and apparitions, there is on hand a vast, worldwide assortment of Marian apparitions and messages. For those seeking the pleasures of life, there is the tradition of Carnival, yearly parish festivals with liquor, parish dances, and parish bingo. For those who need something to do, there are many activities and "good works" in which they can become involved. The Papacy is an organization fully adapted to man. It corresponds with the whole scope of his hopes, fears, desires, passions, quirks, and preferences. The world can find in the Papacy something that matches most tastes and affections.

In the Papacy, flagrant wealth and pomp join hands with poverty and pain. The Pope, in his palace, arrayed with crown, and surrounded with cardinals and archbishops decked out in scarlet and purple, welcomes the poor and suffering of the world, and all are impressed. Nothing seems too exalted for him, while at the same time, nothing is too low to be beneath his care and concern. The Pope's religion is the religion of man and the world loves to have it so. The honor and veneration paid to the Pope is great. The world wonders after him, they admire his power, and policy, and success. So great is the darkness, degeneracy, and madness of the world!

The clinching trap

Papal Rome encourages mankind in its yearning to contact the dead. The Vatican publicly teaches,

> "*Communion with the dead.* In full consciousness of this communion of the whole Mystical Body of Jesus Christ, the Church in its pilgrim members, from the earliest days of the Christian religion, has honored with great respect the memory of the dead...Our prayer for them is capable not only of helping them, but also of making their intercession for us effective."[10] "We can and should ask them to intercede for us and for the whole world."[11]

Supposed communion with the dead and deification of the dead has held a prominent place in nearly every system of paganism. The dead are consulted to give help to the living, which is the alluring charm of the occult. The practice of communicating with the spirits of the departed is sinful, since the Word of the Lord forbids it, "*there shall not be found among you any one...that useth divination ...or a charmer, or a consulter with familiar spirits, or a wizard, or a necromancer,* [one who calls up the dead]."[12] The Papacy's teachings on communion with the dead is quite similar to what one finds in the pages of the occult, "The dead love to celebrate, dance, and cavort with the living, and spirits love spirits, so we invite them with ritual libations..."[13] Nonetheless the Lord Christ Jesus commanded worship in prayer is to God alone, "*thou shalt worship the Lord thy God, and him only shalt thou serve.*"[14] He gave the indispensable command that communication in worship is due to God alone and must not be given to any creature. "*I am the Lord thy God...Thou shalt have no other gods before me.*"[15]

In giving glory, honor, and communion in prayer—which is due to God alone—to the spirits of departed humans, the Papacy flagrantly

---

[10] *Catechism*, Para. 958

[11] *Cathecism*, Para. 2683

[12] Deuteronomy 18:10-11

[13] www.festivalofthedead.com/voodoocemeterygods.html   10/29/03

[14] Matthew 4:10

[15] Exodus 20:2-3

sins against the First Commandment. This prohibition includes a precept that is the foundation of the whole law—that believers know that the Lord is their God, acknowledge that He alone is God, accept Him and worship Him alone in prayer, and learn to set their affections entirely upon Him alone.

A precise portrait

The Catholic Church, while purporting to be Christian, declares its own absolute teachings to be infallible."[16] However, all true believers trust in God and His Written Word alone, *"...the scripture cannot be broken,"*[17] *"Sanctify them through Thy truth: Thy word is truth."*[18] Papal Rome professes to impart Christ by masses, and the Holy Spirit by sacraments. It claims to fortify the faithful with crucifixes, rosaries, statues, holy water and saints. It alleges that they can shorten the sufferings of souls in purgatory by indulgences. It professes to mediate between God and man; to hold the keys of heaven and hell; to forbid the marriage of her priests, and to control lust and sexual scandals by the rule of celibacy. Papal Rome commands abstinence from meats and has clothed its cardinals in purple and scarlet and with fine linen, gold and precious stones. In a word, she has set up a system of unrighteousness and taken to herself the imaginary status of "our holy mother, the Church". The Papacy's presupposition is that the Lord set up a totalitarian hierarchy with the Pope at the top followed by cardinals, patriarchs, major archbishops, archbishops, metropolitans, coadjutor archbishops, diocesan bishops, coadjutor bishops and priests. The biblical organizational structure of the bride of Christ is utterly different. In the true body of Christ, those ordained as elders and deacons are still only brothers within the same body and the one Master is Jesus Christ the Lord, *"for one is your master even Christ and all ye are brethren."*[19]

---

[16] *Catechism,* Para. 891, "..the Supreme Pontiff...enjoys this infallibility in virtue of his office, when...he proclaims by a definitive act a doctrine pertaining to faith or morals....This infallibility extends as far as the deposit of divine Revelation itself."

[17] John 10:35

[18] John. 17:17

[19] Matthew 23:8

As Catholics live their lives under the Church's jurisdiction, they have a long journey through the Sacrifice of the Mass, sacraments, good works, merit, veneration of Mary and the Saints. Each one is required to partake of the sacraments in order to be good enough to die in the state of "sanctifying grace" and then to be saved or at least, it is hoped, to land for a time in purgatory. Even on a natural level one wonders how a Catholic can have any hope. The sacrifice of the Mass and the sacraments are such that the most they can promise is a pseudo-hell called purgatory.

It is time for those who really love the Lord and the truth of the Bible to show where they stand. Each believer is commanded by the Lord not only to contend for the faith, but also he is commanded to separate from those who have already compromised and refuse to repent of their disbelief in the truth of God's own Word. The Lord Jesus Christ's great commandment to give the Gospel is laid on all those who call themselves Christians. To uphold His Gospel of truth based on His written Word alone is what is laid before each one who takes the name of Christian! The Lord Himself warned believers against "other christs", Peter warned of "false teachers", Paul warned of "wolves" within the flock. It is not simply that apostates existed in former days. These warnings are for our day every bit as much as they were for theirs.

The Lord exposed the Pharisees for trying to establish their own righteousness, making the written word of no effect. So also ought the true believers today to oppose the apostate Catholic system—and those who stand with them—because that system officially gainsays the glorious truths of the All Holy God. The salvation of many is involved. The Lord faced the sincere and devout Pharisees with a very strong word. They were looking to their leader and chief, Caiaphas, the High Priest. The Lord said to those Pharisees, *"if ye believe not that I am He, ye shall die in your sins."*[20] Like the Pharisees, many present-day Catholics look to the Pope. And likewise today, as with the Pharisees, if anyone continues to recognize the Pope as "Holy Father," he is in fact denying

---

[20] John 8:24

[21] *"He is antichrist, that denieth the Father and the Son."* I John 2:22

the true Father and the Son."[21] He who persists in his sin will likewise die in his sins. The Lord Christ Jesus died in place of the true believer. His life and finished sacrifice alone are the ransom for the believer. *"The Son of man came not to be ministered unto, but to minister, and to give his life a ransom for many."*[22] This was the price demanded by the All Holy God in order that His justice might be satisfied in the forgiveness of sins. As a result of this payment the true believer on Christ Jesus alone is freed from sin and Satan. *"For the wages of sin is death; but the gift of God is eternal life through Jesus Christ our Lord."*[23]

Living "east of Eden" is futile

Self-salvation by Mass, sacraments, good works, accumulated merit; veneration of Mary and the Saints is a wasteland before the All Holy God. It is thousands of light years away from the conviction of the Holy Spirit that comes through the Scriptures. The advantage of God's written Word is that it is all in black and white, leaving no room to escape. The Catholic Church in contrast tries to control religion, morals, politics, art and education—in a word every aspect of life, and in this endeavor exerts all the power that her "maternal concern" can bring to bear. The bottom line in papal Rome is not the convicting power of the Holy Spirit through the written Word; rather it is the Pontiff, and his bishops and priests, who pronounce on moral questions and preach what is to be to be believed and applied in moral life. Thus Rome proclaims,

"The Roman Pontiff and the bishops, as authentic teachers, preach to the People of God the faith which is to be believed and applied in moral life. It is also encumbent on them to pronounce on moral questions that fall within the natural law and reason."[24]

In stark contrast, the final word in Scripture is that *"He [The Holy Spirit] will reprove the world of sin, and of righteousness, and of judgment."*[25] The Spirit works powerfully, and with evident effects. When a person is brought to truly mourn his sin, and to groan under the

---

[22] Mark 10:45

[23] Romans 6:23

[24] *Catechism,* Para. 2050

[25] John 16:8

burden of his own corruption, to long for Christ Jesus and to cry to the "Abba Father" to rescue him from his helpless state, then he knows that the Spirit of the living God has moved him.

The true focus: looking to the Lord for life

God the Father's will centered and terminated in Christ's sacrifice; it was both an act of His will, and most profitable for His people. The priceless double empowerment of Christ's perfect sacrifice is proclaimed by the Holy Spirit, *"by the which will we are sanctified through the offering of the body of Jesus Christ once for all."*[26] Christ Jesus' sacrifice was vicarious in that He substituted Himself in the place of believing sinners and satisfied the law in their behalf. So authentic was this substitution that His sacrifice for them ruled out all necessity of punishment. In becoming the substitute for His people Christ Jesus took their legal responsibility. In the wonderful words of Scripture, *"when the fullness of the time was come, God sent forth his Son, made of a woman, made under the law, to redeem them that were under the law, that we might receive the adoption of sons."*[27]

Christ Jesus had something even greater than delivering true believers from the bondage of law. He came in human form, consented to suffer and die for believers that He might redeem them from the wrath of God that they might receive the adoption of sons. That is the gracious adoption that Christ's sacrifice brings to believers. As a true believer one is able to experience God as Father. *"And because ye are sons, God hath sent forth the Spirit of his Son into your hearts, crying, Abba, Father."*[28] Under the Gospel, believers are no longer under the servitude of the law, for the law has done its work in convicting them that they are helpless sinners. When they believe that in the place of God's just wrath against them, Christ's sacrifice has been imputed to them—that He has effectually taken their place under God's wrath—they become the children of God. They are accepted by Him, and

---

[26] Hebrews 10:10

[27] Galatians 4:4-5

[28] Galatians 4:6

adopted by Him. They are heirs of God, and are entitled to the heavenly inheritance.

In Scripture the believer looks to Christ Jesus as "*THE LORD OUR RIGHTEOUSNESS.*"[29] The splendor of the Gospel is that the believer's heart is set on Christ, the fountain of life, where he drinks more and more deeply of the rivers of pleasure that are at His right hand. Eternal life is to be found only in Christ Jesus, His perfect life and all sufficient sacrifice. "*But we all, with open face beholding as in a glass the glory of the Lord, are changed into the same image from glory to glory, even as by the Spirit of the Lord.*"[30] This is the true focus, because a believer learns more and more consistently to look always to the Lord Jesus Christ alone for life. How completely different this is from the goal and destiny that Papal Rome holds out to people. Rome directs her people and mankind in general to look to physical sacraments and her ruling hierarchy that upholds her sacraments. The biblical Gospel does not involve looking to physical signs. Rather, believers are to follow the biblical injunction to look "*unto Jesus the author and finisher of our faith; who for the joy that was set before him endured the cross, despising the shame, and is set down at the right hand of the throne of God.*"[31] He is the author and finisher of their faith, its beginning and end. "*Looking to Jesus*" is to trustfully keep one's heart and mind stayed upon Him. In Him is grace. He is the Fountain of all grace and supplies all the needs of each believer. The believer's life is drawn from Christ, and directed to Him. He is its initial principle and the final end of it. True life is that which is lived in personal, intimate communion with Christ, as the Apostle Paul so eloquently stated, "*For to me to live is Christ.*" It means that, as a person justified by the All Holy God alone, he is to walk with the Lord Jesus Christ, taking His yoke upon him and learning of Him, so that he drinks deeply from His Written Word and begins to follow what the Scripture says rather than devising his own ways.

---

[29] Jeremiah 23:6

[30] II Corinthians 3:18

[31] Hebrews 12:2

What a difference it makes when he fixes his eyes intently on the Savior. The more he looks, the more he learns just how wonderful the Lord is. He learns of the sufficiency of His grace and the utter proficiency of the Holy Spirit. It is my ardent desire that the Holy Spirit regenerate you so that you believe on Christ Jesus the Lord alone for your salvation. This has been my purpose and I pray that there will be good fruit to the praise of the glory of God's grace, that His rich grace might be magnified, and appear glorious, and worthy of the highest praise. *"For of him, and through him, and to him, are all things: to whom be glory for ever. Amen."*[32]

A final word

Since I have written personally throughout the book, I would like to finish also on a personal note. What I greatly desire is that the reign of Christ Jesus be the underlying principle of your life, to the praise of the glory of His grace. The Gospel lays before you the solution that is ample to face all evil. The power of it is strong enough to recover our estranged world; and it is destined yet to raise people up to life, and peace, and heaven itself. The same Gospel causes the Lord's redeemed people to rejoice in the glorious grace that flows through the His own plan of eternal life. *"And this is the record, that God hath given to us eternal life, and this life is in his Son."*[33] The Son has eternal life in His own essence and person. From Him eternal life is given to the true believer, both here and in heaven.

I went through great trauma at my father's death. When I heard that my father was nearing his final hours, I was more than 5,000 miles away in Trinidad. I immediately flew back to Dublin. Then came the moving experience of my life at his bedside the evening that he died. I was at one side of his bed and one of my sisters on the other. I put on the priest's stole, and had in my hand the book of the prayers that a priest is supposed to read. But I found I could not read any of those prayers as my heart was melting within me. Then finally I looked down

---

[32] Romans 11:36

[33] I John 5:11

at my father in the bed and, as he regained consciousness, I said clearly and slowly, "Jesus to you I live, Jesus to you I die, Jesus in life and in death I am yours." Then I repeated the same words, and his lips were moving with the same words that I was saying. I do not know what was the spiritual condition of my Father at his death, or if what I had said made any difference. What I do know is that from then onwards the course of my own life was changed. My sister has also been profoundly affected for the rest of her life.

My father's funeral had much pomp and ceremony since he had been a military colonel. My heart, however, was more like the grave itself than the trumpet playing at the graveside. After it was all over, my Dad was gone. Almost unconsciously, he had been an authority figure, the one who to me portrayed courage and decision. Just prior to the Irish civil war, his deliberate decision to follow his conscience rather than his feelings and traditions lead him to change sides—the only man in his battalion to do so. It always struck me as showing a man of great courage and resolve. Now my model of courage and resolve lay dead. The shock of my father's death caused me to begin to search for my true Father. It was then I discovered that *abba* is an Aramaic word that corresponds to our word "daddy" or "papa". I found it three times in the New Testament, first in the Garden of Gethsemane, Jesus prayed, "*Abba, Father*". Then the Apostle Paul linked the Christian's cry of "Abba, Father" with the "Spirit of adoption" when he wrote, "*And because ye are sons, God hath sent forth the Spirit of his Son into your hearts, crying, Abba, Father.*" It was the shock of my father's death that brought me to search for my eternal Abba Father. This has been the most rewarding search I have ever made.

For many years I had greatly longed for a deep personal security that can only be found in God Himself. My heart's cry was not just to be right with God, but also to know intimately the love and the protection of the *Abba Father.* I could believe that God loved others, but I saw no reason why He should turn one thought of love or kindness towards me. I dared not cast myself upon Him. Then I came to realize that no one who believes in such intimate love of God as *Abba Father* and puts his trust in that love is ever deceived. The fact that I desired deeply to turn my affections on the *Abba Father* **showed** me that the heart of the *Abba Father* was first set upon me! Otherwise I would not have wanted and longed for the security of His loving kindness. It was then that the Scripture, like a bright light, opened my mind. *"According as he hath chosen us in him before the foundation of the world, that we should be holy and without blame before him in love: having predestinated us unto the adoption of children by Jesus Christ to himself, according to the good pleasure of his will, to the praise of the glory of his grace, wherein he hath made us accepted in the beloved."*[34] This is love: that God loves us first, and then we respond to His love. Such love draws the believer into a living relationship of contentment, deepest security, thankfulness and praise. When God is seen in Scripture as the *Abba Father*, acting love, you respond to His love. This is, in faith, the ground of all acceptable obedience. To love God is to obey Him. He commands us to rest and delight in His love.

What makes the Papacy's purported method of salvation so horrific is that it is a rejection of the manifest love of God given in the Gospel. The evident truth, however, remains untarnished. God's gratuitous love is made effective in accordance with His supreme purposes, *"In this was manifested the love of God toward us, because that God sent his only begotten Son into the world, that we might live through him. Herein is love, not that we loved God, but that he loved us, and sent his Son to be the propitiation for our sins."*[35]

In Christ Jesus alone the believer beholds the wisdom, goodness, love, grace, mercy, justice and power of the Father! God's grace was planned before it was imparted, as the Scripture says, *"Who hath saved us, and called us with a holy calling, not according to our works,*

---

[34] Ephesians 1:4-6

[35] I John 4:9-10

[36] II Timothy 1:9

but according to His own purpose and grace, which was given us in Christ Jesus before the world began."[36] The purpose and design of God from all eternity was that all gifts should come to sinful man in and through Christ Jesus. Emphatically, grace in its most proper and genuine sense is free, as the Scripture says, *"being justified freely by His grace."*[37] Then finally grace is sovereign—because God bestows it upon whom He pleases. The reign of sin and false religion is overcome by the reign of God's grace, as the Scripture says, *"even so might grace reign!"*[38] The abundance of grace far surpasses the evils of sin. Once a believing sinner accepts Christ Jesus as his only surety before the All Holy God, he finds himself not only freed from his sins, but made to *"reign in life"*, *"For if by one man's offence death reigned by one; much more they which receive abundance of grace and of the gift of righteousness shall reign in life by one, Jesus Christ."*[39] Those who receive the abundant grace given by Christ are not only redeemed from the empire of death, they live and reign with Him as they are sanctified daily through His Word by the Holy Spirit, and by constant fellowship with Him. With Him also they shall forever live and reign, world without end. Through Christ Jesus, grace reigns with sovereign freedom, power, and bounty! *"Blessed be his glorious name for ever: and let the whole earth be filled with his glory; Amen, and Amen."*[40] ◆

---

[37] Romans 3:24

[38] Romans 5:21

[39] Romans 5:17

[40] Psalm 72:19

Appendix I

The Scripture Given to the Early Church

The Church of Rome teaches that the Scriptures were handed on to her as Holy Mother Church. Thus she states:

"For Holy Mother Church, relying on the faith of the apostolic age, accepts as sacred and canonical the books of the Old and the New Testaments, whole and entire, with all their parts, on the grounds that, written under the inspiration of the Holy Spirit, they have God as their author, and have been handed on as such to the Church herself."[1]

"It was by the apostolic Tradition that the Church discerned which writings are to be included in the list of the sacred books."[2]

Thus the Catholic Church associates herself with the early Church and claims that God has handed over Scripture to her. Both of these assertions are false and historically preposterous.

All the books of the Bible were written under the inspiration of the Holy Spirit. They were canonical from the moment they were written. No book became canonical by being discerned by apostolic Tradition and handed on as such to "Holy Mother Church". Rather the leaders of the early Church received the New Testament, as had the Jews the Old Testament. The early Church received the books of the New Testament as divinely inspired, recognizing that the Holy Spirit gave inherent authority and worth to those writings. The New Testament was received as the Word of God as the common property of believers and heritage of the people of God. This was in the manner and humility of faith, as expressed by the Apostle Paul, *"when ye received the word of God which ye heard of us, ye received it not as the word of men, but, as it is in truth, the word of God, which effectually worketh*

---

[1] *Catechism of the Catholic Church* (1994), Para 105

[2] *Catechism*, Para 120

also in you that believe."[3]   This was in the centuries before the dictatorial supremacy of the Church of Rome had been established. These Christians did not look on the church as "Holy Mother"; rather for the most part, their attitude as believers was that expressed by the words of Lord, *"One is your Master, even Christ; and all ye are brethren."*[4]

The appeal to "apostolic Tradition" made by the Church of Rome in this matter is consistent with her constant recourse to apostolic Tradition to prove her doctrine. In particular, the text of Scripture that her apologists fall back on to verify the claim is Thessalonians 2:15, *"Therefore, brethren, stand fast, and hold the traditions which ye have been taught, whether by word, or our epistle."* The Apostle wrote only of what had been delivered to them by himself, whether orally or by letter, not of what was handed down from one to another reportedly as from him. We have neither a single sentence from the Apostles nor any from the Lord Himself apart from what is in the written Word. To appeal to apostolic Tradition is futile. Teachings of "apostolic Tradition" from the Apostles or from the Lord, distinct from Scripture, simply do not exist.

Unlike present day Catholicism, the early Church understood apostolic tradition as apostolic doctrine, in line with the written Word of the Apostles, and not as a source distinct from Scripture.
> "From the very beginning of the post-apostolic age with the writings of what are known as the Apostolic Fathers (Ignatius, Polycarp, Clement, the Didache, and Barnabas) there was an exclusive appeal to the Scriptures for the positive teaching of doctrine and for its defense against heresy. The writings of the Apostolic Fathers literally breathe with the spirit of the Old and New Testaments. In the writings of the apologists such as Justin Martyr and Athenagoras the same thing is found. There is no appeal in any of these writings to the authority of a verbal or extra-biblical tradition as a separate and independent body of revelation. It is with the writings of Irenaeus and Tertullian in the mid to late second century

---

[3] I Thessalonians 2:13
[4] Matthew 23:8

that the concept of an apostolic tradition, which is handed down in the Church in oral form, is first encountered. The word "tradition" simply means teaching. Irenaeus and Tertullian state emphatically that all the teachings of the bishops that were given orally were rooted in Scripture and could be proven from the written Scriptures. Both men give the actual doctrinal content of the apostolic tradition that was orally preached in the churches, and it can be seen clearly that all their doctrine was derived from Scripture. There was no doctrine in what they refer to as apostolic tradition that is not found in Scripture. In other words, the apostolic tradition defined by Irenaeus and Tertullian is simply the teaching of Scripture. It was Irenaeus who stated that while the Apostles at first preached orally, their teaching was later committed to writing, and the Scriptures had since that day become the pillar and ground of the Church's faith."[5]

The evidence we gave in Chapter Two, "The Unshakable Authority of the Scripture", shows clearly that from the earliest times a substantial part of the New Testament was available to the believers. The four Gospels were known and read in the churches. The letters of the Apostles Paul and Peter were circulated and used even while the Apostles lived. These New Testament books did not become authoritative because they were being formally accepted as Scripture by any church or group of churches; rather the believers received them as inspired because under the witness of the indwelling Holy Spirit, they recognized the very Word of God. The life of Christ Jesus, in His role as the final and full revelation of God, culminated in the New Testament canon. It expressed the final prophetic word of grace and truth given in Him. The early believers accepted the Written Word of the New Testament, as the words of Christ Jesus Himself—unchangeable, final, finished and authoritative. In this they were totally unlike Rome, with its unholy tradition equally honored and revered as Scripture, and its cleverly evolving doctrine, including its recent acceptance of Islam.[6]

---

[5] William Webster, "Sola Scriptura and the Early Church" http://www.bereanbeacon.org/ articles/sola_scriptura_early_church.htm
[6] See "The Papacy and Islam" on http://www.bereanbeacon.org/articles/ papacy_and_islam.htm

God's people in the first three centuries after Christ universally accepted what we now know as the New Testament. They *"received it not as the word of men, but as it is in truth, the word of God."* There were indeed controversies over individual books, but this confirmed rather than impeded the certainty that they had God's final Written Word *"which was once delivered unto the saints."*[7] The Lord's people universally knew the contents of the canon of the New Testament well before the local Council of Hippo formally accepted it in 393A.D., and before the provincial Council of Carthage in 397A.D.

The teachings of Rome contradict the New Testament in her hierarchical pyramid of authority beginning in the Pope, her Mary, seven Sacraments, Purgatory and other anti-biblical traditions. In the Vatican's acceptance of the Apocryphal books added to the Old Testament, she also contradicts the teachings of the early Church.

In 1838, George Stanley Faber pointed out in his book, *The History of the Ancient Vallenses and Albigenses*, how the Vaudois withdrew from the areas in and around Rome to the valleys of the Cottian Alps during the persecutions of the early church.[8] These Bible believers always held to the Scripture as their only authority, which was evident in their faith and practice for centuries, from the time of their withdrawal to the valleys of the Cottian Alps through the Reformation of the sixteenth century. Nor did they accept any of the number of traditions that the Papacy increasingly manufactured. Their long testimony includes the centuries of persecution from the Roman Catholic Church precisely because of their faith in the Word of God alone as their authority and the attendant practice of that unmixed biblical faith.

The testimony of their lives over the centuries makes it clear that the Roman Catholic Church was and continues to be schismatic

---

[7] Jude 3

[8] George Stanley Faber, *The History of the Ancient Vallenses and Albigenses* (Fleet Street, London: R. B. Seeley & W. Burnside, 1838) Re-published by Church History Research & Archives, P O Box 38, Dayton, OH 45449 Much of this information comes from the archives of the Roman Catholic Church, who was their persecutor.

from the true faith rather than the Vaudois, the Albigenses and others who have chosen to follow the authority of the Bible, often at great cost to themselves personally, rather than to submit to Rome. Then, too, by the early tenth century the Paulicians, who later became known as the Albigenses, have a similar history of always having had the orthodox Scripture, adhering to it, and through it making many converts to true biblical faith. Such living testimony increasingly incensed the Papacy so that they eventually mounted a crusade that martyred many of the Albigenses and scattered the rest throughout Europe, carrying their Bibles and the Gospel with them.

It is patently obvious, therefore, that the Catholic Church's identification of herself with the early Church and her claim that God has handed over Scripture to her, apparently exclusively, is both false and historically absurd. Over the course of history, she has been an instrument of persecution to those of true biblical faith and consistent in adding her dogmatic traditions to Scripture. In contrast to the dogmas of papal Rome, the Lords' words *"are written that ye might believe that Jesus is the Christ, the Son of God; and that believing ye might have life through his name."*[9] Faith through the written Word is designed and adapted to secure one a place in Christ Jesus. The Lord God performs all that He has promised to us in Christ; and He gives the soul a present fruition of those things that are to come. *"For the Lord is good; his mercy is everlasting; and his truth endureth to all generations."*[10] ◆

---

[9] John 20:31
[10] Psalm 100:5

Appendix II

The Apocrypha

The Apocrypha is the name used for the extra-biblical writings that are contained in the Catholic Bible. The Catholic Church herself refers to these books as the "Deuterocanonical books". They are the books of Tobit, Judith, I and II Maccabees, the Wisdom of Solomon, Sirach (Ecclesiasticus), and Baruch. They also entail aberrations to the book of Daniel: Chapter 13, the story "Susanna"; Chapter 14, the account of "Bel and the Dragon"; and an insertion into Chapter 3 entitled, "The Song of the Three Young Men". Further, the book of Esther is expanded by 107 verses. These books and additions, while interesting in giving the believer insights into the four hundred year period of history between the book of Malachi and the Gospel of Matthew, are not part of the written Word of God, as will be explained.

My own life touched by the Apocrypha
A big part of my life was spent not realizing that the Apocrypha were not in ordinary Christian Bibles. Some of these books had a big influence in my life. When I was about eight years old, I memorized the words of II Maccabees 12:45. The verse says, "It is a holy and a wholesome thought to pray for the dead that they may be loosed from their sins." This I did because it was part of *The Penny Catechism* we memorized at school. It greatly influenced my early years. Each year on November 2nd, All Souls Day, I put the verse into practice. I had been told in the Jesuit school that if I prayed for the souls in Purgatory on each visit to church, saying for them six "Our Fathers", six "Hail Marys" and six "Glory be to the Fathers", each time a soul would be released from Purgatory. I remember on All Souls Day one year, going in and out of our local church forty-seven times, ostensibly to get forty-seven souls out of Purgatory!

In my first year as a Dominican novice, I was introduced to Chapter Thirteen of the book of Daniel. I was scandalized by the story of the two elders' rude and immoral behavior towards Susanna. It is very different in words and moral fiber from the other chapters of the Prophet Daniel. It was only many years later that I realized this chapter is indeed not part of the book of Daniel. Then, too, as a student for the priesthood, I took a big interest in the book of Tobit. That the droppings of sparrows blinded the eyes of Tobit seemed strange to me. Still more bizarre was the fact that the angel Raphael cured him by removing the white spots and at the same time introduced him to his bride to be: Sarah, the daughter of Raguel. This was strange, indeed, since Sarah had had seven previous bridegrooms, each dying before the marriage was consummated. What did please me, however, was the teaching of the angel Raphael, that prayer and alms giving can save the soul! This fitted nicely with my own efforts to gain merit by prayer and penances.

Because the books and portions of the Apocrypha contain errors, I deem them as landmines in the Catholic Bible. Sincere Catholics can come across these books and be damaged by them, not realizing that the Holy Spirit has not inspired them. Because of this, it is extremely important to analyze just what the Catholic Church says about them and how they came to be included in Catholic Scriptures.

Official acceptance of the Apocrypha by Rome
The Vatican's official declaration is as follows:
> "It was by the apostolic Tradition that the Church discerned which writings are to be included in the list of the sacred books. This complete list is called the canon of Scripture. It includes 46 books for the Old Testament (45 if we count Jeremiah and Lamentations as one) and 27 for the New.
> "The Old Testament: Genesis, Exodus, Leviticus, Numbers, Deuteronomy, Joshua, Judges, Ruth, 1 and 2 Samuel, 1 and 2 Kings, 1 and 2 Chronicles, Ezra and Nehemiah, Tobit, Judith, Esther [with 107 extra verses], 1 and 2 Maccabees, Job, Psalms, Proverbs,

Ecclesiastes, the Song of Songs, the Wisdom of Solomon, Sirach (Ecclesiasticus), Isaiah, Jeremiah, Lamentations, Baruch, Ezekiel, Daniel, [including adding vv.4-90 to Chapter 3, and two whole chapters, Ch. 13 and 14] Hosea, Joel, Amos, Obadiah, Jonah, Micah, Nahum, Habakkuk, Zephaniah, Haggai, Zachariah and Malachi."[1]

This statement shows the acceptance of a canon of the books for the Old Testament not recognized by Christ Jesus, the Jews, the Apostles or the early Church. This intrusion of the Apocrypha into the inspired and inerrant Word of God is of utmost consequence. The additions amount to one quarter of the size of the Old Testament in a Catholic Bible. The entire Word of God is thereby polluted. The Lord's gift to the believer is like the Lord Himself—a Word in which there is neither uncertainty nor shadow of deceit, *"Every good gift and every perfect gift is from above, and cometh down from the Father of lights, with whom is no variableness, neither shadow of turning."*[2] Rome's own polluted "scripture" is the clear evidence that there is no continuity between her and the Apostolic Church.

Augustine and Apocrypha

Augustine and two local councils in North Africa[3] were an unusual exception to the general rejection of the Apocrypha by the Early Church[4]; nonetheless the Council of Trent in 1546 accepted and endorsed the Apocrypha as part of God's Holy Word.

Reasons why the Apocrypha cannot be accepted

The four main reasons why the Apocrypha cannot be accepted as part of the Scripture are:

1. The Lord Jesus Christ and the writers of the New Testament never ascribe to any of Apocryphal books the distinctive *"it is written"*

---

[1] *Catechism*, Para 120

[2] James 1:17

[3] Provincial councils of Hippo in 393 A.D. and of Carthage in 397A.D.

[4] It was not even perfectly clear just how much Augustine approved of the Apocrypha. His calling them "Deuterocanonical" could have meant that they were good for church reading while not canonical books.

or the equivalents such as "*thus saith the Lord*". It is extremely significant that although almost all of the canonical books of the Old Testament are thus authenticated in the New Testament, the Lord and the writers of the New Testament never substantiate the Apocrypha as Scripture.

2. God gave the Old Testament to the Jewish people, "*unto them [i.e., the Jews] were committed the oracles of God.*"[5] The Jews have never accepted anything more than the canonical books of the Old Testament. For example, the Jewish scholars of Jamnia in 90 A.D. recognized the books of the Old Testament, as did the Early Church and as do Christians today. They did not recognize the Apocrypha. The Jewish historian, Josephus (30-100 A.D.), explicitly excludes the Apocrypha.

3. There is a conspicuous absence of a claim to be inspired in the books of the Apocrypha themselves; rather, in fact some of the books themselves state that the Lord was not speaking through His prophets at that time, e.g. I Maccabees 9:27, "A terrible oppression began in Israel; there had been nothing like it since the disappearance of prophecy among them."

4. The Apocrypha contains errors, fables, superstitions, magic, deceit, and wrong doctrine such as praying for the dead. All of these things are totally at variance to the pure word of God in the canonical books. For example, in Wisdom 8:19 Solomon is made to say, "I was a boy of happy disposition, I had received a good soul as my lot." But this is at variance with Romans 3:23, "*for all have sinned, and come short of the glory of God.*" Another example is II Maccabees 12:45. This verse is quoted in the *Catechism of the Catholic Church* to justify communion with the dead and prayer for the dead. The official teaching based on the lie of II Maccabees 12:45 is the following:

"*Communion with the dead.* 'In full consciousness of this communion of the whole Mystical Body of Jesus Christ, the

---

[5] Romans 3:2

Church in its pilgrim members, from the very earliest days of the Christian religion, has honored with great respect the memory of the dead; and 'because it is a holy and a wholesome thought to pray for the dead that they may be loosed from their sins' [II Mac. 12:45] she offers her suffrages for them.' Our prayer for them is capable not only of helping them, but also of making their intercession for us effective."[6]

This pagan practice of communion with the dead is forbidden in the Scripture, *"There shall not be found among you any one... that useth divination, or an observer of times, or an enchanter, or a witch, or a charmer, or a consulter with familiar spirits, or a wizard, or a necromancer [one who calls up the dead]."*[7]

There is also the false assumption—that man is left to his own resources when it comes to salvation—that is taught in Ecclesiasticus 15:14 in the Catholic Bible. This deadly error is quoted in the present day Vatican II documents of Rome:

"It is, however, only in freedom that man can turn himself towards what is good....For God willed that man should 'be left in the hand of his own counsel' [Ecclesiasticus 15:14] so that he might of his own accord seek his creator and freely attain his full and blessed perfection by cleaving to him."[8]

This type of soul-damning teaching is unashamedly included in the Catholic Bible. It is in direct contradiction to the scriptural position of being spiritually dead prior to salvation. Ephesians 2:1 states clearly the moral condition of a person before conversion, *"and you hath he quickened who were dead in trespasses and sins."* Colossians 2:13 also clearly states the moral condition of mankind, *"and you, being dead in your sins...."* Because of Adam's sin, mankind is born spiritually dead. Romans 3:10-11 clearly depicts man's state, *"As it is written, there is none righteous, no, not one: there is none that understandeth, there is none that seeketh after God."* Other ghastly

---

[6] *Catechism of the Catholic Church* (1994), Para. 958

[7] Deuteronomy 18:10-11

[8] Flannery, Vatican Council II Document No. 64, *Gaudium et spes*, 7 December 1965, Vol. I, Sec. 17, p.917

errors are found in Tobit 12:9, "Almsgiving saves from death and purges every kind of sin. Those who give alms have their fill of days", and also in Judith 10:11-13 and Baruch 3:4.

Fountain of life poisoned

Deceitful fables, lies and false doctrine have no place in the pure fountain of God's Written Word. The fact that the Roman Catholic Church has added books containing such false doctrine shows that she does not believe in the integrity and absoluteness of the Scripture; rather her love is for her tradition. The enlargement of the Bible to include the Apocrypha was a historical deception formalized at the Council of Trent in 1546. The result was the lessening of the internal consistency of the Holy Scripture. By including these Apocryphal writings in their canon of Scripture, the Catholic hierarchy was able to effectively undermine the confidence of an individual in the work of the Holy Spirit in illuminating His Word. The presence of human error, subsumed into the Written Word of God, attempts to make the Word of God of no effect. The Catholic Church, in empathically stating that it is she who grants authority to books like the second book of Maccabees, high-lights her intention to uphold her traditions such as communion with the dead and prayer for them. This affirmation is given as the reason of its authorization of the second book of Maccabees.[9]

Yet in utter contrast, the author of the second book of Maccabees is quite candid regarding his purpose and ability. At the end of the book he declares, "I shall bring my own work to an end here too. If it is well composed and to the point, that is just what I wanted. If it is worthless and mediocre, that is all I could manage."[10] Would to God that we all had the humility and honesty of this man! A true believer's

---

[9] "Introduction to Maccabees" of the Jerusalem Bible, (Garden City NY: Doubleday & Co. Inc, 1966) states, "The book is important for its affirmation of the resurrection of the dead...sanctions in the afterlife...prayer for the dead...the spiritual fruits of martyrdom...intercession of the Saints. Other Old Testament writings had left these teaching vague: but the latter justify the authority accorded to second Maccabees by the Church" (p. 656).
[10] II Maccabees 15:37-38

desire is for the pure Word of God so that he may grow and be strengthened in grace and the knowledge of his Lord and Savior. In the words of the Apostle Peter, "*desire the sincere milk of the word, that ye may grow thereby: if so be ye have tasted that the Lord is gracious.*"[11] This milk of the Word must be uncontaminated, unadulterated by the mixtures of men. Because "*the law of the Lord is perfect, converting the soul: the testimony of the Lord is sure, making wise the simple. The statutes of the Lord are right, rejoicing the heart: the commandment of the Lord is pure, enlightening the eyes.*"[12] The Word of the Lord is perfect and perfectly fitted to the end for which it was designed. By the Holy Sprit the Word shows us our sinfulness and misery apart from God and the vital necessity of our conversion to Him. The testimony of the Lord is sure and inviolably true. Those who are humbly simple before it become wise now and for eternity. ◆

---

[11] I Peter 2:2-3
[12] Psalm 19:7-8

Appendix III

The Church as the Pillar and Stay of the Truth

I know what it is to hear the words, "the Church is the pillar and support of the truth" and to be told that this church is the Catholic Church, and that I am not to think beyond what the Church has told me. That was the summary of the instruction given to me by a fellow priest when I had written to him advising him to look to the Scriptures for authority. Since the Vatican has no scruples in claiming that the church mentioned in I Timothy 3:15 is herself, it is necessary to examine carefully just what the Lord has given to believers in the I Timothy 3:15 text. The following bold assertion is directed as a requirement binding on those she calls her faithful,

> "The Catholic faithful are required to profess that there is an historical continuity—rooted in the apostolic succession between the Church founded by Christ and the Catholic Church: 'This is the single Church of Christ...which our Saviour, after his resurrection, entrusted to Peter's pastoral care (cf. Jn 21:17), commissioning him and the other Apostles to extend and rule her (cf. Mt 28:18ff.), erected for all ages as 'the pillar and mainstay of the truth' (1 Tim 3:15). This Church, constituted and organized as a society in the present world, subsists in [subsistit in] the Catholic Church, governed by the Successor of Peter and by the Bishops in communion with him'".[1]

Any time Rome argues for her legitimacy, a careful watch must be made for the line of reasoning that undercuts the authority of the Scripture. The Vatican is always seeking to introduce extra-biblical sources to undermine Scriptural authority, and to place herself above the Scripture. In the above quote, it is the notion of "apostolic succession between the

---

[1] Declaration "Dominus Iesus", §16.

Church founded by Christ and the Catholic Church" that accomplishes the diminishment of biblical authority. Rome here actually exposes her deceptive reasoning. She states unequivocally that she requires the "faithful" to put their trust in that notion rather than in the truth so clearly laid out in the inerrant Word of God. Rome here demonstrates again her dependence on "historical continuity," or tradition, rather than on the written Word of the Lord. She has proven abundantly over the centuries, both by her anti-biblical doctrine and practices, that she is not "the pillar and support of the truth".

No continuity between the early church and the Vatican

There is no continuity in faith and practice between the early church and the Vatican, which latterly emerged from Imperial Rome.[2] The Church of Rome must be by her very nature utterly excluded from what is stated in I Timothy 3:15 because the church in question upholds the truth. Given the Catholic Church's superstitions and empty rituals, this would make Rome the last imaginable reference for the Apostle Paul. The text itself states, *"But if I tarry long, that thou mayest know how thou oughtest to behave thyself in the house of God, which is the church of the living God, the pillar and stay of the truth."*[3] The focus of the verse is on the behavior of the believer upholding truth. As with the wise man of Luke chapter six, he is founded on rock when he hears the Word and does what it says; so also in this passage the Apostle Paul is telling Timothy how he ought to behave in the local church at Ephesus. He is to conduct himself in the house of God in such a way that the church of the living God upholds truth and is in fact grounded upon it. In the context, this is the meaning of the verse. The verse cannot be understood to make the church, independent of truth, to be the pillar and support of truth. No other Scripture text says this and in fact, the opposite is stated. Churches that are not rooted in truth are again and again seen failing in conduct, as Paul's letters to the Corinthians and Galatians make clear, and also the book of Revelation, chapters one to three. The church as presented in Scripture is born out of the

---

[2] See Chapter 4, "The Papacy: An Overview of Its History and Nature".

[3] I Timothy 3:15 "Stay" is alternate reading.

written Word of truth. As the Holy Spirit so clearly tells us, "*Of his own will begat he us with the word of truth, that we should be a kind of firstfruits of his creatures.*"[4] Believers are "*born again, not of corruptible seed, but of incorruptible, by the word of God.*"[5] The Lord's Word gave life to the early church, as it does to the true church today. The true church is "the pillar and support of the truth" as the historical demonstration of the truth, on which it rests.[6] It witnesses to and preserves the Word of truth. He who is of the truth belongs by that very fact to the church, for He belongs to Christ, its Head. The Lord Christ Jesus alone is the ground of the truth in the highest sense. "*For other foundation can no man lay than that [which] is laid, which is Jesus Christ.*"[7] The church rests on the truth as it is in Christ and in His Written Word.

---

[4] James 1:18

[5] I Peter 1:23

[6] The Lord Jesus Christ said that He would build His church and the gates of hell would not stand against it. That such a church has in fact existed down through all the centuries is clear from historical records of the Paulicians and Albigenses, and of the Vaudois of the Cottian Alps anterior to the Reformation. Both Roman Catholic and Evangelical historical records show this to be true, although the Papacy has taken great pains to wipe out all such records and to substitute for historical fact her revisionist accounts of the Vaudois and Albigenses. One of the Papacy's known tactics was to destroy all written records and Bibles within her grasp of those it submitted to the Inquisition in the six hundred plus years of its operation. The Papacy has also been quite successful in leveling false charges of heresy against the Paulicians and the Albigenses, and in subtly sending abroad false information to confuse the name of the Vaudois with the Waldenses, who were named after Peter Waldo. See particularly George Stanley Faber, *The History of the Ancient Vallenses and Albigenses* (1838) Reprinted by Church History Research & Archives (CHRAA) P O Box 38, Dayton, OH 45449. See also Jean Paul Perrin, *History of the Ancient Christians Inhabiting the Valleys of the Alps*, in particular "History of the Old Waldenses Anterior to the Reformation" (1618) Reprinted by CHRAA; Sir Samuel Morland, *The History of the Evangelical Churches of the Valleys of Piemont* (1658) Reprinted by The Baptist Standard Bearer, Inc., Paris, AR 72855; J. A. Wylie, *The History of Protestantism* (1878) Republished by Mourne Missionary Trust, Church Road, Carginagh, Kilkeel, Co. Down, N. Ireland, 1985, and by Harland Publications, Rapidan, VA 22733 (2002).

[7] I Corinthians 3:11

The behavior of Timothy and the believers

The Apostle Paul is not claiming that any church is truth or can be "the truth". He shows the failings of particular churches in doctrine as he writes to them concerning these things and the correction of them. He is urging the behavior of the church to be as a placard or billboard upon which the very Word of God is proclaimed in such a way as to be the pillar and support of truth. The Apostle was concerned about the behavior of Timothy and the local believers at Ephesus. He was denying neither what he had declared so consistently in his letters nor the principle highlighted by Christ Jesus and through the whole of Scripture—that God's Word is truth. When a church is "erected for all ages as 'the pillar and mainstay of the truth,'" as is the Vatican's spurious claim, horrendous results become manifest. So for example are the Church of Rome's declarations that the sacraments are necessary for salvation, that Mary is the All Holy One, and that Scripture and Tradition must be honored with equal devotion. If a church is "the pillar and support of truth", it is certain that this is not the Catholic Church, where an avalanche of extra-biblical traditions have completely buried the glorious Gospel of our Lord Jesus Christ under the accumulation of human works. The true church was not instituted to be a chain to bind the body of Christ to idolatry, impiety, ignorance of God, and other kinds of evil. Rather, as the Apostle teaches, it is correct behavior that trains the believers to fear God and uphold the truth! The same Apostle declares that the church is founded on the doctrine of the Apostles and Prophets.[8] The Bride of Christ washed clean in the blood of the Lamb is to be distinguished from the Mother of Harlots drunken with the blood of the saints. The church of the Lord Jesus Christ is to be separated from the conspiracy of Satan by the discriminating test which our Savior has applied to all believers, *"He that is of God heareth God's words: ye therefore hear them not, because ye are not of God."*[9] On this vital test Rome utterly fails. The very fact that the Catholic Church will

---

[8] Ephesians 2:19-20, *"Now therefore ye are no more strangers and foreigners, but fellow citizens with the saints, and of the household of God; and are built upon the foundation of the apostles and prophets, Jesus Christ himself being the chief corner stone."*

[9] John 8:47

not accept the Scriptures as the ultimate authority confirms the fact that she is not of God.

From many years of struggle, I know personally what it is to be torn between the Catholic Church as the ultimate authority and the absolute truth of God's Word. We thank the Lord for the fact that He has clearly shown us that there is no contest whatsoever, for the Scriptures do not simply contain truth—they are truth! No church is the author of salvation, but rather it is the written testimony of the finished work and perfect life of Christ. He is the champion, the model, the inspiration, the author and finisher of our faith. Trust Him alone, and know the joy of being His forever! ◆

The Bible and the *Catechism* Compared

Biblical Truth	Topic	New Catechism
The Light of God's Word		*Catechism of the Catholic Church* (1994)

The Bible only is the Standard for Truth	**The Basis of Truth**	**Truth is based on Scripture, Tradition, and the Pope**

"....the scripture cannot be **broken**." John 10:35
"Sanctify them through Thy truth: **Thy word is truth**." John. 17:17
"That ye might learn in us **not to think...above that which is written**, that no one of you be puffed up for one against another."
I Corinthians 4:6
"**Add thou not unto his words**, lest he reprove thee, and thou be found a liar." Proverbs 30:6

"**All scripture is given by inspiration of God**, and is profitable for doctrine, for reproof, for correction, for instruction in righteousness: **That the man of God may be perfect, throughly furnished unto all good works.**" II Timothy 3:16-17
"**Making the word of God of none effect through your tradition**, which ye have delivered..." Mark 7:13

"**Sacred Tradition** and Sacred Scripture, then, are bound closely together and communicate one with the other." *Catechism of the Catholic Church* Para 80
"And **[Holy] *Tradition*** transmits in its entirety the Word of God which has been entrusted to the apostles by Christ the Lord and the Holy Spirit." Para 81

"As a result the [Roman Catholic] Church...does not derive her certainty about all revealed truths from the holy Scriptures alone. **Both Scripture and Tradition must be accepted** and honored with equal sentiments of devotion and reverence." Para 82
"**The Supreme Pontiff**, in virtue of his office, **possesses infallible teaching authority** when, as supreme pastor and teacher of all the faithful...he proclaims with a definitive act that a doctrine of faith or morals is to be held as such." Para 891

Salvation is by Grace Alone through Faith	**Salvation by Grace Alone**	**For Salvation, Grace becomes merely a help, and is given through the sacraments of the Church**

"**Being justified freely by His grace through the redemption that is in Christ Jesus.**" Romans 3:24

"**For by grace are ye saved through faith**; and that not of yourselves: **It is the gift of God: Not of works**, lest any man should boast." Ephesians 2:8, 9

"For if by one man's offence death reigned by one; much more they which

"Grace is the **help** God gives us to respond to our vocation of becoming his adopted sons. It introduces us into the intimacy of the Trinitarian life." Para2021

"The Church affirms that for believers **the sacraments** of the New Covenant are *necessary for salvation.* 'Sacramental grace' is the grace of the

Biblical Truth	Topic	New Catechism
The Light of God's Word		Catechism of the Catholic Church (1994)

receive **abundance of grace and of the gift of righteousness** shall reign in life **by one, Jesus Christ."** Rom 5:17

"**Not by works of righteousness which we have done**, but according to his mercy he saved us..." Titus 3:5-6

"I do not frustrate the grace of God: **for if righteousness come by the law, then Christ is dead in vain.**" Galatians 2:21

Holy Spirit, given by Christ and proper to each sacrament." Para 1129

"**One who desires to obtain reconciliation with God** and with the Church, **must confess to a priest all the unconfessed grave sins** he remembers after having carefully examined his conscience." Para 1493

Faith is the Gift of God and comes by the Word of God

Topic: Faith is God-given and sustained

Faith comes through the Mother Church

"**Believe on the Lord Jesus Christ, and thou shalt be saved, and thy house.**" Acts 16:31

"For unto you **it is given** in the behalf of Christ, not only **to believe on him,** but also to suffer for his sake." Philippians 1:29

"**So then faith cometh by hearing, and hearing by the word of God.**" Romans 10:17

"**It is the Church that believes first**, and so bears, nourishes and sustains my faith." Para 168

"Salvation comes from God alone; but because we receive the life of **faith through the Church, she is our mother:...**" Para 169
'Believing' is an ecclesial act. The Church's faith precedes, engenders, supports and nourishes our faith. **The Church is the mother of all believers.** 'No one can have God as Father who does not have the Church as Mother.'" Para 181

Christ's Sacrifice was His alone and once offered

Topic: Christ's Sufficient Finished Sacrifice

Christ's Sacrifice continues, and is also of the Church

"...Jesus said, 'It is finished:...'" John. 19:30

"**But this man,** after he had offered one sacrifice for sins for ever, **sat down on the right hand of God"** Hebrews **10:12**

"...when He had **by Himself** purged our sins, sat down on the right hand of the Majesty on high;" Hebrews. 1:3

"In this divine sacrifice which is celebrated in the Mass, the same Christ who offered himself once in a bloody manner on the altar of the cross **is contained and is offered in an unbloody manner.**" Para 1367

"The Eucharist is also the sacrifice of the [Roman Catholic] Church. **The Church which is the Body of Christ participates in the offering of her Head.** With him, **she herself is offered** whole and entire." Para 1368